Naming the World

*first*hand
An imprint of Heinemann
A division of Reed-Elsevier Inc.
361 Hanover Street
Portsmouth, NH 03801-3912
firsthand.heinemann.com
Offices and agents throughout the world

Library of Congress Catalog-in-Publication Data
CIP data on file with the Library of Congress

ISBN 0-325-00746-2

Printed in the United States of America on acid-free paper
10 09 08 07 06 ML 1 2 3 4 5

NAMING THE WORLD
A Year of Poems and Lessons

Nancie Atwell

NAMING THE WORLD
A Year of Poems and Lessons

TABLE OF CONTENTS

XIII. THE LARGER WORLD

What Poetry Can Do:

INTRODUCTION

We begin a year of poetry with selections that demonstrate some of the range of what poems can do. I want students to understand from the start that good poetry isn't obscure, precious, goofy, or hackneyed, that poems can *matter*—can connect with and resonate in the life of every twelve- and thirteen-year-old. So the first ten days of school are devoted to poems that make readers laugh, ponder, envision, empathize, reflect, remember, vent, get political, get personal, and get poetry. By the end of this introductory chunk, I hope every student is sold on the potential of poetry to give voice to something in the experience of his or her life.

On the first day of school, students title a page in their writing-reading handbooks—the hundred-page, spiral-bound notebook they bring to each workshop—with the heading What Poetry Can Do. Then, for the next two weeks, at the end of each poetry discussion, I ask them to add ideas to the list, based on the new poem. I record on chart paper or an overhead transparency, what we decide a poem has done then each student copies it into his or her notebook. They keep this running list in their handbooks all year, adding to it as new poems call for new poetic purposes. At the end of the ninth day of school, the list looks something like this.

What Poetry Can Do:

- Be about anything

- Surprise us

- Tap our senses—make us see, feel, hear, and taste in our imaginations

- Make us laugh

- Make us think

- Connect us with other people at the most essential level: heart and mind to heart and mind

- Express anger and help make sense of a troubling experience

- Define feelings and craft them as art

- Tell stories that point a theme

- Make us look at everyday life through new eyes

- Make us think about the kind of lives we want to live

- Use people, objects, actions, and places as symbols to show something about a life or an experience

- Help capture stages in a life: who we were; who we're becoming

- Help us remember what matters

- Help us commemorate what matters

- Feed us, slake our thirsts, protect us, take us around the world and back in time, heal us, and let us take big chances, yet remain safe

- Reveal the beauty in everyday existence; open our eyes to the poems that hide around us

PRESENTING THE POEM:

You Can't Write a Poem about McDonald's

BY RONALD WALLACE

SETTING THE STAGE: Maybe the most serious misconception about poetry is that its subject matter is narrow. People who don't know poems think poetry is about love, nature, the four seasons, pretty topics like flowers and rainbows, and cute topics like puppies and children.

I think the poems we read together this year, one or two each day, will prove otherwise. Poetry can be about *anything:* there's no subject under the sun that can't be explored and captured as a poem. In terms of its versatility as a genre, poetry can't be beat. We'll read a poem every morning and start our time together in the best way I know.

I'm not dead certain that our first poem began as a response to a dare, but I'd be willing to put money on it. I think someone who didn't get poetry was debating with the poet Ronald Wallace—arguing that there are limits to the subjects a poem can address—and to make the point offered a challenge: "You can't write a poem about *anything.* You can't write a poem about *McDonald's.*" Ronald Wallace could, and he did.

SOME FEATURES TO NOTICE:

- The sensory language: images, descriptions, and comparisons readers can see, feel, taste, and smell
- The similes that compare people to food, like a McDonald's counter girl *as crisp as a pickle*

- The humor: *Suddenly I understand cannibalism*
- The line about *how easy it is to be filled* and the last three lines of the poem: among the most important theme-wise in an ode to the availability and plenty of food in America
- How the first-person voice and the expression of the speaker's emotions make this a *lyric poem*

RESPONSE STANCE: Now it's your turn to read this poem and make it your own. Please go back into "'You Can't Write a Poem about McDonald's'" with a pencil in your hand and read it silently to yourself. Sound each of its words in your head. As you read, *mark the sensory lines in the poem: the lines you can see, smell, taste, and feel.* Also, think about the challenge of the title: can a good poet write a good poem about anything?

BENEDICTION: Something you might try as a poet is a free-verse description of your own outrageous poetic topics. If someone can write a poem about McDonald's, what are other unlikely—and funny—subjects for viewing through the eyes of a poet?

You Can't Write a Poem about McDonald's

Noon. Hunger is the only thing
singing in my belly.
I walk through the blossoming cherry trees
on the library mall,
past the young couples coupling,
by the crazy fanatic
screaming doom and salvation
at a sensation-hungry crowd,
to the Lake Street McDonald's.
It is crowded, the lines long and sluggish.
I wait in the greasy air.
All around me people are eating—
the sizzle of conversation,
the salty odor of sweat,
the warm flesh pressing out of
hip huggers and halter tops.
When I finally reach the cash register,
the counter girl is crisp as a pickle,
her fingers thin as french fries,
her face brown as a bun.
Suddenly I understand cannibalism.
As I reach for her,
she breaks into pieces
wrapped neat and packaged for take-out.
I'm thinking, how amazing it is
to live in this country, how easy
it is to be filled.
We leave together, her warm aroma
close at my side.
I walk back through the cherry trees
blossoming up into pies,
the young couple frying in
the hot, oily sun,
the crowd eating up the fanatic,
singing, my ear, my eye, my tongue
fat with the wonder
of this hungry world.

   –Ronald Wallace

PRESENTING THE POEM:

Maybe Dats Youwr Pwoblem Too

BY JIM HALL

SETTING THE STAGE: Yesterday we began to glimpse what poetry can do as a genre and to understand that its subjects are limitless. Today's poem is so bizarre I don't even have a guess as to how Jim Hall came up with the subject *or* the person. A *persona* is an imagined speaker. The speaker Jim Hall imagines for this poem is Peter Parker, a.k.a. Spiderman, but with a couple of twists: here, Peter is sick to death of the boring routine of a superhero's life, plus, well, Spiderman has a speech impediment.

SOME FEATURES TO NOTICE:
- The voice should be read aloud as written: prepare to become a hyper-emotive Elmer Fudd for the amusement of your students
- The repetition of SPIDERMAN creates a *cadence,* or rhythm
- The conclusion—the last six lines—conveys the poem's theme: each of us is who we are, and none of us can burn our suits/identities

RESPONSE STANCE: Please go back into this funny poem on your own, read it to yourself, and sound its words in your head. This time, please underline your favorite lines—the ones that struck you. Then, would you look for and mark the lines that sum up what this poem is about: *what* is Jim Hall getting at in this deranged monologue?

BENEDICTION: Something you can do as a poet is adopt a persona—choose someone from popular culture, a fairy tale, a myth, a legend—then explore what his or her life is *really* like in a poem.

Maybe Dats Youwr Pwoblem Too

All my pwoblems
who knows, maybe evwybody's pwoblems
is due to da fact, due to da awful twuth
dat I am SPIDERMAN.

I know, I know. All da dumb jokes:
No flies on you, ha ha,
and da ones about what do I do wit all
doze extwa legs in bed. Well, dat's funny yeah.
But you twy being
SPIDERMAN for a month or two. Go ahead.

You get doze cwazy calls fwom da
Gubbener askin you to twap some booglar who's
only twying to wip off color T.V. sets.
Now, what do I cawre about T.V. sets?
But I pull on da suit, da stinkin suit,
wit da sucker cups on da fingers,
and get my wopes and wittle bundle of
equipment and den I go flying like cwazy
acwoss da town fwom woof top to woof top.
Till der he is. Some poor dumb color T.V. slob
and I fall on him and we westle a widdle
until I get him all woped. So big deal.

You tink when you SPIDERMAN
der's sometin big going to happen to you.
Well, I tell you what. It don't happen dat way.
Nuttin happens. Gubbener calls, I go.
Bwing him to powice. Gubbener calls again,
like dat over and over.

I tink I twy sometin diffunt. I tink I twy
sometin excitin like wacing cawrs. Sometin to make
my heart beat at a difwent wate.
But den you just can't quit being sometin like
SPIDERMAN.
You SPIDERMAN for life. Fowever. I can't even
buin my suit. It won't buin. It's fwame wesistent.
So maybe dat's youwr pwoblem too, who knows.
Maybe dat's da whole pwoblem wif evwytin.
Nobody can buin der suits, day all fwame wesistent.
Who knows?

—*Jim Hall*

PRESENTING THE POEM:

Footsteps to Follow

BY KELLI CARTER

SETTING THE STAGE: We've been learning that poems can be about anything. Today we'll begin a new conversation about what poems can be *good for:* why people write them, what poems do for poets, and what poetry does for people who read it.

Kelli was an eighth-grade poet who adored a certain children's book author. He lived in her state and spent a lot of time in local schools, including Kelli's, giving readings and working with kids on their writing. And suddenly, one morning, there he was in the headlines of the local newspaper. He'd been arrested, charged with molesting little boys and girls.

Kelli's response to the bad news about her favorite author was a poem. She wrote it on the bus on the way to school, tore it out of her notebook, folded it about twenty times, and left it on her teacher's desk.

SOME FEATURES TO NOTICE:
- The use of questions—seven of them—to create cadence, build a theme, and suggest the poet's confusion
- The way the pause after *little* in the second-to-last line gives the word a double meaning, about the loss of childhood innocence

- The simple, direct language that gives the poem its emotional power: *Where have all the good guys gone?*
- Because of the coded nature of poetry, Kelli can write about what happened and convey her anguished response to it *indirectly*. The heroes on horseback, knights, and Lone Rangers function as *symbols* for the children's author

RESPONSE STANCE: Please go back into this poem on your own and mark the lines you'd like to talk about. Also, speculate about why you think Kelli wrote this: what might naming and shaping her feelings in a poem have done for her?

BENEDICTION: Something you can do as a poet is express your own strong emotions about a situation that troubles you: use a poem to help you capture, define, and get some control over what hurts.

Footsteps to Follow

What happened to all the Lone Rangers,
the heroes on white stallions,
the knights in white armor
who fought for our honor?
Where have all the good guys gone?
Whose footsteps are we to follow now?
Whose shoes are we to fill?
Mine is the voice of this generation—
the voice of a thousand.
Do you hear our unanswered questions?
Or are you so deaf that you cannot hear?
So what happened to you, Lone Ranger?
Each time you don't answer, a little
part of us dies.

   —*Kelli Carter*

©2006 by Nancie Atwell from *Naming the World: A Year of Poems and Lessons* (Portsmouth, NH: Heinemann)

PRESENTING THE POEM:

SIMS: The Game

BY ELIZABETH SPIRES

SETTING THE STAGE: Today we're back in poems-can-be-about-anything territory. This poem knocked me out for at least ten reasons. At the top of my list was imagining your reactions to it. How many of you have ever played the computer simulation game The Sims? . . . I figured as much. I think you're going to appreciate "SIMS: The Game" and Elizabeth Spires' take on how a little kid might interpret the version of grown-up life it presents.

SOME FEATURES TO NOTICE:

- The persona of the speaker: a child, for whom the poet creates sincere, childlike diction and emotions
- The use of white space to reinforce the voice—to create childlike pauses and emphases—and the lack of punctuation
- The use of stanza breaks to signal and set off categories of information, which function here much as paragraphs do in prose
- The use of *irony*: the humorous differences between real life and the version of real life simulated in SIMS

RESPONSE STANCE: Please go back into this poem on your own and mark the lines that strike you as funny. Then, we'll talk about Spires' use of irony to create humor—about the distance between the child's vision of adult life and the real thing.

BENEDICTION: Something you can do as an adolescent poet is adopt a childlike persona and create your own ironic situation: speak in a little kid's voice about something a little kid doesn't fully understand yet, but you do.

SIMS: The Game

A popular computer game explained by a child

In some ways it's Life   Real Life
        in some ways Yes   in some ways No

You design the people   they can be
        outgoing   nice   playful   active   neat
        but you can't make them be everything
        if they are neat   they will clean up after themselves
        (Charisma is when they talk to themselves
            in front of a mirror)

Adults never get older   & old people can do
        anything young people can do
Adults don't have jobs   they can cheat
        push the rose bud & money appears

        Job objects   like pizza ovens   earn you money
            or you can be   an extra in a movie   a soldier
            a doctor   an astronaut   a human guinea pig

Children get older slowly   every day they get a report card
        children can live in the house without adults
        (a family is anyone who lives in the house with you)

Everyone gets skills points:
        for chess   painting   playing the piano
        gardening   cooking   swimming   mechanics
        (when you get points a circle above your head
            fills up with blue)

& there are goals: not to run out of money   not to die
        & to buy more stuff for the house
        (like a pool table   or an Easy Double Sleeper Bed)

Adults can get married   but it's hard   to get married
        You tell them to propose but they can't   make the decision
        on an empty stomach   or they've just eaten
            & are too tired

To have a Baby   click Yes or No   & a baby carriage
        rolls up

Everyone has to   eat   sleep   go to the bathroom   etc.
        if they live alone   & don't have friends
        they get depressed   & begin waving their arms

If you give them Free Will   you don't have to
      keep track of them
      but it's strange what they'll do:
      once a player fell asleep under the stairs standing up

      & sometimes they go into a bedroom   that isn't theirs
      & sleep in the wrong bed   then you have to tell them:
      Wake up! That is not your bed!

If they are mad they stomp on each other   or put each other
      in wrestling holds   but no one gets hurt

There are different ways to die:
      you can drown in the pool if you swim laps for 24 hours
            (the Disaster Family all drowned in the pool
            except the little girl   who kept going
            to school after they died   she was perfect)

      & the stove   or fireplace   or grill
      can set the house on fire:
            once there was a fire in the kitchen
            eight people rushed in
            yelling *Fire! Fire!*   & blocked the door
            so the firemen couldn't get through
            (after that everyone had to study cooking
            now there are less accidents)

If you have Free Will   you can starve or drown yourself
      then you wander around as a ghost
      until another player agrees   to resurrect you

In some ways it's Life   Real Life
      in some ways Yes   in some ways No
      —*Elizabeth Spires*

"SIMS: The Game," ©April, 2004 by Elizabeth Spires
and The Poetry Foundation.

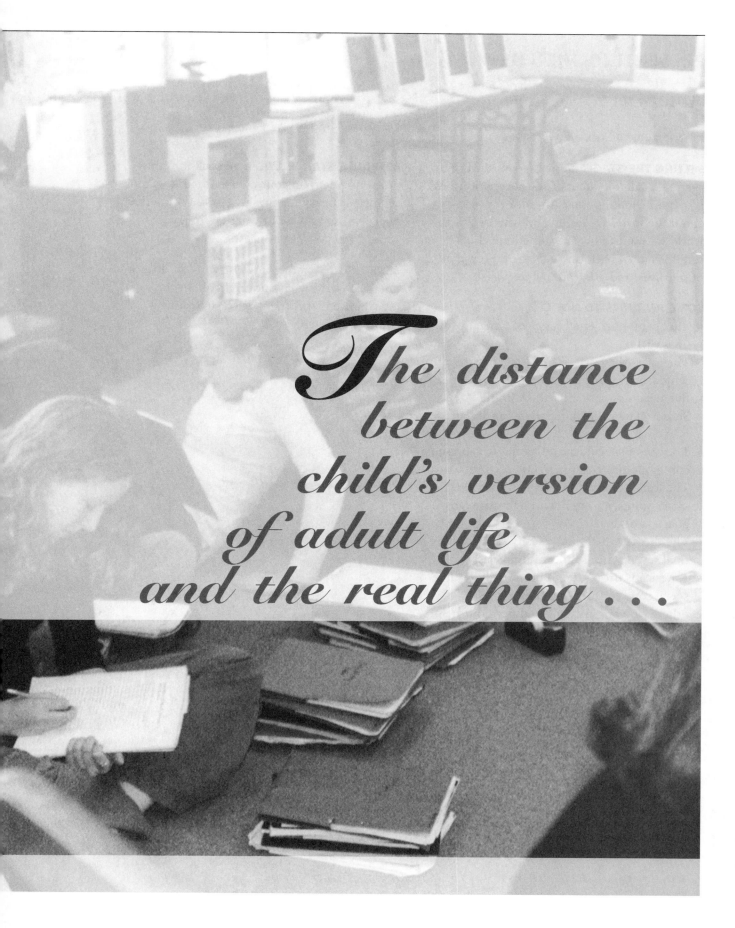

*The distance
between the
child's version
of adult life
and the real thing . . .*

PRESENTING THE POEM:

America

BY TONY HOAGLAND

SETTING THE STAGE: Today's poem shifts gears again. I'd call it a poem of social consciousness. It's about contemporary American society—about the world we live in and whether it's the world we want to live in. Something else a poem can do is draw back, show us the bigger picture of our lives, and ask *what's wrong here?*

SOME FEATURES TO NOTICE:

- The form: unrhymed *couplets:* stanzas of two lines each
- The form: the poem is one long, interrogative sentence; the only end-stop punctuation is the question mark after the last line
- Sensory language that readers can see and hear
- The use of specific brand names to represent contemporary consumerism
- The tone: conversational and informal at some points, and rich with figurative language at others
- The theme, which is especially clear in the final seven stanzas: how middle-class Americans use stuff and noise to dull our social consciousness—our awareness of others who are suffering and need our help

RESPONSE STANCE: Please go back into this powerful poem on your own and mark its most important lines: the lines where you think the poet's meaning—about what's wrong with America today—is strongest.

BENEDICTION: Something else you can do as a poet is observe what's not right about the society you live in, protest it, even show how it could be different.

America

Then one of the students with blue hair and a tongue stud
Says that America is for him a maximum-security prison

Whose walls are made of Radio Shacks and Burger Kings, and MTV episodes
Where you can't tell the show from the commercials,

And as I consider how to express how full of **it I think he is,
He says that even when he's driving to the mall in his Isuzu

Trooper with a gang of his friends, letting rap music pour over them
Like a boiling Jacuzzi full of ballpeen hammers, even then he feels

Buried alive, captured and suffocated in the folds
Of the thick satin quilt of America

And I wonder if this is a legitimate category of pain,
Or whether he is just spin doctoring a better grade,

And then I remember that when I stabbed my father in the dream last night,
It was not blood but money

That gushed out of him, bright green hundred-dollar bills
Spilling from his wounds, and—this is the weird part—,

He gasped, "Thank god—those Ben Franklins were
Clogging up my heart—

And so I perish happily,
Freed from that which kept me from my liberty"—

Which is when I knew it was a dream, since my dad
Would never speak in rhymed couplets,

And I look at the student with his acne and cell phone and phony ghetto clothes
And I think, "I am asleep in America too,

And I don't know how to wake myself either,"
And I remember what Marx said near the end of his life:

"I was listening to the cries of the past,
When I should have been listening to the cries of the future."

But how could he have imagined 100 channels of 24-hour cable
Or what kind of nightmare it might be

When each day you watch rivers of bright merchandise run past you
And you are floating in your pleasure boat upon this river

Even while others are drowning underneath you
And you see their faces twisting in the surface of the waters

And yet it seems to be your own hand
Which turns the volume higher?

   —Tony Hoagland

PRESENTING THE POEMS:

My Room

BY JOE POWNING

&

Patterns

BY ANNE ATWELL-MCLEOD

SETTING THE STAGE: I remember my bedroom from when I was your age so well that I can close my eyes and *feel* myself there. I've never enjoyed a more intense or complicated relationship with a physical space. My room was my haven. It was where I pretended I was adopted, wrote my first poems, tried to keep diaries, taught myself to play the guitar, learned how to apply mascara, listened to the Beatles and Bob Dylan, ate candy, plucked my eyebrows, and fantasized about boys: guys I knew and guys I knew I'd never meet. My bedroom was also the place I was banished to after I mouthed off at my parents, the place where I cried about my disloyal friends and embarrassing body and terrible clothes, the place where I wondered, *what's wrong with me?*

Like I said, it was an intense and unique relationship with a physical space. It's also a perfect subject for poets your age. As seventh graders, Joe and Anne each wrote poems about their bedrooms.

SOME FEATURES TO NOTICE—"MY ROOM":

- The form: how Joe crafted each stanza as four lines except the last, which allows the poem to build momentum at its conclusion; how he used almost no punctuation and let his line breaks do the work of voice marks; how his capitalization of *My* emphasizes the personal nature of his subject
- The way the language is cut to the bone
- The humor
- How Joe's description of his room reveals a lot about who he is

SOME FEATURES TO NOTICE—"PATTERNS":

- The form: how Anne crafted each stanza as eight lines, except for the last
- How the title captures what the poem is about without labeling it, e.g., "My Bedroom"
- The sensory details that a reader can see
- The concrete nature of the details: objects that suggest who the poet is and what's important to her
- The theme: the comfort people derive from familiarity and routine
- How Anne's description of her room reveals a lot about who she is

RESPONSE STANCE: Please choose which one of these two poems you'd like to go back into on your own. Then mark the lines you'd like to talk about. We'll discuss Joe's poem first, then Anne's.

BENEDICTION: Something you can do as a poet, and an adolescent, is capture your own remarkable, idiosyncratic, unique bedroom and what it shows about who you once were and who you are right now.

My Room

My room
My haven
My block of peace
in a hectic world

My room
My personal disaster area
of piled clothing and blaring music
of comfortable chaos

My room
My harbor of fantasies
"Gee whiz, Ace, what kinda room is this?" asked Ace Detective's sidekick
"I don't know," Ace replied, "but I like it"

My room
My ongoing rationalization
Joe's brain: Joe's room is messy
Joe: What's new?

My room
My responsibility
the subject of many
"Go Clean Yours"

My room
My prison
the subject of many
"Go to Yours"

My room
My cubicle of terror
zone of nightmares
shelter of my angst

My room
My haven
My organized chaos
My ongoing rationalization
My responsibility
My harbor of fantasies
My prison
My terror
My block of peace
in a hectic world

  —Joe Powning

Patterns

Late afternoon light
kisses translucent curtains
the way it has year after year,
as familiar as the wallpaper
I chose from a patchwork quilt of samples
back when I couldn't imagine a time
I'd want to look
at anything else.

The wallpaper frames a sampler embroidered
Friendship, Love, and Truth:
words that take on new meanings
as friends come, go, stay.
And the books overflowing their shelves—
each is a relic left behind
as a timeline of this room
and the person who lives here.

A life hides
in a jumble of outgrown running shoes,
the blank pages of journals too beautiful to write in,
the empty windows of a dollhouse too precious to put away,
a dusty pink boa framing a cloudy mirror,
the collection of boxes, each housing a story, a memory,
the worn red collar of the dog that died,
and, under the bed, a puppy's lost tennis ball.

Darkness will come soon.
I know, because it has every other night.
I'll rest my head upon a pillow
that witnessed a thousand emotions.
I'll blink into the orange glow of the streetlight
until my eyelids close
and I dream amidst the pinks and blues
of my past,
my present,
my room.

   —*Anne Atwell-McLeod*

Anne's description of her room reveals a lot about who she is.

PRESENTING THE POEM:

Remembrance of a Friend

BY BENJAMIN F. WILLIAMS

SETTING THE STAGE: Today's poem is an *elegy;* that is, it's a poem that mourns a death. This is a sad poem about a sad subject, but it also does the work of a good elegy: it brings some measure of comfort to the poet. Something else poetry can do is help us remember, capture, and celebrate what matters to us, before the essential details slip away.

SOME FEATURES TO NOTICE:

- The way Ben informs the reader indirectly, through an accumulation of details, that the deceased friend is his dog
- The voice: an *I* speaking to a *you*
- The use of *vignettes*: little stories that show Ben and Buster in action and suggest what their relationship was like
- The sensory language, especially the verbs
- The evocative *things* of the final stanza: the field, the dog's bed, the piano, the dandelions, and the grave

RESPONSE STANCE: Please go back into this poem on your own and mark your favorite lines and words—the ones that struck you deepest.

BENEDICTION: Something else you can do as a poet is to use your poetry to remember and celebrate the ones you loved who are gone. What are the moments and sensations you need to capture, before they slip away?

Remembrance of a Friend

My sight is blurred by tears
as we walk to the field.
I wish you were beside me,
your paws padding the ground,
your pink tongue tasting the air.

Your life was long.
You, who babysat me
when I was nine months old,
watching me bounce
in my johnny-jump-up,
only your eyes moving
as you pretended not to notice
when I landed on your snout.

You, who Dad lifted
and plopped on the sled
so you could slide down
the driveway with me,
my hands burrowed
in black fur,
your ears drawn back
by the icy wind.

You, my dog Buster,
who will be buried in the field
along with your bed that lived
under the piano,
so in the springtime
dandelions will grow
over your grave.

    —Benjamin F. Williams

©2006 by Nancie Atwell from *Naming the World: A Year of Poems and Lessons*
(Portsmouth, NH: Heinemann)

The Little Boy

BY HELEN E. BUCKLEY

SETTING THE STAGE: I have a collection of teacher poetry—poems that help me remember what school can be like for kids and keep in mind, as a teacher, what it *should* be like. "The Little Boy" comes from that file. Every time I read this poem it reminds me why we have writing workshop: what it means to kids to make their own creative decisions and to be seen and respected as *themselves.*

SOME FEATURES TO NOTICE:
- The parallel structure: the repetition of elements—of language, events, and dialogue—from one episode to another
- The childlike voice created by the simple language: how the diction consists of words of one or two syllables
- A few telling specifics, like the door from the outside directly into the classroom, that turn this from a fable into what feels like the story of an actual little boy
- The two classroom doors as symbols for the difference between the two schools: the first, seeking to make things easy for children, thwarts their independence; the second gives children responsibilities, which increases their independence
- The red flower with a green stem as a symbol of how denying kids choice and independence destroys their creativity/individuality/sense of initiative

RESPONSE STANCE: Please go back into this poem on your own and mark what you think are its most important lines. Then, would you write a sentence or two about what you think the *themes* of this poem might be? By *theme*, I mean the poet's ideas about life—in this case about school—that are conveyed through the poem.

BENEDICTION: Something else you can do as a poet is to tell a story, about your own experience or someone else's, that points a theme—a story that shows how you feel about some aspect of life, say, school, growing up, parents, siblings, stereotyping, friendship, a sport you played.

The Little Boy

Once a little boy went to school.
He was quite a little boy,
and it was quite a big school.
But when the little boy
found that he could go to his room
by walking right in from the door outside,
he was happy.
And the school did not seem
quite so big any more.

One morning,
when the little boy had been in school a while,
the teacher said,
"Today we are going to make a picture."
"Good!" thought the little boy.
He liked to make pictures.
He could make all kinds:
lions and tigers,
chickens and cows,
trains and boats.
And he took out his box of crayons
and began to draw.

But the teacher said, "Wait!
It is not time to begin."
And she waited until everyone looked ready.

"Now," said the teacher,
"we are going to make flowers."
"Good!" thought the little boy.
He liked to make flowers,
and he began to make beautiful ones
with his pink and orange and blue crayons.

But the teacher said, "Wait!
And I will show you how."
And she drew a flower on the blackboard.
It was red, with a green stem.
"There," said the teacher.
"Now you may begin."

The little boy looked at the teacher's flower.
Then he looked at his own flower.
He liked his flower better than the teacher's.
But he did not say this.
He just turned his paper over
and made a flower like the teacher's.
It was red, with a green stem.

On another day,
when the little boy had opened
the door from the outside all by himself,
the teacher said,
"Today we are going to make something with clay."
"Good!" thought the little boy.
He liked clay.
He could make all kinds of things with clay:
snakes and snowmen,
elephants and mice,
cars and trucks—
and he began to pull and pinch
his ball of clay.

But the teacher said, "Wait!
It is not time to begin."
And she waited until everyone looked ready.

"Now," said the teacher,
"we are going to make a dish."
"Good!" thought the little boy.
He liked to make dishes.
And he began to make some.
They were all shapes and sizes.

But the teacher said, "Wait!
And I will show you how."
And she showed everyone how to make
one deep dish.
"There," said the teacher.
"Now you may begin."

The little boy looked at the teacher's dish.
Then he looked at his own.
He liked his dishes better than the teacher's.
But he did not say this.
He just rolled his clay into a big ball again
and made a dish like the teacher's.
It was a deep dish.

And pretty soon
the little boy learned to wait
and to watch
and to make things just like the teacher.
And pretty soon
he didn't make things of his own anymore.

Then it happened
that the little boy and his family
moved to another house
in another city,
and the little boy
had to go to another school.

This school was even bigger
than the other one,
and there was no door from the outside
into his room.
He had to go up more big steps
and walk down a long hall.
And the very first day
he was there
the teacher said,
"Today we are going to make a picture."

"Good!" thought the little boy.
And he waited for the teacher
to tell him what to do.
But the teacher didn't say anything.
She just walked around the room.

When she came to the little boy
she said, "Don't you want to make a picture?"
"Yes," said the little boy.
"What are we going to make?"
"I don't know until you make it," said the teacher.
"How shall I make it?" asked the little boy.
"Why, any way you like," said the teacher.
"And any color?" asked the little boy.
"Any color," said the teacher.
"If everyone made the same picture
and used the same colors,
how would I know who made what
and which is which?"
"I don't know," said the little boy.
And he began to draw a flower.
It was red, with a green stem.
        —Helen E. Buckley

Defining the Magic

BY CHARLES BUKOWSKI

SETTING THE STAGE: Since we've been considering and naming what a good poem does, I thought we should consult an expert. Charles Bukowski wrote forty books of good poems. He was famous for living on the edge and writing about it. In Bukowski's poems you'll meet gamblers, hoods, working-class people down on their luck, outright bums, prostitutes, and other Americans trying to survive life on the margins of America.

SOME FEATURES TO NOTICE:

- The humor
- The similes, metaphors, and personifications, all framed in strong, simple, direct language
- The nature of the comparisons: what they show or suggest about who the speaker is
- The way the repetition of the phrase "a good poem" creates a cadence
- How the title fits the poem without labeling it
- The short, strong lines
- The lack of capital letters, except on proper nouns, and the single period after *stop*

RESPONSE STANCE: Please go back into the poem on your own and mark your three favorite comparisons. Then, write a few words next to each about *why* this simile, metaphor, or personification resonates for you.

BENEDICTION: Something else you might do as a poet is consider what a good poem represents for you—or a good book, a good song, a good movie, good french fries, a good dog or cat, a good friend. What's it *like* for you?

Defining the Magic

a good poem is like a cold beer
when you need it,
a good poem is a hot turkey
sandwich when you're
hungry,
a good poem is a gun when
the mob corners you,
a good poem is something that
allows you to walk through the streets of
death,
a good poem can make death melt like
hot butter,
a good poem can frame agony and
hang it on a wall,
a good poem can let your feet touch
China,
a good poem can make a broken mind
fly,
a good poem can let you shake hands
with Mozart,
a good poem can let you shoot craps
with the devil
and win,
a good poem can do almost anything,
and most important
a good poem knows when to
stop.

—*Charles Bukowski*

Valentine for Ernest Mann

BY NAOMI SHIHAB NYE

SETTING THE STAGE: We'll round out this first grouping of poems—free verse that shows some of the range of what poetry can do—with a poem that might remind you of our first, Ronald Wallace's "'You Can't Write a Poem about McDonald's.'" That poem read like a response to a challenge from a reader. This poem reads like a response to a *demand* from a reader.

It seems that someone named Ernest Mann— probably a kid—said to Naomi Shihab Nye, "Okay, so you're a poet. Here's my address. Write me a poem." As a writer who's serious about poetry, Nye knows it doesn't work that way.

So, where do poems come from?

SOME FEATURES TO NOTICE:

- The way the poem begins in the midst of its meaning, without an introduction or preamble
- The direct language and conversational tone: an *I* speaking to a *you*
- The poet's use of concrete objects to exemplify her meaning: the two skunks show how poems are hiding in our lives, if only we'll look for them, better than a wordy explanation ever could
- The purposeful, effective repetition of the word *serious*

RESPONSE STANCE: Please underline the most important lines in this poem—where the strongest meanings reside. Mark your favorite lines, too.

BENEDICTION: Something else you can do as a poet is "check your garage, the odd sock in your drawer, the person you almost like, but not quite"—as well as your closet, your kitchen table, the top of your bureau, your box of junk, your dog's mouth, your cat's eyes, your old toys, your everyday life—and find your poems.

Valentine for Ernest Mann

You can't order a poem like you order a taco.
Walk up to the counter, say, "I'll take two"
and expect it to be handed back to you
on a shiny plate.

Still, I like your spirit.
Anyone who says, "Here's my address,
write me a poem," deserves something in reply.
So I'll tell you a secret instead:
poems hide. In the bottoms of our shoes,
they are sleeping. They are the shadows
drifting across our ceilings the moment
before we wake up. What we have to do
is live in a way that lets us find them.

Once I knew a man who gave his wife
two skunks for a valentine.
He couldn't understand why she was crying.
"I thought they had such beautiful eyes."

And he was serious. He was a serious man
who lived in a serious way. Nothing was ugly
just because the world said so. He really
liked those skunks. So, he re-invented them
as valentines and they became beautiful.
At least, to him. And the poems that had been hiding
in the eyes of skunks for centuries
crawled out and curled up at his feet.

Maybe if we re-invent whatever our lives give us
we find poems. Check your garage, the odd sock
in your drawer, the person you almost like, but not quite.

And let me know.
            —*Naomi Shihab Nye*

This group...
middle schoo...
identity—ab...
now, who the...
see themselve...
to be seen, ar...

Your Life:
INTRODUCTION

This group of poems helps middle school students think about identity—about who they are now, who they were, how they see themselves, how they wish to be seen, and how they see others—in short, to think about *what matters* in the life of an individual. Twin themes of choice and reconsideration run through these poems, as the poets explore first thoughts, then second thoughts, about what's important, what's not, and why.

PRESENTING THE POEM:

Autobiography in Five Short Chapters

BY PORTIA NELSON

SETTING THE STAGE: There's a scene in the movie *Good Will Hunting,* set in a psychologist's office, in which the Matt Damon character is talking about the choices he made in his life and the outcomes that he is—and isn't—responsible for. On the wall behind him hangs a poster version of this poem. When I caught a glimpse of it, I thought, "Smart set decoration—not only did someone in Hollywood know this poem, they *got* the theme of this poem."

SOME FEATURES TO NOTICE:

- How the chapter headings on the stanzas separate them and give each the weight of a distinct episode in an autobiography or phase in a life
- The use of repetition to create patterns, both in the structure of the poem and the actions of its speaker
- The sustained metaphor: engaging in a harmful behavior is encoded as walking down the same street
- The open-endedness of the imagery: *the street* can be interpreted in myriad ways

RESPONSE STANCE: Please go back into the poem and mark what you think are its most important lines. Then, write a sentence or two: what, for you, is this poem *about?*

BENEDICTION: We'll never know exactly what the speaker's problem is in "Autobiography in Five Short Chapters." Nelson's sustained metaphor—the same street, then another one—is generous: it accepts multiple interpretations. But we can be pretty sure there *was* a problem, something concrete from a real life that led to this coded imagery. As poets, consider what you might be able to do with a sustained metaphor. What if you wrote at length about something from your real life as if it were something else?

Autobiography in Five Short Chapters

Chapter I

I walk down the street.
There is a deep hole in the sidewalk.
I fall in.
I am lost…I am helpless.
It isn't my fault.
It takes forever to find a way out.

Chapter II

I walk down the same street.
There is a deep hole in the sidewalk.
I *pretend* I don't see it.
I fall in again.
I can't believe I'm in this same place.
But it isn't my fault.
It still takes a long time to get out.

Chapter III

I walk down the same street.
There is a deep hole in the sidewalk.
I see it there.
I still fall in…it's a habit…but,
my eyes are open.
I know where I am.
It is *my* fault.
I get out immediately.

Chapter IV

I walk down the same street.
There is a deep hole in the sidewalk.
I walk around it.

Chapter V

I walk down another street.

—*Portia Nelson*

"Autobiography in Five Short Chapters," ©1993 Portia Nelson

PRESENTING THE POEMS:

Fat Man
BY NIALL JANNEY

&

New Eyes
BY ADRIENNE JAEGER

SETTING THE STAGE: In these poems, seventh graders Niall and Adrienne tell stories of chance encounters—Niall's with, as he puts it, a fat man, and Adrienne's with someone who is homeless. A shift in their perspectives shifts their attitudes, and as Niall and Adrienne are surprised and changed, so are we.

SOME FEATURES TO NOTICE—"FAT MAN":

- How the lead and conclusion echo one another, with an intentional shift in the verb tense from present to past and the addition of two lines at the end that imply Niall's shift in perspective
- How the repetition of *fat man* and *fatter* in the third stanza conveys Niall's initial impression of disgust
- How Niall doesn't need to describe his reaction, once he realizes the fat man's purpose and recognizes that the man isn't a stereotype; Niall lets the reader connect the dots

SOME FEATURES TO NOTICE—"NEW EYES":

- How the lead and conclusion echo one another, with the addition of two lines that imply Adrienne's shift in perspective
- The strength and specificity of the verbs, nouns, and adjectives: we can see and feel what Adrienne saw and felt
- How Adrienne doesn't need to spell out her reactions, once she recognizes that the young man isn't a stereotype—how, like her, he is a reader and has a rich inner life; how Adrienne lets the reader connect the dots

RESPONSE STANCE: Please go back into one of these two poems on your own—your choice—and mark the phrases and lines that struck you. Then, would you write a sentence or two about why you think Niall or Adrienne wrote it?

BENEDICTION: Something else your poems can do is help capture times when you discovered you were mistaken—when you misjudged or stereotyped someone. These are poems that will help you grow up—and help others, too.

Fat Man

I catch sight of the man
on route to the mountain's summit.
He carries with him a recycled Coke bottle
secured to a small pack.

But the man also hefts his weight
inside a sweat-stained XXXL red tee shirt.
He's what I call a fat man—

a fat man who doesn't exercise,
a fat man who engulfs food,
a fat man who lives only to become fatter and fatter.

He turns at my approach
then drops his eyes
as they meet the expression in mine.

I pass the fat man swiftly, with disgust,
wondering what could drive him
to attempt the summit.

When I glance back with this question in mind,
my eyes drop to the legend on the red tee shirt:
I'm hiking for the National Cancer Foundation.

I caught sight of the man
on route to the mountain's summit.
He carried with him a recycled Coke bottle
secured to a small pack.

He was heading upward.
He was on a mission.

    —Niall Janney

New Eyes

Shuffling through the crowds—
a sea of shorts and tank tops—
hot sun beating down on a packed Madison Avenue,

I tighten my grip on my sister's hand
and push through the mob.
From behind us stalks a young man,
trailing in back of him a cart.

He flips his head
to wipe unkempt hair out of his face.
Grubby, torn clothes
swallow a frail body.

He curses
as he drops the remnants of a sandwich
and, without a flinch, picks it up
and stuffs his mouth. I look away in disgust.

But as he passes us,
I spy books
scattered through his pile of belongings,

each with a tattered binding
or missing cover,
but every page well loved.

I watch him disappear into swarms of people,
embarrassed that with one look,
I knew everything.

I trudge on
through a sea of shorts and tank tops,
hot sun beating down on a packed Madison Avenue,
looking ahead

with new eyes.

—*Adrienne Jaeger*

*These are poems
that will help you
grow up —
and help others, too.*

PRESENTING THE POEM:

Unlucky

BY MICHAEL CONLEY CARTER

&

Family

BY ANNA JAEGER

SETTING THE STAGE: Sometimes a poet's reconsideration of the past doesn't involve a difficult life lesson. Sometimes reconsideration means measuring the distance between a childhood perspective and a new level of awareness that comes with adolescence.

SOME FEATURES TO NOTICE—"UNLUCKY":

- How the line breaks give the poem voice and emphasize Michael's emotions
- The sensory images
- The diction
- The humor
- How the conclusion echoes the lead; how both connect with the title

SOME FEATURES TO NOTICE—"FAMILY":

- How Anna uses italics rather than quotation marks to indicate spoken dialogue
- The sensory details
- The contrast between life in the photo—*they had to rent shoes*—and Anna's life: *my aunt's wide screen television*
- How the conclusion refers to the lead: Anna is back in the present at her aunt's house

RESPONSE STANCE: Please go back into one of these two poems—your choice—and mark the lines you want to talk about—because you can see them, because they strike you as effective, because you can identify with the feelings or ideas expressed in them.

BENEDICTION: What did *you* believe or understand when you were little? As a poet, can you look back on your childhood fantasy life and measure the distance, as Michael did, or on your old and new perspectives, as Anna did?

Unlucky

How did all those nearsighted kids
get so lucky?

When I was little,
I wanted
glasses.
Call me naïve,
but I thought it'd be cool
to own a sleek pair of glasses
and a big, snapping case
to protect them.

Imagine: this small,
sight-enhancing device
could change my whole identity:
a costume of smartness.
I pictured my face in the mirror,
a new me with a cool pair of glasses
resting on my nose.
Wow.

I guess a few
"Hey, four-eyes!"
might have made me want to reconsider,
but who says that anymore, anyway?
And I knew all the lucky people
wearing glasses
would have told me I was crazy,
that wearing glasses
was the worst.
But dreams of transformation
still tempted me.

Now I've outgrown
my childish ideas.
Why would I ever want glasses?
With my twenty-twenty vision,
I can finally see
how lucky I am.

          —*Michael Conley Carter*

Family

Each time we visited my aunt
my mom told me the story
of the photo:

That's your great-grandfather Julius
and his mom, your great-great-grandmother.
This photo was taken in Russia.
They were so poor
they had to rent shoes for this picture.

I never thought much of it
until now.
In school I study people
coming to America
in hope of a better life.

That is what they did.

I stare hard into the picture:
their faces stiff with fear,
their eyes that resemble Adrienne's,

the mother,
arms wrapped around
her daughter's frail body.

I wonder:
did they ever imagine
that some of them wouldn't survive?
That the two boys
would be forced
to fend for themselves?
Start a new life,
alone,
in a strange new world?

I change the channel
on my aunt's wide screen television.
I glance back at the photo.

Before, all I saw were strangers
in odd, old clothes.
Now, I see my family.

          —*Anna Jaeger*

PRESENTING THE POEM:

Guilt

BY JED CHAMBERS

SETTING THE STAGE: Have you ever been persuaded to do something that made you uncomfortable? Something "everyone" did and "everyone" enjoyed, but you hesitated? For Jed, the something was fishing.

SOME FEATURES TO NOTICE:
- The specific descriptions, sensory language, and strong verbs
- How the manner in which Jeb broke the lines of the last stanza slows down the conclusion and emphasize his feelings
- The unidentified *you:* how the device of a friend to whom Jed addresses the poem, without naming him, helps prevent the poem from turning into a story; instead, it's a lament

RESPONSE STANCE: Please go back into this sensory poem and mark the lines you can see, that put you *there* in the scene, and also what seem to you to be its most important lines.

BENEDICTION: Something else you can do as a poet is to reconsider a time "everyone" was doing something—when you felt pressured by a peer or an adult to behave in a way that didn't jibe with your values or character. How did it feel? How did you act? How do you *wish* you'd acted?

Guilt

We would fish,
and we would enjoy it.
That's what my mother said.
I had never fished before,
so I called you.

At the pier we baited our hooks—

slipped barbs into rancid shrimp.
The shining silver pierced one side
and emerged,
glistening, on the other.

Then we cast.
Yours landed far away
near one of the fishing boats,
but mine landed close—
too close perhaps—
to the solitary black cormorant
who clumsily flapped away
and screamed at me in its foreign tongue.

Then came reluctant waiting.

Finally, I felt a sharp tug
and I saw it—
the blue-white streak
cut through the brine
like harnessed lightning.
A mackerel.

The monofilament stretched taut.
Slowly I reeled it in.
As it lay there,
staining the dock crimson,
you killed it.
"Just a fish," you claimed.

But when it was cooked
for our dinner
I tasted
guilt.

—*Jed Chambers*

PRESENTING THE POEM:

Mail Call

BY ADRIENNE JAEGER

SETTING THE STAGE: This is another student poem about reconsideration. We get to witness the change as Adrienne realizes—then acknowledges—that something she has taken for granted is important to her.

SOME FEATURES TO NOTICE:
- How the reader has to infer to whom the poem is addressed, but how we can unpack the clues and understand the *you* is Adrienne's mother
- How the simple noun-verb constructions at the start of the first, third, and fourth stanzas give the poem its form
- How the fifth stanza shifts the setting—away from a close-up of Adrienne on her bunk, to a wide-angle shot, then to a flashback
- The powerful, one-line-stanza conclusion

RESPONSE STANCE: When you go back into this visual poem on your own, please mark the lines you can see; then, mark the lines that help you understand who the *you* is that Adrienne is acknowledging here.

BENEDICTION: As a poet, you may want to consider and capture one of the times when you realized your appreciation of your mom, dad or someone else who has had an influence on your life. A poem about that moment would make a wonderful gift of writing. That's what Adrienne did with "Mail Call"—she gave it to her mom for Mother's Day.

Mail Call

I wait
at the foot of my cot
for the arrival of the mail.
I watch
as the counselor paces,
distributing letters to giddy campers.

Finally
four envelopes drop
onto my scratchy blanket.
I sift through the pile
and find three
are from you—
all bright and colorful cards.

I laugh
as I read your version
of Anna's experience at sailing camp
and for a moment
wish I was back home.

I gaze
at the rainbow wall
pasted with other cards,
all from you.
Then I look at my bunkmates'
barren walls,
and I understand how you are different.

Outside tall ferns sway in the wind
and the sun is alone in a flawless blue sky
like the day when you and I said good-bye
and I told you I don't miss you when I'm at camp.

Well, I do.

   —*Adrienne Jaeger*

Long Dream

&

Someday

BY MICHAEL STOLTZ

SETTING THE STAGE: Sometimes a poet finds a subject, dream, or theme in his or her life that's central, one so important to the poet's identity that it's worth revisiting. For Michael, a seventh grader, that obsession was his guitar.

SOME FEATURES TO NOTICE—"LONG DREAM":

- The form: five stanzas of five lines each
- The sensory verbs and nouns
- How the single-word lines in the last stanza slow down and emphasize Michael's conclusion

SOME FEATURES TO NOTICE —"SOMEDAY":

- How the repetition of the same two lines at the start of each stanza creates a cadence, moves the poem, and builds to Michael's concluding sentiment
- How Michael includes vocabulary and references that are specific to the world of heavy metal music

RESPONSE STANCE: Please go back into Michael's odes to his obsession and mark the lines you like, plus the lines you think best express his obsession.

BENEDICTION: So what's your obsession, your dream, your theme? Have you written a poem about it yet? And have you considered writing another? And another?

Long Dream

Sweat
makes it hard
to hold the chords.
My fingers kill.
New blisters pop.

The neck of the guitar squeaks
as I force myself to finish the song.
My mind a wild blur,
oblivious to the outside world,
I slam the last note.

The amp changes from roar to buzz,
while my imaginary crowd cheers.
I switch it off
and snap back to reality.
"Just another day of practice,"

I say to myself—
one more step
toward fulfilling my long dream
to join one more famous band
and become

one
more
famous
guitar
player.

       —Michael Stoltz

Someday

No one matches the skill
of John 5—
the easy glide of his fingers
from fret to fret,
string to string,
punching out riffs one after another.

No one matches the skill
of John 5—
from blue grass to metal
to intense country shred,
the ex-Manson musical genius
is unstoppable.

No one matches the skill
of John 5—
the ominous chords,
the heavy tuning,
always changing,
always different.

No one matches the skill
of John 5—
but someday
I will.

       —Michael Stoltz

PRESENTING THE POEMS:

Where I'm From
BY GEORGE ELLA LYON

&

Where I'm From
BY JACOB MILLER

&

where i'm from
HALLIE HERZ

SETTING THE STAGE: George Ella Lyon's poem "Where I'm From" isn't about the place she was born. Instead, it's about the specific world she was born into: the landscape, people, food, expressions, and stories that are her heritage as a member of a particular community. Read along with me, and see what I mean . . .

Some seventh-grade poets were intrigued by Lyon's poem, by the odd and telling particulars of family and background that she captured. They developed a questionnaire of information they could ask their parents, to help them gather similar particulars about the things, people, music, food, and pastimes they were born into. Then they selected and crafted the data. Here are two of their poems, about where Jacob and Hallie are from.

SOME FEATURES TO NOTICE:

- The specifics: how books, candy brands, television shows, musical groups, etc., are *named*
- How Jacob and Hallie are inspired by Lyon without plagiarizing her poem: the particulars make their poems their own
- How Hallie decided to forgo capital letters
- How each student poet ended the list with a satisfying concluding stanza, in the mood of Lyon but distinctly his or her own

RESPONSE STANCE: Please go back into Hallie's and Jacob's poems. First, mark the references you understand—that anyone could. Then, mark the period references you think your own parents might get, that you could ask them about tonight at home.

BENEDICTION: Poetry can help you discover where you're from and express this other kind of family tree. If you'd like to interview your parents and gather data for a "Where I'm From" of your own, I have copies of the questionnaire that Jacob and Hallie's class devised.

Where I'm From

I am from clothespins,
from Clorox and carbon-tetrachloride,
I am from the dirt under the back porch.
(Black, glistening,
it tasted like beets.)
I am from the forsythia bush,
the Dutch elm
whose long-gone limbs I remember
as if they were my own.

I'm from fudge and eyeglasses,
        from Imogene and Alafair.
I'm from the know-it-alls
        and the pass-it-ons,
from Perk up! and Pipe down!
I'm from He restoreth my soul
        with a cottonball lamb
        and ten verses I can say myself.

I'm from Artemus and Billie's Branch,
fried corn and strong coffee.
From the finger my grandfather lost
        to the auger,
the eye my father shut to keep his sight.

Under my bed was a dress box
spilling old pictures,
a sift of lost faces
to drift beneath my dreams.
I am from those moments—
snapped before I budded—
leaf-fall from the family tree.

    —*George Ella Lyon*

Where I'm From

I am from kettle chips,
from the rock I used to keep under my bed,
and from the Beatles, especially Paul.
I am from the catnip plant in the garden
whose triangular leaves I remember
as if they are my own.

I am from Pay Days and Nik-L-Nips,
from Clyde Dexter and Larry Bird,
from "Take a chill pill" and the Boston Red Sox.

I am from the Brady Bunch
and the scar on my finger.
I am from rec league soccer,
from Antoine Walker and Paul Pierce.

In the closet are ancient scrolls,
mementoes of my lost ages.
I am from those memories.
Scribed down before this age,
they waited for our family tree
to grow me.

　　　　　—Jacob Miller

where i'm from

i'm from cub scouts
and demolay,
from tiddlywinks,
black licorice,
and bazooka bubblegum,
from "squeeze my finger"
and "just try it—you'll like it,"
from *harriet the spy*,
lacrosse,
and blackberries behind the house,
from baseball games in hip-high grass,
from crosby, stills, and nash,
robison and friedman,
elvis,
and dinah washington.

i'm from thirty years in california,
smiles in a pink photo album,
the twinkle in your eye.

　　　　　—Hallie Herz

FIGURE X — **STUDENT HANDOUT**

Cross-Generational Questionnaire

Your name _____

The year you were twelve _____

1. What toys did you play with?

2. What sports and games did you play?

3. What else did you do in your spare time? What were your hobbies?

4. What singers or groups did you listen to?

5. What celebrity or public figure did you admire or have a crush on?

6. What candy did you buy?

7. What was your favorite TV show?

8. What was your favorite book or series of books?

9. What was a saying or expression that adults or other kids were using?

10. What did you want to be when you grew up?

PRESENTING THE POEMS:

What's in My Journal

BY WILLIAM STAFFORD

&

What's in My Journal

BY NIALL JANNEY

&

What's in My Journal

ANNA JAEGER

SETTING THE STAGE: William Stafford's poems knock me out. He wrote about the experiences of his life and his feelings about them with clarity, honesty, and humor. In this poem he opens up his journal to us and describes what he finds there—except it's a metaphoric journal: its contents are images, objects, jokes, and quirks of personality that, taken together, tell a lot about who William Stafford was . . .

Niall and Anna were two students who liked Stafford's idea and tried it for themselves. By identifying the objects, images, quirks, and emotions that might be found in the pages of their imaginary journals, they captured who they are.

SOME FEATURES TO NOTICE:
- How the poems consist of lists that answer the question of the title but require no other introduction
- How Niall and Anna borrow Stafford's caesuras

- The mixture of serious and humorous elements
- The idiosyncrasy of the lists
- Three different tones in three poems with the same title, each reflecting the personality of its poet

RESPONSE STANCE: Please go back into one of these three poems on your own—your choice—and mark the lines that reveal the most to you about who the poet is, about what he or she is like.

BENEDICTION: You're probably already thinking about what's in your journal. This is a great technique for you to try as a poet: take a verbal snapshot of who you are right now.

What's in My Journal

Odd things, like a button drawer. Mean
things, fishhooks, barbs in your hand.
But marbles too. A genius for being agreeable.
Junkyard crucifixes, voluptuous
discards. Space for knickknacks and for
Alaska. Evidence to hang me, or to beatify.
Clues that lead nowhere, that never connected
anyway. Deliberate obfuscation, the kind
that takes genius. Chasms in character.
Loud omissions. Mornings that yawn above
a new grave. Pages you know exist
but you can't find them. Someone's terribly
inevitable life story, maybe mine.

—*William Stafford*

What's in My Journal

A Brinks truck on its side, greenbacks
and Ben Franklins pouring
from smashed safes. Blades of knives,
a smoking gun, and a flame
that never dims or fades.
Cats prowling around an eight-lane
pool filled to the brim with lemonade.
On the serious side: sick humor—
a destructive passion Satan himself can't
     match.
But also the side of the room
draped in shadow—a foreboding mix
of darkness and deceit. Well,
kind of.

    —Niall Janney

What's in My Journal

Spit-drenched tennis balls and a pungent
stench. "Lost" with a heart drawn around it on every
blank surface. The lingering scent of Burberry Brit
that stains our upstairs for all eternity. Quizzes
from trashy magazines–
Who's Your Celebrity Sister?
And, Are You the Party Girl or the Wet Blanket?
Dead goldfish: Judy, Whoopie, Francis. Camp memories:
sailing with Schmidt and Olivia; plunging
into the gleotricia-infested lake. Page upon page
of possible future signatures. Sketches
of celebrities from the best-dressed section of *Teen People*.
And still sleeping soundly when the clocks read 11:30 am:
a glance into my twelve pages.

    —Anna Jaeger

What's in your journal? Take a verbal snapshot of who you are right now.

PRESENTING THE POEM:

Famous

BY NAOMI SHIHAB NYE

SETTING THE STAGE: I love this poet, and I love this poem. We'll talk about it today as the last in a sequence of poems that have helped us think about the kinds of lives we want to lead. I think "Famous" is a perfect bookend to Portia Nelson's "Autobiography in Five Short Chapters." In a society obsessed with celebrity, Naomi Shihab Nye redefines what it means to be famous.

SOME FEATURES TO NOTICE:

- How, with the first, one-line stanza, Shihab Nye jumps right into the conceit of this poem: her redefinition of fame
- The separate images that express variations on a theme: the idea of fame as *worth*
- The powerful concluding stanza, about wanting to live a life of usefulness

RESPONSE STANCE: Please go back into "Famous" and underline your favorite versions of fame.

BENEDICTION: This is a poem to put up on your bulletin board or your bedroom wall; I think the last stanza—at least—is one to memorize. Poetry is useful. It can help us live our lives. This poem will remind you not to forget what matters, what lasts, what *you* can do to matter.

Famous

The river is famous to the fish.

The loud voice is famous to silence,
which knew it would inherit the earth
before anybody said so.

The cat sleeping on the fence is famous to the birds
watching him from the birdhouse.

The tear is famous, briefly, to the cheek.

The idea you carry close to your bosom
is famous to your bosom.

The boot is famous to the earth,
more famous than the dress shoe,
which is famous only to floors.

The bent photograph is famous to the one who carries it
and not at all famous to the one who is pictured.

I want to be famous to shuffling men
who smile while crossing streets,
sticky children in grocery lines,
famous as the one who smiled back.

I want to be famous the way a pulley is famous,
or a buttonhole,
not because it did anything spectacular,
but because it never forgot what it could do.

—*Naomi Shihab Nye*

The poetic

William Car

great twenti

was "Say it—

things." "Will

the concrete

Ideas *in* Things:

INTRODUCTION

The poetic mantra of William Carlos Williams, the great twentieth century poet, was "Say it—no ideas but in things." Williams focused on the concrete particulars of the world as the basis for his vision as a writer. Although my students don't end up writing like Williams—no one will ever match his style, diction, or perspective—they learn from him about the need for a poet to focus on "things," on real people and objects and events.

Student poets are drawn to broad topics: snow, love, autumn, music, war, nature. But the strongest student poems, theme-wise and craft-wise, address specific moments and objects, not universal ideas or feelings. The details of a particular writer's particular experience touch our senses, involve us, and create a feeling of shared meaning.

PRESENTING THE POEMS:

The Red Wheelbarrow,
Poem,
&
Between Walls

BY WILLIAM CARLOS WILLIAMS

SETTING THE SCENE:
If I had to name the most important poem of the twentieth century—important because of its influence on poets who followed—it would be "The Red Wheelbarrow" by William Carlos Williams. In sixteen words it expresses a view of the world—a writer's *vision*—that helped every poet since Williams understand that poetry begins as an act of perception. Read along with me . . .

"So much depends upon" *noticing*, in other words—upon using our senses to appreciate the details of the world around us. For Williams, the quest for meaning begins with noticing. *Look*, he says. Stop and perceive everyday life. Take in the fact of "a red wheelbarrow glazed with rain water beside the white chickens." And then, what else can you notice?

I love two things that Williams said about poetry. The first is an admonition to other poets: "Say it—no ideas but in things." He's reminding us that specific objects and moments best reveal life and our attitudes toward it. The second quote is "Perception is the first act of the imagination." In other words, look around you; notice the physical world. This is where you'll find your voice and vision as a poet.

Let's look together at two more short, famous poems by William Carlos Williams. The first, titled "Poem," exemplifies his poetic theory: in the way his cat scales the furniture in his kitchen,

Williams sees a living poem. When I read aloud the second, "Between Walls," it might interest you to know that Williams, in addition to being a poet, was a family physician who delivered over two thousand babies in his medical career. He often "saw" poems as he made his hospital rounds, and he jotted down his perceptions on the pages of his prescription pad. I think that's where "Between Walls" might have begun.

**SOME FEATURES TO NOTICE
IN ALL THREE POEMS:**
- The simple, everyday diction
- Williams' use of strong, unadorned color words to create visuals: *red, white, green*
- How the language is cut to the bone
- How he invents a form for each poem
- How each poem consists of just one sentence
- His omission of punctuation
- The lack of figurative language; instead, direct descriptions
- Visual/sensory nouns, adjectives, and verbs
- Poetry grounded in the concrete: in observations of "things" and actions, which function as poetic snapshots

RESPONSE STANCE: Please go back into "Poem" or "Between Walls" on your own—your choice—and mark the images you can see in your mind's eye.

BENEDICTION: So "say it—no ideas but in *things*." And remember: "*Perception* is the first act of the imagination." You'll hear those two Williams quotes a lot in the next week, as we read the poems of poets who paid attention to them. To help remember Williams' theory of good poems, tonight for homework, would you please memorize "The Red Wheelbarrow"?

The Red Wheelbarrow

so much depends
upon

the red wheel
barrow

glazed with rain
water

beside the white
chickens.

— *William Carlos Williams*

Poem

As the cat
climbed over
the top of

the jamcloset
first the right
forefoot

carefully
then the hind
stepped down

into the pit of
the empty
flowerpot

— *William Carlos Williams*

Between Walls

the back wings
of the

hospital where
nothing

will grow lie
cinders

in which shine
the broken

pieces of a green
bottle

— *William Carlos Williams*

PRESENTING THE POEMS:

The Tree

&

Seasons of the School Oak

BY EBEN COURT

SETTING THE SCENE: Yesterday I told you that poetry was transformed by William Carlos Williams' idea that a poet's vision begins in actual vision: in looking at and noticing the real world. Here's a student poem—or, rather, two drafts of the same poem—that shows what I mean by transformation.

Eben was an eighth-grade poet. Read his first draft of "The Tree" with me . . .

It's not a terrible poem, but it is a general one. The problem is that the subject could be any deciduous tree anywhere. We can't see it, so we don't get much meaning from a poem about it. It's a standard, stereotyped tree.

When I talked with Eben about "The Tree," I explained that as a reader, I couldn't see this tree in my mind's eye or feel it in my heart. I made a suggestion: "You know, Eben, there's a big oak on the edge of the soccer field. I wonder what would happen if your next draft of a poem about a tree over the four seasons began with observations of our oak—if you grounded your poem in the images that a real tree brings to mind."

So Eben went outside with a clipboard and pencil, looked hard at the old oak, and took notes about the images and memories that came to him during this act of perception. The final draft of his poem is no longer about *any* tree; it's about the essence and meaning of one oak tree. Listen to "Seasons of the School Oak" . . .

SOME FEATURES TO NOTICE—"SEASONS OF THE SCHOOL OAK:—

- Specific, concrete details in each stanza, which evoke images and feelings in the reader and convey Eben's attitude toward the tree
- Strong, sensory nouns, adjectives, and adverbs
- Eben's use of unadorned color words: *green* vs. *a brilliant shade of green*; *golden* vs. *beautiful shades of red and orange*
- How he invents a form and sticks with it: a stanza for each season and seven lines per stanza

RESPONSE STANCE: Please go back into "Seasons of the School Oak" and mark the lines you can see and feel.

BENEDICTION: Say it with me: "The Red Wheelbarrow" by William Carlos Williams . . .

So much depends on noticing the qualities of *a* tree vs. general principles of treeness. As poets, try to make this distinction: *look before you write*. Recognize that perception is a way to kickstart your poet's imagination.

The Tree

In spring
your leaves start to come back
and the forest grows with color.
In summer
your leaves turn a brilliant shade of green
and your branches reach for the sky.
In fall
your leaves turn beautiful
shades of orange and red,
filling the air with color.
And then they begin to fall
slowly downwards,
making the ground
crunch beneath my feet.
In winter
all your leaves are gone.
Just skeletons live in this age.
The seasons—
they are different to a tree,
but all of them are beautiful.

—*Eben Court*

Seasons of the School Oak

In fall
the children rest under you,
backs
against your massive trunk,
books in hand,
as you drop golden leaves and acorns
and decorate what lies beneath.

In winter,
a tall skeleton
dressed in white,
you watch car pools and children
come and go,
while snow buries everything
and you wait.

In spring
your leaves fill the air
with green
as you watch the children
in the field play soccer
and everything—including you—
comes back to life.

In summer,
when the kids are gone
and the heat grows,
you enjoy the silence
while it lasts
but miss the company
of the children.

—*Eben Court*

Watermelon

BY NORA BRADFORD

SETTING THE SCENE: Nora, a seventh grader, took William Carlos Williams seriously. As a poet she looked for ideas in things. Here, she found one in the first watermelon feast of the season on her family's back deck.

SOME FEATURES TO NOTICE:
- The specific, observed details that evoke a sensory response and create the mood of summer
- Strong, sensory nouns, adjectives, and adverbs
- Nora's use of color words: *reddest, green*
- How she invents a form and sticks with it, apart from a purposeful shift in the last stanza

RESPONSE STANCE: Please go back into this sensory poem and mark the language you can *perceive*—words and phrases you can see, feel, taste. Would you also mark the diction—the choices of language—that you like and want to talk about?

BENEDICTION: Say it with me again: "The Red Wheelbarrow" . . .

For Nora, so much depends on a red slice of watermelon, its *green rind,* and a dog with *mighty jaws.* What does so much depend on for you, in your world of sight, sound, taste, touch, and smell? Go home and look, listen, taste, feel, and sniff. Take notes on your perceptions. As poets, find where *your* acts of imagination are hiding.

Watermelon

I watch Mom cut five slices,
then take the largest and reddest.
When I sink my teeth into solid juice,
the melon squirts its fireworks.

I swallow a seed—
that's one I won't spit
into the bowl
beyond the deck railing.

When I finish the delightful redness
I throw the green rind to Hobo,
who waits his turn.
He grabs the crust in his mighty jaws

and runs away
with its sweetness.

    —*Nora Bradford*

©2006 by Nancie Atwell from *Naming the World: A Year of Poems and Lessons*
(Portsmouth, NH: Heinemann)

What Came to Me

BY JANE KENYON

&

Shell

BY HARRIET BROWN

SETTING THE SCENE: Here are two more poems that show the influence of William Carlos Williams. Both are about a big idea: grief. And each focuses on what might seem to be a mundane thing—a gravy boat, a seashell—to evoke the feeling and meaning of loss.

SOME FEATURES TO NOTICE—"WHAT CAME TO ME":

- How the gravy boat and the remains of a family dinner—the "hard, brown drop of gravy"—summon up for the poet the reality of her mother's death
- How Kenyon encodes the identity of the *you* to whom she is speaking
- How the title has a double meaning: what she inherited from her mother, as well as what she recognized and acknowledged about the loss as she unpacked her inheritance
- The simple diction
- The strong visual detail
- A strong color word: *brown*

SOME FEATURES TO NOTICE—"THE SHELL":

- How the shell had become for the poet a symbol of her grief over the death of someone she loved; how the passage of time and the innocence of new life—the child who picked up the shell and left it in her pocket—erode grief

- How Brown encodes in the first stanza the identity of the *you* to whom she is speaking: her own mother or grandmother
- *The use of calcareous,* meaning *containing calcium carbonate* or lime, a shell's main ingredient
- The alliteration of *clean, calcareous curve*
- The comparison of the shape of the shell to *a palm open to nothing,* which creates an image of emptiness
- A strong color word: *orange*
- How she invents a form and sticks with it, apart from a purposeful shift in the final stanza

RESPONSE STANCE: Please go back into one of these two poems—your choice—and think about two questions as you read it. Who might be the *you* the poet's addressing? Then, what do you understand as the *so what?* or theme: what's the *idea* that's discovered in the *thing?* Write a few notes to yourself about your theory.

BENEDICTION: Again, look for the *things* of your life—the events, experiences, objects, people, and animals that signify. Write about your attitude by focusing on the imagery of the *thing.*

What Came to Me

I took the last
dusty piece of china
out of the barrel.
It was your gravy boat,
with a hard, brown
drop of gravy still
on the porcelain lip.
I grieved for you then
as I never had before.

      —Jane Kenyon

Shell

I found it in the wash, the orange
shell I picked up on the beach
that last time. One of my girls—
the one named after you—

must have found it in my room
and wanted it. Clean calcareous
curve, a palm open to nothing,
reeking of sunshine

and your death. For years
I didn't know what to do with it.
You would have liked
this story: how a child

slips grief into a careless pocket.
Breaks it to pieces. Lets it go.

      —Harriet Brown

PRESENTING THE POEM:

Puddle

BY SIOBHAN ANDERSON

SETTING THE SCENE: After a summer thunderstorm, have you ever noticed your reflection in a puddle? Siobhan (Shuh-VON), an eighth grader, did. Her perception became an opportunity to consider herself—to wonder who she is—from a new perspective.

SOME FEATURES TO NOTICE:
- The strong imagery
- The strong verbs and nouns
- Siobhan's *tone* or mood: contemplative and pensive
- The double meaning of the last line: she recognizes in the reflection of a blue sky her own blue mood

RESPONSE STANCE: Please go back into this thoughtful poem on your own and mark the lines you want to talk about.

BENEDICTION: A poem like this one is especially important for poets your age, when one of your jobs is to figure out who you are. Siobhan's poem about her identity was triggered by a rain puddle. What *thing* will trigger your poem about you? Keep looking.

Puddle

A drop of sky falls to the earth
and nestles among the slopes of the asphalt.
I trace my finger through the clouds
and along the ridged mark
a bicycle made.
Sun pours color
into this one place

and my world is caught in the crystal
between light
and water.

My toes send ripples
that touch the reflection
of a jet winding along.
I wonder:
how many faces tilt toward the ground
to watch a plane pass overhead?

I stare at someone who is not yet me,
a girl with clouds among her fingers,
leaves near her lips,
airplanes in her hair,
gardens over her shoulders.

And all she sees

is blue.

—*Siobhan Anderson*

©2006 by Nancie Atwell from *Naming the World: A Year of Poems and Lessons*
(Portsmouth, NH: Heinemann)

The Bowl

BY CARL JOHANSON

&

Seven in the Morning

BY ZOË MASON

SETTING THE SCENE: Yesterday we saw how Siobhan wrote about her sense of herself by focusing on her reflection in a puddle. Today we'll look at how two eighth graders wrote about their relationships with their moms by finding ideas in things. Carl focused on the bowl his mother used for whipping cream; Zoë centered her poem on the braids her mother plaits into her hair every morning.

SOME FEATURES TO NOTICE—"THE BOWL":
- How the poem begins inside the experience
- How Carl encodes the identity of the *you* to whom he is speaking
- The sensory details
- The specific, strong nouns (*shards*, *tile*) and verbs (*crashes*, *seep*)
- A strong color word: *red*
- How the repetition of the word *your* builds and emphasizes the significance of the bowl
- How the last line implies Carl's sense of regret: there is nothing else to do but sweep it up; there are no words

SOME FEATURES TO NOTICE—"SEVEN IN THE MORNING":
- How describing this ritual becomes a vehicle for Zoë to express her love for and appreciation of her mother
- How Zoë encodes the identity of the *you* to whom she is speaking

- The strong, sensory diction: *six slices of thick curl*
- The strong figurative language: *I'm cradled in my own hair,/ a nest you've made for me*
- How the language of the poem repeats and winds in and out, like a braid
- How Zoë invents a form and sticks with it

RESPONSE STANCE: Please go back into one of these sensory poems—your choice—and mark the lines that evoke a feeling in you. Would you also mark any other lines you like and want to talk about?

BENEDICTION: Poems like these, that begin in a concrete experience, are the best vehicle to show your feelings. Look for the experiences—the isolated moments as well as the traditions and rituals—that capture your relationships with your mom, dad, siblings, friends.

The Bowl

In a second
it leaves my clumsy fingers
and crashes to the floor.
You turn at the sound
to find shards of the little red bowl
scattered across the tile.
I look up from the remains
and watch sadness seep
into your face.
And then I realize:
to me it was the whipped cream bowl,
to you it was a bowl of memories,
a tie to your childhood, your children,
your own mother.
I look down at the pieces
of a life
lying in front of me.
Then I turn
to get
the broom.

—*Carl Johanson*

©2006 by Nancie Atwell from *Naming the World: A Year of Poems and Lessons*
(Portsmouth, NH: Heinemann)

Seven in the Morning

When you braided my hair
and only we two knew the ups and downs—this morning
it was worth the laughter for the day.
What's the pleasure you take in these tasks for me?

When I'm older I'll understand.

This morning
you did the part for you, I did the part for me—
as always—followed by the six slices of thick curl. Our day
has begun on a note of good hair—

and for you, I'm beginning to understand.

I'm cradled in my own hair,
a nest you've made for me.
The ends are frayed and sudden to the flow and the morning.
Time winds the tassels together. The day—

which I'm beginning to understand—

is one thick ringlet of love frayed and joined again and again for me—
for you. The tassels forgive and forget, day
after day. This morning
I was in such a rush, I forget to thank you for everything,

but especially for braiding my hair.

    —Zoë Mason

Poems that begin in a concrete experience are the best vehicle to show your feelings.

PRESENTING THE POEM:

Deer Print

BY BENJAMIN F. WILLIAMS

SETTING THE SCENE: Ben, a seventh grader, wrote a poem about something he *didn't* see. Because he uses such sensory language to invent such concrete details, we get to see what he didn't. More importantly, we get to feel what Ben felt.

SOME FEATURES TO NOTICE:
- The strong, sensory nouns, verbs, and adjectives
- The use of alliteration (*marvel . . . muddy; steam streaming*)
- The visual imagery
- How the poem moves in a circle: it begins with Ben spying the two-toed hoof print and ends with him imagining the deer making the print as she bounds away
- A strong color word: *brown*

RESPONSE STANCE: Please go back into this sensory poem and mark the phrases and lines you can see, and the ones you like, too.

BENEDICTION: Poems like Ben's are the best nature poems. They begin with a real observation of, or experience with, the natural world, then respond to it in a personal way. Get yourself outside, into whatever nature is available to you, and open your senses. Can you notice a poem?

Deer Print

A soft indentation—
two toes—
marks the ground,
a blank reminder
of what has been here before me.
I try to feel amazed,
to marvel at this muddy imprint,
to feel lucky at my chance notice—
but I want to see the deer,
steam streaming from her nostrils
as she stares at me,
thin legs threatening
to give way,
small brown head
trembling in the cold.
I want to see her bound away,
her tail high in the air,
her two-toed hooves
marking the ground.

—*Benjamin F. Williams*

PRESENTING THE POEM:

The Swingset

BY GRACE WALTON

SETTING THE SCENE: Some of the most evocative poems that are grounded in things describe moments and objects from a poet's childhood. The particular images of a toy or stuffie, a game or storybook, summon up who the poet was—and who she is now, too. For Grace, a seventh grader, the thing that measured the distance between her childhood and right now was her swingset.

SOME FEATURES TO NOTICE:
- How Grace uses the swingset to represent her attitude toward growing up
- The specificity of the swingset memories that Grace describes
- The simple, strong noun-verb combinations of the first four lines
- The strength of the verbs: *cease, sulk, preen, shed, cart away, shredded*

RESPONSE STANCE: Please go back into Grace's poem and mark the lines you *get*—the lines where you understand or recognize what she's feeling and writing about. And mark anything else you like and want to talk about, too.

BENEDICTION: Again, what are your *things?* Or, in this case, what *were* they? What's the one thing that will help you measure the distance between who you were and who you're becoming? Go home tonight and look for your version of the swingset.

The Swingset

Wood rots,
ropes fray,
metal rusts,

memories stay.

It stands there
deserted in the midst
of many times climbed
and swung from.

Sometimes it was a ship
escaping from the storm.
Other times, many times,
it was the Saab convertible a friend and I
drove to McDonald's.

Now years of playing cease.
It's just the goal for flashlight tag,
where people sulk after losing
or
preen after winning.

At times I want to shed
my childhood,
but somehow I can't cart it away
to the dump, where
swingsets are shredded, where
times past
can't ever
return.

—*Grace Walton*

©2006 by Nancie Atwell from *Naming the World: A Year of Poems and Lessons*
(Portsmouth, NH: Heinemann)

This collec

the poetry al

other physic

both boy an

liked best, bu

boys were m

Games:
INTRODUCTION

This collection represents the poetry about sports and other activities that both boy and girl students liked best, but I confess that boys were my target audience as I searched for these poems. Jocks, too, need to know that they can find their feelings and experiences spoken for in poetry, and that their own poems are a way for them to consider and name the satisfactions of movement, speed, power, competition, and fandom, as well as the heartaches of the sporting life.

PRESENTING THE POEM:

First Love

BY CARL LINDER

SETTING THE STAGE: At recess I watch you out front, playing four square or shooting hoops, and I know you've learned how to read every crack and ripple in that patch of asphalt. I think lots of kids have similar patches of asphalt. Carl Linder wrote a poem about his.

SOME FEATURES TO NOTICE:

- How the diction is specific to the sport—it's the language of basketball—and gives the poem its authority
- The strong verbs
- How the title, the last line, and the verbs combine to make this a love poem

RESPONSE STANCE: Please go back into "First Love" on your own and consider two questions: How does the title fit the poem? How does the title connect with the poem's conclusion? Write a few notes for yourself.

BENEDICTION: As people who exist in that timeframe known as *before sixteen,* you have your own first loves—each of you—that isn't a boy or a girl. Think about the poem you've yet to write about your own first source of excitement and self-confidence and comfort and love.

First Love

Before sixteen
I was fast
enough to fake
my shadow out
and I could read
every crack and ripple
in that patch of asphalt.
I owned
the slanted rim
knew
the dead spot in the backboard.
Always the ball
came back.

Every day I loved
to sharpen
my shooting eye,
waiting
for the touch.
Set shot, jump shot,
layup, hook—
after a while
I could feel
the ball hunger-
ing to clear
the lip of the rim,
the two of us
falling through.

> —Carl Linder

PRESENTING THE POEMS:

Six Minutes Twenty-Six Seconds

BY JAMES MORRILL

&

Speed

BY DAVID MACDONALD

SETTING THE STAGE: In today's poems, two seventh-grade boys take us along with them as they push their bodies to the limit and craft poems that mimic their physical exertions.

SOME FEATURES TO NOTICE:

- How short lines make the poems move fast and mimic the action and/or feeling being described
- How the omission of unnecessary words (e.g., pronouns) helps the poems pick up speed
- How present-tense verbs help make the action immediate
- How the stanza breaks divide the action into phases or stages
- How Jim's use of repetition mimics hard breathing

RESPONSE STANCE: Please go back into one of these two workouts of a poem—your choice—and mark what the poet did to make the poem *move,* to make it feel like bike-jumping or long-distance running.

BENEDICTION: This is something you could try as a poet—an interior monologue about what it feels like when you jog, dance, come up to bat, make a lay-up, intercept a pass, dribble the soccer ball down the field, you name it. Put your reader inside your mind and body *in the moment.*

Six Minutes
Twenty-Six Seconds

Throat scorched.
Chest burning.
Fast jogging.
Keep up, keep up—
two hundred
meters behind.

Breath fast.
Breath shallow.
I'm short distance.
Thought
I was on a roll:
beat my time
in hurdles,
beat my height
in high jump.

Last lap.
Breath fire.
Finish hard.
Last to cross
but get my time.

Win.

—James Morrill

Speed

0 MPH

I mount my bike.
Both feet hit the pedals at once
as I launch myself forward
and shoot down the steep hill.
5 MPH

Lean forward.
Pedal harder.
15 MPH
Wind hits my face,
and my eyes blur.

25 MPH

Then 30.

I hit the first jump.
My wheels leave the ground behind
as I fly through the air

for two seconds

before I'm jolted
by a rough landing
back to Earth.
The excitement ends
when I stand on the brakes
and skid to a stop.

0 MPH

—David MacDonald

The Double Play

BY ROBERT WALLACE

SETTING THE STAGE: This is one of the greatest poems ever about baseball. It moves on the page like a classic double play: all the action takes place almost at once, and Robert Wallace imitates it with form and language.

SOME FEATURES TO NOTICE:
- How this poem needs to be read fast and with familiarity: how the abrupt shifts from object to subject mimic the almost simultaneous action on the field, and how the last two stanzas slow down the action by reverting to conventional grammar
- The similes
- The visual verbs
- The sensory details
- The two main metaphors: the double play is a *dance;* afterwards, it is a *poem*

RESPONSE STANCE: Please go back into "The Double-Play" and mark what you like and want to talk about.

BENEDICTION: As a fan or as an athlete yourself, what's a moment in the action you'd like to capture and reinterpret as a dance, as a battle, as a conversation, as a poem?

The Double Play

In his sea-lit
distance, the pitcher winding
like a clock about to chime comes down with

the ball, hit
sharply, under the artificial
banks of arc lights, bounds like a vanishing string

over the green
to the shortstop magically
scoops to his right whirling above his invisible

shadows
in the dust redirects
its flight to the running poised second baseman

pirouettes
leaping, above the slide, to throw
from mid-air, across the color tightened interval,

to the leaning-
out first baseman ends the dance
drawing it disappearing into his long brown glove

stretches. What
is too swift for deception
is final, lost, among the loosened figures

jogging off the field
(the pitcher walks), casual
in the space where the poem has happened.

    —Robert Wallace

PRESENTING THE POEM:

A Sestina for Michael Jordan

BY JAY SPOON

SETTING THE STAGE: Fans write some of the great poems about sports. Jay, an eighth grader, loved pro-basketball great Michael Jordan. The first—of several—times that Jordan retired, Jay captured his feelings in a sestina. A sestina is a repeating poem that's based on six: six words end each of the six lines in the first six stanzas in a set order, followed by an envoy of three lines, each of which includes two of the six words. You'll see what I mean. The six words Jay chose for his fan poem were *Michael*, *GAME*, *game*, *shoes*, *dunks*, and *moves*.

SOME FEATURES TO NOTICE:
- The sestina form
- How Jay works, mostly successfully, to say something slightly different in each stanza
- How a form that uses repetition suits the purpose and subject of the poem: a fan's praise— and lament—for Michael Jordan

RESPONSE STANCE: Please go back into Jay's sestina and mark the words, phrases, and lines that you like. And when you're done, see if you can figure out the form—the order of the six end words in each stanza.

BENEDICTION: Here are two new possibilities for you as poets: maybe a sestina? maybe a fan poem, instead of a fan letter, about an athlete you admire?

A Sestina for Michael Jordan

The NBA wasn't the same without Michael.
What was THE GAME
Became just a game.
I missed watching him in his hundred dollar shoes
Do his million dollar dunks
After pulling some of his million dollar moves.

Other people tried the same moves,
But they couldn't make them as smoothly as Michael.
They tried to copy his dunks,
To make it more of a GAME.
Some of them even wore his shoes.
But without him it was always, only, a game.

It got boring just watching a game,
Even if there were a few good moves,
And someone was wearing some really nice shoes.
In our hearts the fans knew that without Michael
There would never be a great GAME—
Just lay-ups and shots from outside, but no great dunks.

Sure, they all tried to do powerful dunks,
But they could never make it more than a game.
The only event that would make it a GAME
Again were the magnificent moves
Of the fabulous Michael—
With or without his overpriced shoes.

Some say it was the shoes,
And some say it was the dunks,
But everyone loved to watch Michael.
Coaches don't like coaching a game.
They want steals, dunks, exciting moves—
They want a GAME.

The only way it could ever be a GAME
Again was him, wearing his hundred dollar shoes,
Pulling his million dollar moves,
Then going up for his million dollar dunks.
Without him on the starting five it was an amateur's game.
The playoffs, the steals, the fouls were nothing without Michael.

The plain truth is that before Michael there was no GAME.
It was just a predictable game played in boring shoes.
I'm relieved to have him back; I missed those dunks and moves.

—Jay Spoon

PRESENTING THE POEM:

Execution

BY EDWARD HIRSCH

SETTING THE STAGE: In this poem, Edward Hirsch tells us about a great high school football coach—his old coach—and the man's favorite word, *execution*, by which the coach means, to accomplish a play according to the plan. But *execution* has other meanings, too.

SOME FEATURES TO NOTICE:
- The visual similes and metaphors
- The precise and sensory diction
- The double meaning of *execute:* to achieve, but also to kill
- How the poet's high school team tried to execute their coach's plan; how the downstate team executed *them;* how cancer is executing a coach who seemed, back then, to be larger than life

RESPONSE STANCE: Please go back into "Execution" and mark the words and lines you think are strong and that you want to talk about.

BENEDICTION: Sometimes, as athletes, the people you play with or the coaches you play for are a story waiting for someone to tell. *You* could tell the story, as a poem.

Execution

The last time I saw my high school football coach
He had cancer stenciled into his face
Like pencil marks from the sun, like intricate
Drawings on the chalkboard, small x's and o's
That he copied down in a neat numerical hand
Before practice in the morning. By day's end
The board was a spiderweb of options and counters,
Blasts and sweeps, a constellation of players
Shining under his favorite word, *Execution,*
Underlined in the upper right-hand corner of things.
He believed in football like a new religion
And had perfect unquestioning faith in the fundamentals
Of blocking and tackling, the idea of warfare
Without suffering or death, the concept of teammates
Moving in harmony like the planets—and yet
Our awkward adolescent bodies were always canceling
The flawless beauty of Saturday afternoons in September,
Falling away from the particular grace of autumn,
The clear weather, the ideal game he imagined.
And so he drove us through punishing drills
On weekday afternoons, and doubled our practice time,
And challenged us to hammer him with forearms,
And devised elaborate, last-second plays—a flea-
Flicker, a triple reverse—to save us from defeat.
Almost always they worked. He despised losing
And loved winning more than his own body, maybe even
More than himself. But the last time I saw him
He looked wobbly and stunned by illness,
And I remembered the game in my senior year
When we met a downstate team who loved hitting
More than we did, who battered us all afternoon
With a vengeance, who destroyed us with timing
And power, with deadly, impersonal authority,
Machine-like fury, perfect execution.

—*Edward Hirsch*

Elegy for a Diver

BY PETER MEINKE

SETTING THE STAGE: This is the best-loved poem about an athlete I've ever taught. It is gorgeous, heartbreaking, and haunting. In "Elegy for a Diver," Peter Meinke sings to an athlete whose body had betrayed him, as all bodies must.

SOME FEATURES TO NOTICE:

- The poem's structure: Part I describes the diver in life; the italics of Part II describe the poet's vision of the diver in death
- How the vocabulary of diving—*jackknife swandive gainer twist*—gives the poem its authority
- How the repetition of that phrase in each stanza in Part I stresses the diver's skill, then his loss of skill
- The strict, but different, meaning-driven, and natural-sounding rhyme schemes in Part I and Part II
- The allusions to the story of William Tell and the myth of Icarus and Daedalus
- The gorgeous diction
- The powerful figurative language
- How the poet addresses the elegy to the diver, to a *you*

RESPONSE STANCE: Please go back into "Elegy for a Diver" and mark everything that Peter Meinke did here as a poet that knocks you out.

BENEDICTION: Some of your own experiences with sports or sports fandom may have had an edge to them—a sense of what happens when the body can't do what an athlete wants it to. These are poems, too.

Elegy for a Diver

I

Jackknife swandive gainer twist
high off the board you'd pierce the sky
& split the apple of the devil sun
& spit in the sun's fierce eye.
When you were young you never missed,
archer-diver who flew too high
so everything later became undone.

Later everything burned to ash
wings too close to the sun broke down
jackknife swandive gainer twist
can't be done on the ground
and nothing in your diver's past
had warned you that a diver drowns
when nothing replaces what is missed.

Everything beautiful falls away
jackknife swandive gainer twist
muscles drop and skin turns coarse
even the skin the sun has kissed.
You drank the sun down every day
until the sun no longer existed
and only the drink had any force.

Only the drink had any force
archer-diver who flew too high
when you were young you never missed
& spit in the sun's fierce eye.
Later everything burned to ash:
everything beautiful falls away
even the skin the sun has kissed
jackknife swandive gainer & twist

II

and now I see your bones in dreams
turning and twisting below our feet
fingerbones bending out like wings
as once again your body sings
swandiving through the stone
that sparks your skull and shoulder bones
layer by layer and over and over
you flash through the limestone sand & lava
feet together and backbone arched
like an arrow aimed at the devil's heart
the dead are watching your perfect dive
clicking their fingers as if alive
high off the board & the hell with the chances
once again your body dances
anything done well shines forever
only polished by death's dark weather
diver diver diving still
now & forever I praise your skill

—*Peter Meinke*

To an Athlete Dying Young

BY A. E. HOUSMAN

SETTING THE STAGE: A. E. Housman (1859–1936) was an English writer and scholar whose most famous book was *A Shropshire Lad*. This is a collection of poems that are set in the British countryside and tell stories about the local people, often in the voice of one of them—a farm boy or a soldier. The language is nineteenth century, so this poem is going to be a little more difficult than what we're used to. But it's worth it. This is one of Housman's saddest and most famous poems. Here, a local man tells us about the fastest runner in his town, the young champion in the county competition who won for them the long-distance race and the challenge cup, and who is, suddenly, inexplicably, dead.

SOME FEATURES TO NOTICE — VOCABULARY:

- **chaired:** placed or seated in a chair and carried aloft by others in celebration (vs. later, when the runner is carried aloft *shoulder high* in a coffin)
- **betimes:** early
- **laurel:** the foliage of the laurel tree, an emblem of athletic victory
- **rout:** a group of defeated people
- **renown:** fame
- **sill of shade:** the doorstep of the abode of the dead, i.e., the grave
- **low lintel:** the top of the entrance to the grave
- **still-defended:** the championship hasn't yet been challenged in another race
- **garland:** the crown of laurel
- **briefer:** worn for a short duration
- **girl:** child (Middle English)

RESPONSE STANCE: Please go back into this difficult poem on your own and mark the lines and words you want to talk about because they confuse you and you want to understand them.

BENEDICTION: In "Elegy for a Diver," Peter Meinke spoke to an old athlete whose body had outlived his athletic skill. Housman spoke to a young athlete who died in his prime. Both poets show us that there's more to sports than wins and losses—that there are ideas and dreams and ironies to consider, too.

To an Athlete Dying Young

The time you won your town the race
We chaired you through the market-place;
Man and boy stood cheering by,
And home we brought you shoulder-high.

Today, the road all runners come,
Shoulder-high we bring you home,
And set you at your threshold down,
Townsman of a stiller town.

Smart lad, to slip betimes away
From fields where glory does not stay,
And early though the laurel grows
It withers quicker than the rose.

Eyes the shady night has shut
Cannot see the record cut,
And silence sounds no worse than cheers
After earth has stopped the ears:

Now you will not swell the rout
Of lads that wore their honors out,
Runners whom renown outran
And the name died before the man.

So set, before its echoes fade,
The fleet foot on the sill of shade,
And hold to the low lintel up
The still-defended challenge-cup.

And round that early-laureled head
Will flock to gaze the strengthless dead,
And find unwithered on its curls
The garland briefer than a girl's.

    —A. E. Housman

PRESENTING THE POEM:

Ping-Pong Alfresco

BY CAMERON BLAKE

SETTING THE STAGE: This poem reminds me of times when I was a kid, when we wanted to play a game and didn't have the equipment, so we made do—like the baseball games we played with a hunk of tree limb and an apple, with piles of stones as bases. Cameron, a seventh grader, and his little brother found a couple of old paddles and wanted to play table tennis. So they improvised.

SOME FEATURES TO NOTICE:
- The visual details
- Cam's use of repetition—of *paddle* in the first stanza, *two* in the second, and *one* in the third—to create a cadence
- His use of assonance (e.g., *creates crazy ricochets as we play)*
- How separating the last line as a stanza gives it emphasis
- *Alfresco* means out-of-doors
- *Ping-Pong* is capitalized and hyphenated because it's a trademark

RESPONSE STANCE: Please go back into "Ping-Pong Alfresco" and mark the lines you can see, plus anything else Cam did here as a poet that you like.

BENEDICTION: Your poems about competing with others don't have to be about the day you suited up for The Big Game. Look for your own everyday moments: Monopoly tournaments, games of four square on the playground, times you shot hoops with a friend.

Ping-Pong Alfresco

I grab my paddle
and slam out the door.
My brother and I take our sides
and prepare for the match.
To see who serves,
I spin the paddle—
the paddle with electrical tape
wrapped around the handle,
the paddle covered
with scrapes and tears
from various "incidents."

I serve the ball
over the wooden net
and onto the grooved table
fashioned from
two sawhorses
and two old doors
we found behind the house,
which creates crazy ricochets
as we play.

I wait for a real
Ping-Pong table,
one with a reliable surface
and soft net,
one with official lines
and even sides,
one that's actually green.
But until then

this one's perfect.
             —Cameron Blake

©2006 by Nancie Atwell from *Naming the World: A Year of Poems and Lessons* (Portsmouth, NH: Heinemann)

PRESENTING THE POEM:

What's Not to Like?

BY MICHAEL CONLEY CARTER

SETTING THE STAGE: I asked for this poem when I announced in class one day that I hated board games, especially Monopoly. Lots of students agreed with me, about Monopoly anyway, but Michael rose to its defense with a poem.

SOME FEATURES TO NOTICE:
- The humor
- The diction: the word choices, tone, and voice are those of an enthusiastic kid
- The effective use of repetition
- The strong conclusion
- The form Michael invented: opening and closing stanzas of four lines, with three-line stanzas otherwise

RESPONSE STANCE: Please go back into Michael's diatribe and mark the lines and language that ring true for you as someone who has played a board game.

BENEDICTION: So, what's your game? Uno? Clue? Cranium? Chess? Poker? Scrabble? Boggle? *Twister?* Is there a poem in you about its rituals, challenges, and pleasures?

What's Not to Like?

I don't get it.
Almost everyone I know
hates Monopoly.
What's not to like?

I love the cool
metallic figures.
The race car is mine.

You can buy property,
just like real life.
I buy the orange squares.

You can go to jail and get out,
trespass on other people's land,
buy houses and even hotels.

And you use real money!
Well, it looks real at least.
Sorta.

But the best part is the end,
when the game's over
and one player has it all:

all the property,
all the money,
all the houses and hotels—

and he's spewing out insults
like a broken brag machine.
That's when the magic happens.

Because even if
you're one of the losers,
you didn't lose a thing.

In real life, you didn't spend a penny.
And that braying millionaire
across from you?
He didn't gain a thing, either.

 —*Michael Conley Carter*

Mystery Baseball

BY PHILIP DACEY

SETTING THE STAGE: The first and second times I read this poem, I didn't know what to make of it. Finally I understood: Philip Dacey had crossed two genres, pro baseball and mystery stories, and come up with "Mystery Baseball."

SOME FEATURES TO NOTICE:

- How each stanza tells the story of a different mysterious person or event
- The humor, as some of the mysteries "explain" conventions of baseball, like why a batter strikes out or why players *pull at the bills of their caps.*

RESPONSE STANCE: Please go back into "Mystery Baseball" and mark your favorite stanza/mystery.

BENEDICTION: Think about it: if a poet can cross mystery and baseball, what genres could you cross, as a sports fan and a poet? Mystery and basketball? Soap opera and baseball? Fairy tales and football? What else is a possibility?

Mystery Baseball

No one knows the man who throws out the season's first ball.
   His face has never appeared in the newspapers,
      except in crowd scenes, blurred.
   Asked his name, he mumbles something
      about loneliness,
      about the beginnings of hard times.

Each team fields an extra player, tenth man.
   This is the invisible player,
      assigned to no particular position.
   Runners edging off base feel a tap on their shoulders,
      turn, see no one.
   Or a batter, the count against him, will hear whispered
      in his ear vague, dark
      rumors of his wife, and go down.

Vendors move through the stands
   selling unmarked sacks,
   never disclosing their contents,
   never having been told.
   People buy, hoping.

Pitchers stay busy
   getting signs.
   They are everywhere.

One man rounds third base, pumping hard,
   and is never seen again.
   Teammates and relatives wait years at the plate,
      uneasy, fearful.

An outfielder goes for a ball on the warning track.
   He leaps into the air and keeps rising,
      beyond himself, past
      the limp flag.
   Days later he is discovered,
      descended, wandering dazed
      in centerfield.

Deep under second base lives an old man,
   bearded, said to be
   a hundred. All through the game,
   players pull at the bills of their caps,
   acknowledging him.

   —*Philip Dacey*

This is ano

poems with

but it's deep

Almost every

had—a pet h

—a soulmate

Dogs & Cats:

INTRODUCTION

This is another group of poems with broad appeal, but it's deep appeal, too. Almost every kid has—or had—a pet he or she adores, a soulmate who listens, loves, comforts, entertains, and never judges. These are the easiest and most relevant love poems for my middle school students to read and to write.

PRESENTING THE POEMS:

Dharma

BY BILLY COLLINS

&

Man and Dog

BY SIEGFRIED SASSOON

SETTING THE STAGE: Poets, like just about every human on the face of the earth, love their pets. I've collected hundreds of poems about cats and dogs, and I've written a few, about my springer spaniels. It's easy to fall in love with a pet, and it's satisfying, fun, and easy to write a love poem about that relationship.

We'll start with two love poems to dogs. The first was written a few years ago by Billy Collins, an American and our former poet laureate. The second, by the British poet Siegfried Sassoon, is almost a hundred years old. The voices, styles, sentiments, and techniques are worlds apart, but the subjects are the same: a dog and his man.

It'll be helpful to you to know that Dharma isn't the name of Billy Collins' dog. *Dharma* is a word from Sanskrit that means someone's essential spiritual state. At a reading, Collins introduced the poem by saying it was an attempt "to investigate the spiritual possibilities of this creature," his dog.

SOME FEATURES TO NOTICE—"DHARMA":
- The humor
- Collins' use of metaphor: *the saucer of my heart*
- His ironical attempt to compare the dog's virtue with that of Thoreau and Gandhi
- The visual imagery and color words
- The amused, wry, detached tone: a contemporary voice that observes his dog from a sardonic distance
- The way the tone shifts in the last stanza, with the list of "if onlys"

SOME FEATURES TO NOTICE—"MAN AND DOG":
- The conventional form: four-line stanzas of rhyming couplets
- The simple, elemental diction, which suggests the simple, elemental relationship between man and dog
- The *we* voice, the tone of devotion, and the theme of loyalty: here, man and dog are one

RESPONSE STANCE: Please go back into one of these two poems—your choice—and mark the lines you like, the language and perspectives that appeal to you.

BENEDICTION: Think about your attitude, as a poet, toward your dog or cat. Are you an observer, like Collins? A partner, like Sassoon? Or sometimes one and sometimes the other?

Dharma

The way the dog trots out the front door
every morning
without a hat or an umbrella,
without any money
or the keys to her doghouse
never fails to fill the saucer of my heart
with milky admiration.

Who provides a finer example
of a life without encumbrance—
Thoreau in his curtainless hut
with a single plate, a single spoon?
Ghandi with his staff and his holy diapers?

Off she goes into the material world
with nothing but her brown coat
and her modest blue collar,
following only her wet nose,
the twin portals of her steady breathing,
followed only by the plume of her tail.

If only she did not shove the cat aside
every morning
and eat all his food
what a model of self-containment she would be,
what a paragon of earthly detachment.
If only she were not so eager
for a rub behind the ears,
so acrobatic in her welcomes,
if only I were not her god.

—*Billy Collins*

"Dharma," ©2001 Billy Collins

Man and Dog

Who's this—alone with stone and sky?
It's only my old dog and I—
It's only him; it's only me;
Alone with stone and grass and tree.

What share we most—we two together?
Smells, and awareness of the weather.
What is it makes us more than dust?
My trust in him; in me his trust.

Here's anyhow one decent thing
That life to man and dog can bring;
One decent thing, remultiplied
Till earth's last dog and man have died.

—*Siegfried Sassoon*

   "Man and Dog," by Siegfried Sassoon, ©1957 by the Viking Press

Are you an observer like Collins? A partner, like Sassoon?

PRESENTING THE POEMS:

Love That Cat

BY MICHAEL STOLTZ

&

Cat Smile

BY NIALL JANNEY

SETTING THE STAGE: Today's poems are about cat comfort. Two macho, seventh-grade guys—one a skateboarder and heavy metal guitarist, the other a champion swimmer—recognize the pleasure and the solace to be found in feline companionship.

SOME FEATURES TO NOTICE—"LOVE THAT CAT":

- How the poem is about a particular experience with a particular cat
- The sensory details, visual imagery, and color words
- The alliteration: *curls up on the corner/ of a creamy couch*
- The line breaks that create emphases
- The strong, visual verbs: *curls up, stretch, arching, slips, tiptoes, wait, stare, leaps, hinting*

SOME FEATURES TO NOTICE—"CAT SMILE":

- How the poem is about a particular experience with a particular cat
- The poet's shift in tone, from oppressed to relieved
- The use of figurative language: a day *littered with bad luck*
- How breaking the last two lines as two stanzas mimics the action of a cloud drifting away

RESPONSE STANCE: Please go back into these two short poems and mark what Michael and Niall did here, as poets and pet lovers, that you can appreciate.

BENEDICTION: As poets, look for *particular* moments with your cat or dog. These are the poems that will reveal who your pet is and what your relationship is like.

Love That Cat

Velvet-black fur
curls up in the corner
of a creamy couch.
White tipped paws
stretch
past white tipped whiskers.
Arching his back,
he slips off the cushion
and tiptoes
across the wooden floor
to where I wait.
Glowing eyes stare into mine
before he leaps to my chest,
hinting,
until I stroke his soft coat.
He purrs his love
for me.
I pet my love
for him.

   —Michael Stoltz

Cat Smile

My mood is not good:
tired, frustrated, angry.
The day has been hard and saddening,
littered with bad luck and shame.

I collapse on the couch with a sigh
beside my sleeping cat.
She wakes, yawns, stares at me expectantly.
I scratch her ears; she smiles with pleasure.

The cloud that has hung over me

drifts away.

   —Niall Janney

Dog in Bed
BY JOYCE SIDMAN

&

Primetime
BY TESS MCKECHNIE

&

A Reason for Black
BY LINCOLN BLISS

SETTING THE STAGE: In today's poems, two dog lovers and a cat lover use figurative language to tell us about their pets. They write about a dog in bed, a cat on the prowl, and a black Lab in the nighttime as if they're something other than dogs or cats, in order to show us the essential natures of their pets, as well as their own feelings. And it works, beautifully.

SOME FEATURES TO NOTICE:
- The strong, sensory verbs
- The visual details and descriptions
- The metaphors: *planet; movie star; tuxedoed; coat of bright obsidian; inky suit; ocean of soft stealth*
- The similes: *black silk ears/ feel like happiness; black like sweet licorice,/ the shiny polish on the shoe,/ the velvet curtain*

- The personifications: *love . . . steps in gently; James Bond; handsome face; manicured paws; night that captures/ with its cold embrace*

RESPONSE STANCE: Please go back into these three poems and mark your favorite figurative language—the best comparisons—and your favorite descriptions, too.

BENEDICTION: So here's another technique you can try. Watch your cat or dog. What is he or she *like?* What else? And what else?

Dog in Bed

Nose tucked under tail,
you are a warm, furred planet
centered in my bed.
All night I orbit, tangle-limbed,
in the slim space
allotted to me.

If I accidentally
bump you from sleep,
you shift, groan,
drape your chin on my hip.

O, that languid, movie-star drape!
I can never resist it.
Digging my fingers into your fur,
kneading,
        I wonder:
How do you dream?
What do you adore?
Why should your black silk ears
feel like happiness?

This is how it is with love.
Once invited,
it steps in gently,
circles twice,
and takes up as much space
as you will give it.

        —*Joyce Sidman*

"Dog in Bed," ©2003 by Joyce Sidman

Primetime

Through the black
my midnight marauder lurks,
darts,
strolls idly,
slinks through moonstruck patches
into darkness,
to the beat of his Pink Panther
soundtrack.

He is the white-whiskered James Bond,
tuxedoed to the max.
His inky suit glints
with moonshine,
transforms his coat
to bright obsidian.
Glowing green orbs
scour the world.
He creeps while he can.

In morning
his adventures cease.
He'll rest his handsome face
in manicured paws
while the missions of nighttime
pass through his dreams,
until pitch blackness spreads
itself through the air again
and he disappears into dark.

–*Tess McKechnie*

©2006 by Nancie Atwell from *Naming the World: A Year of Poems and Lessons*
(Portsmouth, NH: Heinemann)

A Reason for Black

His tail wags furiously
through the night,
black against black.
The silky, inky appendage
flits in and out of vision—
an ocean of soft stealth.

I love the black.

The click of claws against tar
bounces around my pitch surroundings,
sparking light
in the dark.

I love the black,

not deep night that captures
with its cold embrace.
I love the black sheen of glossy fur.
I love his black like sweet licorice,
the shiny polish on the shoe,
the velvet curtain
that separates the audience from the actors.

I love the black.

—*Lincoln Bliss*

PRESENTING THE POEMS:

Cat

BY J. R. R. TOLKIEN

&

Dogs

BY MARY OLIVER

SETTING THE STAGE: Today's poems consider the essential natures of the two major domestic pets. We humans anthropomorphize our dogs and cats—we give them our feelings and needs and reactions. But underneath, in their ancestries, in their blood, our dogs and cats are beasts. In two very different styles and voices, the contemporary American poet Mary Oliver and J. R. R. Tolkien, British author of *The Lord of the Rings*, remind us of the genealogy of our darling dogs and our cuddly cats.

SOME FEATURES TO NOTICE—"CAT":

- The tight rhyme scheme
- The internal rhymes within lines
- *Pard* means a leopard or panther in Middle English
- How Tolkien imagines the tamed house cat's inner life: how the pet "walks in thought" and recalls his kin, the lion and the leopard, hunting and killing prey, including humans

SOME FEATURES TO NOTICE—"DOGS":

- The form: stanzas of unrhymed couplets
- The strong, sensory verbs: *screaming, lunging, buckling, leaped, plunged, tearing, clambered,* etc.
- How, stanza by stanza, Oliver tells the story of her dogs chasing the deer, then, in the final five stanzas, brings meaning to her observations: in the dogs' eyes, she sees everything she loves about them *and* everything about them, nature, and the world that is vicious, brutal, and hopeless

RESPONSE STANCE: Please go back into one of these poems on your own—your choice—and mark what you think are the most important lines in the poem. Would you also underline any words, phrases, and lines that struck you and that you want to talk about?

BENEDICTION: I adore my cuddly, stuffie toy of a spaniel dog, but I've also seen her pick up another, smaller dog by the throat and try to break its neck. Sometimes loving a pet isn't simple and uncomplicated. As poets, look for these moments, too, when you're forced to recognize and acknowledge the beast in your favorite beast.

Cat

The fat cat on the mat
may seem to dream
of nice mice that suffice
for him, or cream;
but he free, maybe,
walks in thought
unbowed, proud, where loud
roared and fought
his kin, lean and slim,
or deep in den
in the East feasted on beasts
and tender men.
The giant lion with iron
claw in paw,
and huge ruthless tooth
in gory jaw;
the pard dark-starred,
fleet upon feet,
that oft soft from aloft
leaps on his meat
where woods loom in gloom—
far now they be,
fierce and free,
and tamed as he;
but fat cat on the mat
kept as a pet,
he does not forget.
                    —*J. R. R. Tolkien*

Dogs

Over
the wide field

the dark deer
went running,

five dogs
screaming

at his flanks,
at his heels,

my own two darlings
among them

lunging and buckling
with desire

as they leaped
for the throat

as they tried
and tried again

to bring him down.
At the lake

the deer
plunged—

I could hear
the green wind

of his breath
tearing

but the long legs
never stopped

till he clambered
up the far shore.

The dogs
moaned and screeched

they flung themselves
on the grass

panting
and steaming.

It took hours
but finally

in the half-drowned light
in the silence

of the summer evening
they woke

from fitful naps,
they stepped

in their old good natures
toward us

look look
into their eyes

bright as planets
under the long lashes

here is such happiness when you speak their names!
here is such unforced love!

here is such shyness under courage!
here is the shining rudimentary soul

here is hope retching, the world as it is
here is the black the red the bottomless pool.

—*Mary Oliver*

Look for these moments, when you're forced to recognize the beast in your favorite beast.

Dog's Death

BY JOHN UPDIKE

SETTING THE STAGE: Some of the saddest poems I know are about the deaths of our cats and dogs. Humans feel so helpless to offer comfort or relief when dumb animals suffer. In this haunting poem, John Updike tells the story of a puppy that couldn't tell her people that something was wrong.

SOME FEATURES TO NOTICE:
- How Updike chose, through the title and the first line, to begin the poem with the fact of the dog's injury and death and, instead, to make the subject of the poem his and his wife's observations and reactions
- The irony and poignancy of the last two words of the poem: even though she was dying, the *good dog* found a piece of newspaper on which to relieve herself
- The subtle rhyming
- *Malaise* means physical weakness or discomfort
- Here, *imperious* means urgent
- Here, *dissolution* means death

RESPONSE STANCE: Please go back into this eloquent poem and mark the lines and language that touched your heart.

BENEDICTION: If you come from a pet-owning family, it's likely you have your own story to tell about the end of the life of a beloved cat or dog. A poem is the perfect genre to tell that story.

Dog's Death

She must have been kicked unseen or brushed by a car.
Too young to know much, she was beginning to learn
To use the newspapers spread on the kitchen floor
And to win, wetting there, the words, "Good dog! Good dog!"

We thought her shy malaise was a shot reaction.
The autopsy disclosed a rupture in her liver.
As we teased her with play, blood was filling her skin
And her heart was learning to lie down forever.

Monday morning, as the children were noisily fed
And sent to school, she crawled beneath the youngest's bed.
We found her twisted and limp but still alive.
In the car to the vet's, on my lap, she tried

To bite my hand and died. I stroked her warm fur
And my wife called in a voice imperious with tears.
Though surrounded by love that would have upheld her,
Nevertheless she sank and, stiffening, disappeared.

Back home, we found that in the night her frame,
Drawing near to dissolution, had endured the shame
Of diarrhea and had dragged across the floor
To a newspaper carelessly left there. *Good dog.*

    —*John Updike*

PRESENTING THE POEMS:

Birch

BY KAREN SHEPARD

&

Shelter

BY R. S. JONES

SETTING THE STAGE: Today's poems come from one of my favorite anthologies ever: *Unleashed: Poems by Writers' Dogs*. The editors, Amy Hempel and Jim Shepard, asked a bunch of dog-owning poets to write poems as if they were their own dogs. The results are funny, also thought-provoking, also moving.

SOME FEATURES TO NOTICE—"BIRCH":
- How the repetition suggests the cadence of a panting, begging dog and also creates a strong visual
- Its brevity
- Its humor

SOME FEATURES TO NOTICE—"SHELTER":
- How the title has a double meaning: the dog, rescued from the shelter, seeks shelter with the poet
- The specific, evocative images of life at a pound; the visual details
- How the information that the poet did, in fact, adopt the dog is revealed indirectly, inside parentheses
- The richness of the old dog's voice
- The poem's tone of yearning

RESPONSE STANCE: First, let's go back into "Birch" all together. What do you *see?* How are we getting such a strong visual image from just two lines? Now, enter "Shelter" again, on you own. This is such a *yearning* poem. Mark the lines where you get a sense of just how much this dog is yearning to be owned.

BENEDICTION: If your cat or dog could talk, what would be its message? Its tone? Its point of view? Its imagery? These could be funny poems, or thoughtful poems, or moving poems.

Birch

You gonna eat that?

You gonna eat that?

You gonna eat that?

I'll eat that.

—*Karen Shepard*

Shelter

You paused outside
to look into my cage.
I tried to play it right,
wanting to catch your eye
with a shy glint in my own,
     a soft bark
that said, "Choose me,"
in a canine grammar
I hoped you'd understand.

Your face held nothing
(pity, maybe)
that let me believe
you would ever want
a dog like me.

You turned once,
twice,
a hundred times,
coming and going
the length of my cage.
(Coming and going
like you do now,
ten times a day.)
Then walked away.

I could not stand another day
of strangers coming to stare,
passing me over for younger dogs who
knew too little to have the strange
     look of longing
I could not keep from my eyes.

I could not stand another night
alone in that place—
     the cracked cement floor,
     the howls and whines that kept me sleepless.
(Did you know that sound is still the one I hear
when you wake me kicking from dreams,
sleeping in your bed?)

Then suddenly you were back.
I saw you glance at the card
hung onto my gate—
        a false name, a date of arrival,
otherwise a blank
        no age, no history,
        nothing
that would let you know
I would stay with you forever
and never go.

You leaned your face into the fence,
curling your hand through the wires,
        blinking in the sun.
(Neither one of us so young
in the bright, spring light
yet wanting to be.)

I let one paw
hover in the air
but looked away,
not wanting to show my eagerness,
        but wanting
to find a way to tell you
that I would be a good dog
and how much I wanted to be owned.
(A dog is only half himself
without a master.
Unfinished, half-alive.)

I could not move
        nor speak
but when you dropped to your knees
and reached two fingers towards my fur
I felt myself fall,
(oh god I could not help myself)
letting my body form the words
        head back, eyes closed,
            throat exposed,
        legs flailing in the air.
"Please," I said. "Yes, please.
Take me. Yes."

        —R. S. Jones

PRESENTING THE POEM:

Sonnet for Shoelace

BY BENJAMIN F. WILLIAMS

SETTING THE STAGE: An Elizabethan sonnet, which dates from the age of Queen Elizabeth I of England, is a highly structured kind of love poem. William Shakespeare wrote a famous sequence of Elizabethan love sonnets, each one fourteen lines long, with ten syllables per line and a rhyme scheme of ABAB, CDCD, EFEF, GG.

Ben, a seventh grader, decided to try an Elizabethan sonnet. The object of his affections is his new kitten, Shoelace. Ben's sonnet observes Shoelace's first encounter with snow.

SOME FEATURES TO NOTICE:
- The sensory details and visual imagery
- The strong, sensory verbs, nouns, and adjectives
- Ben's adherence to the Elizabethan sonnet form

RESPONSE STANCE: Please go back into Ben's sonnet on your own and mark the lines you can see, hear, and feel.

BENEDICTION: Again, look for specific moments of your pet in action, ones you can describe in sensory language that captures the action and the essence, and preserves the moment like a snapshot. And if you want to try to craft it as an Elizabethan sonnet, that's fine, too.

Sonnet for Shoelace

The ice crystals on your coat make you glow.
Giant eyes reflect a cold March moonlight.
You prance over the ice, up on your toes.
Your nose twitches to feel the air's cold bite.
The gleaming snow swirls around you like mist.
Your velvet fur is coated in its clean.
You scout all around with a face moon-kissed,
filled up with wonder at all that's unseen.
A shiver sends snow from you to the ground.
Your thirst for warmth—urgent now—must be quenched.
You stop your play, and to the house you bound.
From your throat an inhuman cry is wrenched.
You fly inside when I open the door.
Four paws skitter across a warm oak floor.

—*Benjamin F. Williams*

©2006 by Nancie Atwell from *Naming the World: A Year of Poems and Lessons*
(Portsmouth, NH: Heinemann)

I love the [...]
eye. I think [...]
joined in Eng[...]
by mind's ear[...]
mind's tongu[e]
nose. Well-ch[...]

The *Senses:*
INTRODUCTION

I love the phrase *mind's eye.* I think it should be joined in English vocabulary by *mind's ear, mind's skin, mind's tongue,* and *mind's nose.* Well-chosen words have the power to evoke the senses and invite us to see, hear, feel, taste, and smell the physical world. Although the term *imagery* suggests pictures only, most critics agree that words and phrases that call up other sensory experiences are images, too, in the sense that all of these are versions of *imaginative thought.*

The poems in this section are rich in diction that leads to imaginative thought. The poets use such specific language to describe their experiences that they move their poems beyond mere description to become our imaginative sights, sounds, textures, tastes, and aromas.

The Fish

BY ELIZABETH BISHOP

SETTING THE STAGE: "The Fish" by Elizabeth Bishop may well be the most visual poem ever written in the English language. The diction is so rich that we are *there*, with Bishop, in a little rented boat, seeing through her eyes as she catches the ultimate one that got away.

SOME FEATURES TO NOTICE:

- How Bishop opens the poem in the moment *after* she has landed the "tremendous fish"
- The evocative metaphors (*fine rosettes of lime*) and similes (*brown skin . . . like ancient wallpaper*) throughout the poem
- The poet's realization: this fish had been caught by five others and had broken free each time
- How Bishop's vision transforms the experience into something like a religious epiphany: *rainbow, rainbow, rainbow!* suggests the "Sanctus, sanctus, sanctus" (Holy, holy, holy) of a Catholic mass
- *Venerable* means someone or something worthy of respect because of his/her/its age
- *Isinglass* is a transparent form of gelatin made from the air bladders of fish; it was used as a substitute for glass

RESPONSE STANCE: Please go back into this glorious visual feast and mark every phrase or line you can *see*. Then, write a sentence or two: why do you think she let the fish go?

BENEDICTION: One of the most powerful things a poet can do is, through his or her diction, *evoke* the physical world—touch our senses and elicit sights, sounds, tastes, odors, and tactile feelings in our imaginations. All this week we'll enjoy the experience of sensory poems, talk about *how* they evoke, and consider how you can summon up sensations in others through sensory poems of your own.

The Fish

I caught a tremendous fish
and held him beside the boat
half out of water, with my hook
fast in a corner of his mouth.
He didn't fight.
He hadn't fought at all.
He hung a grunting weight,
battered and venerable
and homely. Here and there
his brown skin hung in strips
like ancient wallpaper,
and its pattern of darker brown
was like wallpaper:
shapes like full-blown roses
stained and lost through age.
He was speckled with barnacles,
fine rosettes of lime,
and infested
with tiny white sea-lice,
and underneath two or three
rags of green weed hung down.
While his gills were breathing in
the terrible oxygen
—the frightening gills,
fresh and crisp with blood,
that can cut so badly—
I thought of the coarse white flesh
packed in like feathers,
the big bones and the little bones,
the dramatic reds and blacks
of his shiny entrails,
and the pink swim-bladder
like a big peony.
I looked into his eyes
which were far larger than mine
but shallower, and yellowed,
the irises backed and packed
with tarnished tinfoil
seen through the lenses
of old scratched isinglass.
They shifted a little, but not
to return my stare.

—It was more like the tipping
of an object toward the light.
I admired his sullen face,
the mechanism of his jaw,
and then I saw
that from his lower lip
—if you could call it a lip—
grim, wet, and weaponlike,
hung five old pieces of fish-line,
or four and a wire leader
with the swivel still attached,
with all their five big hooks
grown firmly in his mouth.
A green line, frayed at the end
where he broke it, two heavier lines,
and a fine black thread
still crimped from the strain and snap
when it broke and he got away.
Like medals with their ribbons
frayed and wavering,
a five-haired beard of wisdom
trailing from his aching jaw.
I stared and stared
and victory filled up
the little rented boat,
from the pool of bilge
where oil had spread a rainbow
around the rusted engine
to the bailer rusted orange,
the sun-cracked thwarts,
the oarlocks on their strings,
the gunnels—until everything
was rainbow, rainbow, rainbow!
And I let the fish go.

—*Elizabeth Bishop*

PRESENTING THE POEM:

Tree Heartbeat

SETTING THE STAGE: In this poem, Siobhan, a seventh grader, tells the story of the tree that grew outside her bedroom window. Stanza by stanza, she takes us through the four seasons and the sensations she associates with her tree.

SOME FEATURES TO NOTICE:

- How each season gets a stanza—fall, to winter, to spring, to summer
- The surprise of the fifth stanza: this poem is an *elegy* for a dying tree that Siobhan's father is about to chop down
- How much Siobhan *implies* without naming it: each season, the tree's fate, her feelings
- The visual imagery throughout
- The aural imagery: *tap, tap, tapping*
- The visceral imagery: she leans against bark that's *rough, snowy, soft, wet,* and *cool*
- The repetition of *Listened for a heartbeat. Tree heartbeat* mimics the sound of a human heart beating
- The alliteration: *balloons, blossoms, and buds*
- The metaphors (*pointy red treasures; a lighted match*) and personifications (*Dressed in silver; tree's embrace*)

RESPONSE STANCE: Please go back into this sensory poem and underline all the phrases and lines that touch your senses—that you can see, hear, or feel. Then, think about the other kind of feelings—the emotions—that Siobhan's sensory imagery evokes in you.

BENEDICTION: Sensory imagery, combined with her specific memories of the tree, made Siobhan's poem a great one. As poets who are trying to find ideas in things, think now about how you can describe what you *see, feel, hear, taste,* and *smell* so that you can put others *there,* inside the world of your poem.

126 | A YEAR OF POEMS AND LESSONS

Tree Heartbeat

The tree was there. It was always there,
gently *tap tap tapping* at my window
for me to come and play.
A warm breeze lingered in its branches,
a leftover of summer,
as it dropped pointy red treasures in my hair.
I leaned against the rough autumn bark.
Remembered when my dad said the tree was alive.
Listened for a heartbeat. *Tree heartbeat.*

Dressed in silver, she twirled her branches,
dumping snow when least expected.
I climbed up up up
where, nestled among branches, I stayed all afternoon.
I leaned against the snowy bark.
Listened for a heartbeat. *Tree heartbeat.*

Red blossoms burst from limbs,
fireworks in April.
I caught them in my shirt
only to throw them back up to the tree's embrace.
I leaned my head against the soft, wet bark.
Listened for a heartbeat. *Tree heartbeat.*

The only shady place on the lawn
but with room enough for everyone.
A hole on the left for waterballoons,
when brothers were around.
I leaned my face against the cool bark.
Listened for a heartbeat. *Tree heartbeat.*

Now, a lighted match against pale blue sky,
it waits for my father, knowing its life is at an end.
A life of snow, balloons, blossoms, and buds.
I lean once more against the bark.
I remember how my dad told me it was alive.
Listen for a heartbeat. *Tree heartbeat.*

    —Siobhan Anderson

©2006 by Nancie Atwell from *Naming the World: A Year of Poems and Lessons*
(Portsmouth, NH: Heinemann)

PRESENTING THE POEMS:

Campfire Lullaby

BY ZOË MASON

&

night songs

BY MOLLY JORDAN

SETTING THE STAGE: Here are two poems that almost put me to sleep—*not* because they're boring, but because both eighth-grade poets used such sensory language that their poems work like lullabies.

SOME FEATURES TO NOTICE—"CAMPFIRE LULLABY":
- How Zoë invents a form and sticks with it: stanzas of four short lines, mostly noun-verb clauses
- The attention to diction: strong, sensory verbs, adjectives, and nouns

SOME FEATURES TO NOTICE—"NIGHT SONGS":
- How Molly invents a form and sticks with it: no caps, and stanzas of four lines each
- How lower-case letters add a calm, quiet tone to the poem
- The attention to diction: strong, sensory verbs, adjectives, and nouns
- The onomatopoeia of *hooting, creaking, click of computer keys, rustles, whispering, lull, doze*

RESPONSE STANCE: Please go back into these two poems and mark the lines you can feel, see, and hear; also, note anything else the poets did that you like.

BENEDICTION: Every part of speech is important in good writing across the genres, but nouns and verbs are the workhorses. Nothing beats a specific noun combined with a sensory verb. When you revise and polish your poems, look at your verbs. Are they strong, evocative? Should you consult a thesaurus for verb help?

Campfire Lullaby

Eyelids heavy,
arms hang,
legs numb,
jaw drops.

Fire blinds,
eyes stare,
drums beat   constant,
lulling, lulling.

Dog's stroked,
hand's licked,
head's propped
and caught as it slips.

Moon's out,
sun's down,
voices sparkle
lake's reflection.

Body melts,
pine needles sting,
darkness falls,
eyes stop.

—Zoë Mason

night songs

unable to sleep
i face the ceiling
and listen
to the night.

owls
sing outside,
hooting soft solos,
then duets.

the house sings
a creaking song
of heaters and pipes
as i wait.

my sister breathes
deeply
deeply
in the next room.

from downstairs
a click of computer keys
serenades me
and joins the song.

wind rustles through
pine trees
in the darkness
outside my window.

a choir of whispering
voices begins.
night songs
lull me

from wandering thoughts
into the comfortable doze
between consciousness and sleep.
soon i am gone:

faded into dream.
but
the night songs
play on.

—Molly Jordan

Peaches

BY PETER DAVISON

&

Craisins

BY MICHAEL CONLEY CARTER

SETTING THE STAGE: Today's poems play with the *sounds* of words. They're just for fun, but they make a point, too. As Peter Davison put it, it's awesome *What English can do*. These poems *dance*.

SOME FEATURES TO NOTICE:

- The word play and patterns
- The versatility of the English language
- The power of words to evoke sensations—and get salivary glands flowing
- The alliteration: *tart texture; hauled... haunches... hunched*
- The assonance: *beach, sweet... breaches... pleached*
- Here, *plashy* means wet or marshy
- Here, *pleached* means interwoven, like branches in a hedge or arbor
- Michael, an eighth grader, wrote "Craisins" after reading "Peaches"

RESPONSE STANCE: Please go back into these two poems and mark the words and lines you like the sound of.

BENEDICTION: As poets, don't be afraid to play with words, to take pleasure in exploring the relationships between sound and meaning. See if you can tickle your readers' ears.

Peaches

A mouthful of language to swallow:
stretches of beach, sweet clinches,
breaches in walls, pleached branches;
britches hauled over haunches;
hunched leeches, wrenched teachers.
What English can do: ransack
the warmth that chuckles beneath
fuzzed surfaces, smooth velvet
richness, plashy juices.
I beseech you, peach,
clench me into the sweetness
of your reaches.

—Peter Davison

Craisins

A sweetness
of the sour kind
can make whole worlds
with a fruity lust:
"Craisins or Bust!"
I need
that mouthful of tart
texture and absolute
flavor;
the juicy burst
that ripens beneath
the wrinkled layer
of newborn fruit—
the one that I'm cravin',
the cranberry of all raisins:
The Craisin.

—Michael Conley Carter

©2006 by Nancie Atwell from *Naming
the World: A Year of Poems and Lessons*
(Portsmouth, NH: Heinemann)

I Can't Forget You.

BY LEN ROBERTS

SETTING THE STAGE: Today's poem tells a story of graffiti. The official, primary sense that's tapped here is the visual. But if there is such a thing as a sixth sense, I think it's what the *heart* perceives. This poem taps that sense, too.

SOME FEATURES TO NOTICE:

● How almost the whole poem is visual
● The specific details of the visual images
● How the poet describes not only what he saw—the graffiti—but what the sight inspired him to imagine in his mind's eye
● *Hyperbole* (hi-PUR-bo-lee) means exaggerated for effect

RESPONSE STANCE: Please go back into "I Can't Forget You." and mark the lines and phrases you can see.

BENEDICTION: There's a lot to be said for careful visual imagery, combined with the poet's imagination. Again, begin with the *thing*—the visual perception; then bring to it your poet's vision and invention.

I Can't Forget You.

spray-painted high on the overpass,
each letter a good foot long,
and I try to picture the writer
    hanging from a rope
between midnight and dawn
the weight of his love swaying,
    making a trembling
N and G, his mind at work
    with the apostrophe—
    the grammar of loss—
and his resistance to hyperbole,
    no exclamation point
    but a period at the end
that shows a heart not given
    to exaggeration,
a heart that's direct with a no-
    fooling around approach,
and I wonder if he tested the rope
before tying it to the only tree I can see
    that would bear his weight,
or if he didn't care about the free-
    fall of thirty or more feet
as he locked his wrist to form such
    straight T's,
and still managed, dangling, to flex
    for the C and G,
knowing as he did, I'm sure,
the lover would ride this way each day
until she found a way around,
a winding back road with trees
    and roadside
tiger lilies, maybe a stream, a
    white house, white fence,
    a dog in the yard
      miles
from this black-letter, open-book
    in-your-face missing
that the rain or Turnpike road
    crew
will soon wash off.

    —Len Roberts

"I Can't Forget You," ©February 2003. by Len Roberts and The Poetry Foundation

PRESENTING THE POEM:

Afternoon Beach

BY MOLLY JORDAN

SETTING THE STAGE: Molly, an eighth-grade poet, is taking us to the beach today. Trust me: regardless of what's going on outside our window, in two minutes it's going to feel like a ninety-degree August afternoon in this classroom.

SOME FEATURES TO NOTICE:
- The alliteration: *Home is hot./ The family fries*
- The strong, sensory verbs: *pull on, grab, pile, taunts, blaze*
- The experiments with word and line placement that emphasize Molly's actions and attitudes
- The purposeful repetition
- How the imagery at the beginning of the poem is hot; how it's cooled off by the *blue* at the end

RESPONSE STANCE: Please go back into "Afternoon Beach" and mark the lines you can see and feel, plus anything else Molly has done here that you like.

BENEDICTION: Molly wrote this poem in the middle of winter. She closed her eyes, brought back the sensations of a summer day at the beach, and drafted, revised, and polished her verbs until her language and line breaks matched the intensity of her memory. Slow down your poems about your experiences and focus on the sensory details, on the way the moment felt, looked, sounded, and tasted.

Afternoon Beach

Home is hot.
The family fries
until we summon
the energy
to pull on stretchy suits,
grab towels,
and pile into the car,
    which is an oven.
We drive
until a roar of waves
    taunts us
from a parking lot.

On the beach
sand and sun
    blaze hot,
but welcome breezes
play with my hair
until I pull it back,
away from their grasp.
I shed shorts and shirt
and
sprint to the water.

I push my way out
against crashing waves
and
    dive
        into
            pure
                cool
                    salty
                        pleasure.

Silence.

Silence until
I surface.
    The roar
of ocean
fills my ears.

I stand,
wipe salt from my eyes,
and divethroughawave,
then ride the next
as it races to shore.
I get knocked flat,
float over more waves,
let them
                push me
            pull me
take me wherever
they want to go.
I dive over, under,
            through.
I lose the time.

And suddenly
I've lost the time—
        we need to leave.
I stagger onto the fiery sand
and wait
for my land legs to return.
My hair is salty.
    My skin is sticky
as I survey my crashing waves
my oceansky
my blue
beneath blue.

    —*Molly Jordan*

©2006 by Nancie Atwell from *Naming the World: A Year of Poems and Lessons* (Portsmouth, NH: Heinemann)

PRESENTING THE POEM:

Lines

BY MARTHA COLLINS

SETTING THE STAGE: Something I love about the English language is its versatility—how one word, through its range of definitions, can do the work of many. For example, the word *play* has sixty-seven definitions in my college dictionary; the word *die* has twenty. *Line* has fifty-four, and in her poem "Lines," Martha Collins plays with some of them.

SOME FEATURES TO NOTICE:
- How the purposeful repetition of *line* creates a cadence and moves the poem
- The humor
- The alliteration: *corners, cross, cut in*

RESPONSE STANCE: Please go back into this linear poem and mark your favorite phrases and lines about lines.

BENEDICTION: You could do this: scan the dictionary for a word that's followed by a chunk of definitions and go to work—or play—with sound patterns and meanings.

Lines

Draw a line. Write a line. There.
Stay in line, hold the line, a glance
between the lines is fine but don't
turn corners, cross, cut in, go over
or out, between two points of no
return's a line of flight, between
two points of view's a line of vision.
But a line of thought is rarely
straight, an open line's no party
line, however fine your point.
A line of fire communicates, but drop
your weapons and drop your line,
consider the shortest distance from x
to y, let x be me, let y be you.

—*Martha Collins*

Let Evening Come

BY JANE KENYON

SETTING THE STAGE: Jane Kenyon was a great poet who died too young, of cancer. She lived on a farm in New Hampshire with her husband, the poet Donald Hall. In this beautiful poem filled with rural imagery, Kenyon uses a sound pattern—the repetition of the word *let*—to try to convince us not to be afraid of the dark, or of what lies beyond it.

SOME FEATURES TO NOTICE:
- How the soothing repetition of *let* gives the poem the sound of an incantation or prayer
- The concreteness of the things Kenyon names in her prayer: a place, a person, objects, animals
- The gorgeous diction
- How Kenyon invents a form and sticks with it: three-line stanzas

RESPONSE STANCE: Please go back into "Let Evening Come" and mark the lines you can see, hear, and feel, plus anything else Kenyon has done here that you love.

BENEDICTION: There's nothing poetry can't do, and that includes giving us comfort. As readers of poetry, look for—and hold onto—the poems that comfort you.

Let Evening Come

Let the light of late afternoon
shine through chinks in the barn, moving
up the bales as the sun moves down.

Let the crickets take up chafing
as a woman takes up her needles
and her yarn. Let evening come.

Let dew collect on the hoe abandoned
in long grass. Let the stars appear
and the moon disclose her silver horn.

Let the fox go back to its sandy den.
Let the wind die down. Let the shed
go black inside. Let evening come.

To the bottle in the ditch, to the scoop
in the oats, to air in the lung
let evening come.

Let it come, as it will, and don't
be afraid. God does not leave us
comfortless, so let evening come.

   —Jane Kenyon

These are t

students said

most keenly

of adulthood

as adolescen

To find their

Growing Up:
INTRODUCTION

These are the poems my students said spoke to them most keenly about the onset of adulthood and their identities as adolescents on the cusp. To find their phase of life spoken for in poetry surprised and gratified them. To speak as poets themselves about this moment—when Frost's "gold" slips away, as it must—helps give some perspective on what's happening to them, and inspires a sense of confidence in the self they are today and the adult who is beginning to emerge.

PRESENTING THE POEM:

Nothing Gold Can Stay

BY ROBERT FROST

NOTE: If your students don't know the Old Testament story of Genesis and Adam and Eve's banishment from Eden—mine never seem to these days—a quick read-aloud of *Adam and Eve*, a children's picture book by Warwick Hutton, provides essential background. I do think kids need to know Bible stories, as well as Greek myths, in order to get the allusions that surround them in our culture.

SETTING THE STAGE: We tend to categorize Robert Frost as a nature poet, and he does write powerfully about the natural world. But it's the complexity of human nature that's his real subject—our fears, desires, tragedies, and surprises. Nature may be the prism, but the focus is us. Frost's "Nothing Gold Can Stay" is probably the most famous poem ever written about the need for all things to grow up.

SOME FEATURES TO NOTICE:
- How, in early spring, the first buds to appear on deciduous trees aren't green, but, rather, golden in color. This *hue* is nature's hardest to hold onto because it lasts such a short time
- How a tree's first *leaves* also aren't green; these are its blossoms, and they, too, last for just a brief time: *only so an hour*
- How the regular, mature, green leaves of summer soon emerge and take over: *then leaf subsides to leaf*
- How this natural process of maturation resembles the Biblical loss of Paradise: Adam and Eve had to sin, had to lose their innocence, mature, and become part of the mortal world: *So Eden sank to grief*

- How every dawn mirrors this process, as the glory and newness of a sunrise last for only a moment before it *goes down to day*
- How this is nature's way: the evanescent, innocent beauty of new life cannot last; it would be *un*natural to stay gold
- How Frost's choice of the word *gold* to describe this stage is an allusion to the first of the five ages of mankind in Greek mythology, beginning with the Golden Age and ending with the Iron Age, as described by Hesiod. The Golden Age was the period after Kronus first created man on earth, when spring was never-ending, streams of milk and nectar flowed, laws and wars weren't necessary, and no one grew old, worked, or felt unhappy.

RESPONSE STANCE: Please go back into "Nothing Gold Can Stay" and mark the words and lines you want us to talk about together because they confuse you and you want to understand them. Then we'll unpack this poem together.

BENEDICTION: This is a poem to memorize—to take into your life to help you understand that growing up is inevitable: *Nothing gold can stay*. But it's also a chance to think about what will replace your gold, your sense of innocence. It could be cynicism. It could also be—should be, I think—knowledge, self-knowledge, and hope.

Nothing Gold Can Stay

Nature's first green is gold,
Her hardest hue to hold.
Her early leaf's a flower;
But only so an hour.
Then leaf subsides to leaf.
So Eden sank to grief,
So dawn goes down to day.
Nothing gold can stay.

—*Robert Frost*

The Death of Santa Claus

BY CHARLES WEBB

SETTING THE STAGE: This poem about growing up captures what I think of as the quintessential event, the one that begins the end of childhood. Almost everyone your age has a story to tell about *the moment*: the awful dawning of the awful truth about Santa Claus.

SOME FEATURES TO NOTICE:

- How Webb spins and sustains the metaphor: describes in vivid detail the story of Santa's heart attack to suggest the power, to a child, of the death of this myth
- The humor
- The similes
- The sensory verbs
- The eight-year-old's voice that takes over in the stanzas second and third from the end
- How the conclusion leaves readers writing in our heads: we can imagine what's going to happen next in that tract house in Houston
- How the poet invents a form: stanzas of three lines

RESPONSE STANCE: Please go back into this funny, heartbreaking poem on your own and underline and make notes to yourself about *what surprises you* and *what you like* in Charles Webb's way of depicting the quintessential event.

BENEDICTION: This may be a story you can tell as a poem, too—a funny one, a heartbreaking one, or, like "The Death of Santa Claus," both: your free-verse version of the moment *you knew*.

The Death of Santa Claus

He's had the chest pains for weeks,
        but doctors don't make house
        calls to the North Pole,

he's let his Blue Cross lapse,
        blood tests make him faint,
        hospital gowns always flap

open, waiting rooms upset
        his stomach, and it's only
        indigestion anyway, he thinks,

until, feeding the reindeer,
        he feels as if a monster fist
        has grabbed his heart and won't

stop squeezing. He can't
        breathe, and the beautiful white
        world he loves goes black,

and he drops on his jelly belly
        in the snow and Mrs. Claus
        tears out of the toy factory

wailing, and the elves wring
        their little hands, and Rudolph's
        nose blinks like a sad ambulance

light, and in a tract house
        in Houston, Texas, I'm 8,
        telling my mom that stupid

kids at school say Santa's a big
        fake, and she sits with me
        on our purple-flowered couch,

and takes my hand, tears
        in her throat, the terrible
        news rising in her eyes.

        —Charles Webb

After Watching
Peter Pan *Again*

BY MARLEY WITHAM

SETTING THE STAGE: Santa Claus is a standard story character icon of childhood. Beyond him, most of us, as kids, had other characters from storybooks or movies or TV who we identified with, fantasized about, even loved. I wanted to be Jo March in *Little Women*. I daydreamed about being a friend of Timmy, the boy who owned Lassie, and accompanying them on their adventures, and of running away with Circus Boy—don't ask. For Marley, an eighth grader, her object of fantasy was—and sometimes still is—Peter Pan, the boy who wouldn't grow up.

SOME FEATURES TO NOTICE:
- The specificity of Marley's Peter Pan fantasies as well as her descriptions of this evening
- How the stanzas break the action and indicate the changes in Marley's attitude
- The contrast in the third stanza between the realistic natural imagery and the Peter Pan fantasy
- The self-deprecating humor
- How the title works as part of the first line of the poem
- How the conclusion implies the death of the fantasy

RESPONSE STANCE: Please go back into Marley's poem on your own and mark the lines where you can recognize what she's feeling.

BENEDICTION: The specifics of Marley's poem brought her childhood fantasy and her feelings, then and now, to life for us. What's the childhood fantasy—and what are the feelings—you'd like to remember and bring to life as a poem?

After Watching
Peter Pan *Again*

I return to my room with tears in my eyes.
When I was little, this was pure adventure.
Now
I stare out the open window
and begin to imagine.
The unreasonable part of me—
the part that
once upon a time
let me be a princess,
let me sail with pirates,
the part that believes good
always
triumphs over evil—
hopes that Pan himself
will come swooping to my window
and take me away,
take me,
so I will never, ever become a grown-up.

But the reasonable part of me—
the part that concedes
it's just a movie,
that shouts everyone must grow up,
the part that helps me with math—
that side states in a calm voice:
You need to get over it.

Tonight I ignore the voice of reason.
I continue to gaze out my window.
Warm summer air drifts in.
I can smell the night on it
and the subtle scent of fresh cut grass.
Thin clouds stretch over stars,
ghostly and pale.
I strain my neck till I'm dangling out the window,
searching for some sign of a flying boy.
Of course, there is none,
just as there never was.

Still, I stay like this
until my mother yells to me to get ready for bed.
I replace the screen,
step away,
and, earthbound,
move on.

     —*Marley Witham*

©2006 by Nancie Atwell from *Naming the World: A Year of Poems and Lessons*
(Portsmouth, NH: Heinemann)

PRESENTING THE POEMS:

Quotes

BY BENJAMIN F. WILLIAMS

&

Living in Rings

BY ANNE ATWELL-MCLEOD

SETTING THE STAGE: Two seventh-grade poets, Ben and Anne, used collections of *things* as a way to take stock of who they are and how they're growing up. Ben collects quotes that appeal to him; Anne is a collector of rings.

SOME FEATURES TO NOTICE:

- The specifics of each poem: Ben gives us the words of the quotes he loves; Anne describes each of the rings in her jewelry box
- How the quotes Ben selects and the rings Anne chooses show aspects of their personalities and what they care about
- How each poem ends without closure: both poets know their identities are still in flux

RESPONSE STANCE: Please go back into one of these collectors' poems—your choice—and mark the lines you can identify with, as someone else who is growing up.

BENEDICTION: What do you collect? What did you collect? What might you find out about yourself through writing a poem about your collection?

Quotes

My room is a home
for other people's words,
a haven for ideas and thoughts
that weren't my own
until I pinned them on my wall
or penciled them on my desk
so I could see them,
remember each one.

They aren't inspirational—
not most of them, anyway.
Bill Watterson uttered the best,
but there are others:

Personal grooming is completely overrated
by M. T. Anderson;

Hollow heroes separate as they run
by Breaking Benjamin;

Trust me, I'm a genius
by Eoin Colfer
as Artemis Fowl;

Hi
by Everyone,
translated
into a million languages.

Most of them
have no meaning to anyone
except me.
Most of them
I am still figuring out.

But for me
they are a life line,
a way to change bad moods
to good,
a way to borrow
other people
to express who I am
until I know
for sure.

　　　—*Benjamin F. Williams*

Living in Rings

I slip it on my finger,
a perfect circle
(the circle itself a symbol
in its continuity,
its endlessness,
its connection and relevance to everything).
It fits
although differently than it did
during the phase of signet jewelry
when it echoed my name,
an early assurance of who I was.

Now I try on
the years when garnets adorned my fingers.
I remember each ring better
than memory can recall myself
at that age.
I treasure garnet as something
that symbolized me—
for a time.

The rings of fleeting fads
that slid on and off my fingers
until the silver wore off
make me laugh.
The Fimo ring,
the twenty-five-cent painted tin,
the stone that promised to know my mood
blend together in an image of hope
outgrown by the end of the week.

Next I roll between my fingers
intricate rings of silver floral.
Their idealized nature gave me summer
through months of snow,
a promise
that a time must come when they'd be laid aside,
paling in comparison to Earth's real beauty.

Now I look at my hands
bereft of silver, gold, tin—
only hands
with fingers that provided the background
to rings
linked together in the chain of a lifetime—
the circles I have made it with this far.

I gather up these pieces of my life.
I put them away in a box of jewels.
I wait for the next ring to fall into place.

—Anne Atwell-McLeod

©2006 by Nancie Atwell from *Naming the World: A Year of Poems and Lessons* (Portsmouth, NH: Heinemann)

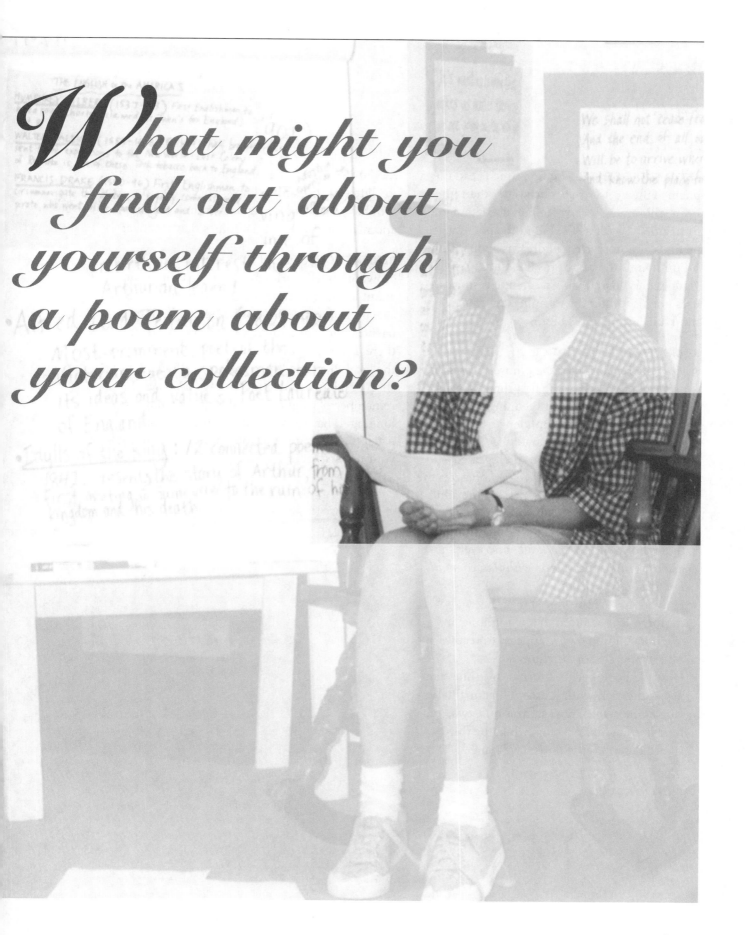

*What might you
find out about
yourself through
a poem about
your collection?*

PRESENTING THE POEM:

Fifteen

BY WILLIAM STAFFORD

SETTING THE STAGE: The first time I read the poem "Fifteen" I wasn't much older than fifteen. I can still remember my feeling of excitement, as I imagined myself as the kid in the poem when he finds a motorcycle and dreams about taking off on it, into the rest of his life, until . . . well, you'll see. William Stafford often tells stories—uses poems to find the meanings in events. I think this is one of his best.

SOME FEATURES TO NOTICE:
- How the repetition of the phrase *I was fifteen* at the end of each of the first three stanzas emphasizes the poet's burgeoning sense of power, ambition, and confidence: his *forward feeling* about becoming an adult
- How the final variation on the repeated phrase—*I stood there, fifteen*—emphasizes the poet's youth and powerlessness, as the adult owner of the motorcycle *roared away*
- How in the second stanza Stafford animates the motorcycle: gives it *flanks* and eyelashes; leads it *gently;* and stands *with that companion, ready and friendly*
- How in the last five-line stanza the motorcycle is reduced to a *machine* again when its injured owner appears to recover it
- The strong, sensory diction
- How the poet invents a form—five-line stanzas—and sticks with it except for the final, single-line stanza; how stanzas one, two, and four narrate literal action, while the third stanza describes the boy's daydream

RESPONSE STANCE: There's so much to admire in "Fifteen," it's hard to know where to begin. Would you start by going back in on your own and marking the words and lines that you like?

BENEDICTION: Some of the best poems about growing up tell stories not about triumphs but about longings. I can remember myself at your age, pumping my bike up the steep hill to my friend's house and longing to be able to drive there. I remember browsing for exotic stuff at the local Pier One Imports store and longing to shop in genuinely exotic Greenwich Village. I remember playing my guitar, singing along, and longing to have a voice, to become someone to listen to. What are your longings? These are your poems, too.

Fifteen

South of the bridge on Seventeenth
I found back of the willows one summer
day a motorcycle with engine running
as it lay on its side, ticking over
slowly in the high grass. I was fifteen.

I admired all that pulsating gleam, the
shiny flanks, the demure headlights
fringed where it lay; I led it gently
to the road and stood with that
companion, ready and friendly. I was fifteen.

We could find the end of the road, meet
the sky on out Seventeenth. I thought about
hills, and patting the handle got back a
confident opinion. On the bridge we indulged
a forward feeling, a tremble. I was fifteen.

Thinking, back farther in the grass I found
the owner, just coming to, where he had flipped
over the rail. He had blood on his hand, was pale—
I helped him walk to his machine. He ran his hand
over it, called me a good man, roared away.

I stood there, fifteen.

—William Stafford

Evening on the Lawn

BY GARY SOTO

SETTING THE STAGE: I don't know about you, but I spent a chunk of my adolescence feeling irked by my parents because our perspectives and perceptions were so different—because, in general, they just didn't *get it*. They didn't get watching for shooting stars for hours. They didn't get why figuring out song lyrics mattered, or how someone could spend a whole day in her bedroom drawing or reading or, worst of all from their perspective, daydreaming. In "Evening on the Lawn," Gary Soto tells a story that measures the difference between the adult he felt himself becoming and the perspectives of the adults he lived with who didn't *get it*.

SOME FEATURES TO NOTICE:

- The contrast between the beautiful diction that describes the poet's perception of the night sky and the mundane language that characterizes the actions and speech of the mother and stepfather
- The strong, visual verbs: the cloud is *boiling, churning, washing*
- The metaphors that capture how young the poet is: *My stomach a valley, my arms twisted with new rope*
- The appropriateness of the simile *the screen door closing like a sigh*
- The humor and anger in the last six lines

RESPONSE STANCE: Please go back into Soto's "Evening on the Lawn" and mark the lines that surprised you. Plus note anything else he did here, as a poet, that you'd like to talk about.

BENEDICTION: Moving from childhood to adulthood means defining yourself. Sometimes that means comparing and contrasting the personal identity you're defining with that of the people around you, including your parents. At some junctures, there may not be a close fit between what you find yourself caring about and what your significant adults do. These points of tension are also subjects for poems about growing up.

Evening on the Lawn

I sat on the lawn watching the half-hearted moon rise,
The gnats orbiting the peach pit that I spat out
When the sweetness was gone. I was twenty,
Wet behind the ears from my car wash job,
And suddenly rising to my feet when I saw in early evening
A cloud roll over a section of stars.
It was boiling, a cloud
Churning in one place and washing those three or four stars.
Excited, I lay back down,
My stomach a valley, my arms twisted with new rope,
My hair a youthful black. I called my mother and stepfather
And said something amazing was happening up there.
They shaded their eyes from the porch light.
They looked and looked before my mom turned
The garden hose onto a rosebush and my stepfather scolded the cat
To get the hell off the car. The old man grumbled
About missing something on TV,
The old lady made a face
When mud splashed her slippers. How you bother,
She said for the last time, the screen door closing like a sigh.
I turned off the porch light, undid my shoes.
The cloud boiled over those stars until it was burned by their icy fire.
The night was now clear. The wind brought me a scent
Of a place where I would go alone,
Then find others, all barefoot.
In time, each of us would boil clouds
And strike our childhood houses
With lightning.

    —*Gary Soto*

Practically Triplets

BY HALLIE HERZ

&

Call Me

BY CHRIS KUNITZ

SETTING THE STAGE: Maybe the most painful part of growing up—I know it was for me—is the childhood friendships that don't stick. One kid grows one way, and his best friend grows another. Or a girl decides her closest friend isn't cool and walks away from her forever. The feelings of loss and betrayal are intense, but poetry can help. Chris and Hallie, two eighth graders, got some control over the experience and their feelings by crafting them as poems.

SOME FEATURES TO NOTICE—"PRACTICALLY TRIPLETS":

- The powerful repetition of *remember?* and *practically triplets*
- The specific experiences Hallie describes, which call up visual images for the reader
- How Hallie addresses the poem to her ex-friend as a *you*

SOME FEATURES TO NOTICE—"CALL ME":

- The powerful repetition of *You don't call me./ I don't call you.*
- The subtle rhyming
- How Chris addresses the poem to his ex-friend as a *you*

RESPONSE STANCE: Please go back into one of these two thoughtful poems on your own—your choice—and mark the lines and words you'd like to talk about—as a reader of poems, but also as someone who may have had a similar experience.

BENEDICTION: Writing poetry can do lots of things for us. Maybe one of the best is the way a poem can turn pain and confusion into art. I know that Chris and Hallie were helped by crafting their growing-apart experiences as poems. As poets yourselves, know this, remember this.

Practically Triplets

Do you remember?
We were practically triplets,
so close
that the only way to separate us
would be
a long and painful surgery.

Now, when you see me,
you won't even glance my way.
You and your friends with your
tiny, stylish bikinis
make me feel childish
and ashamed of my green
flowered suit.
I stay underwater
so you won't laugh at me.

Don't you remember
the shoe-flinging game
on the swings,
when we
hid our
bare feet
from the passing recess monitor?
I do.

Remember when we drew portraits
of each other
in third grade,
mine with a starry background,
yours sunny,
Siobhan's rainy?
Our crayon faces,
mismatched and lopsided,
looked nothing like our real ones.

But you must remember,
after our separation,
the only words you said to me
that whole year
were
I like your shirt.

We were practically triplets,
so close.

Don't you remember?

　　　—Hallie Herz

Call Me

You don't call me.
I don't call you.

We grew up laughing and playing,
so why do you keep saying
I'm so different from you?

I looked at you,
you looked at me,
and then you turned away.
When you're smoking with your friends,
what am I supposed to say?

You don't call me.
I don't call you.

I'm into punk,
you're into beer.
When you see my clothes
you laugh
and sneer with *the guys*.

I don't need to inhale anything to be cool.
I don't need to go drinking after school.
Where, oh, where did the good times go?
When you call me names,
how do I go with the flow?
You make fun of the way I act.
You need to keep your new image intact. And

you don't call me.
I don't call you.

　　　—Chris Kunitz

PRESENTING THE POEMS:

the drum

BY NIKKI GIOVANNI

&

On the Road

BY TED KOOSER

SETTING THE STAGE: I thought we'd talk about these two poems together because each is short and packed, and each poet uses a *thing*—nikki giovanni, a drum; Ted Kooser, a pebble—to show how he or she wants to look at life and live it.

SOME FEATURES TO NOTICE:

- How the speaker in "the drum" determines to rise to the challenge of life in a world her father warns her is *tight and hard* by finding her own way of living in it: *i'm gonna beat / out my own rhythm*
- How the speaker in "On the Road" *almost* glimpses the answer to the question of the meaning of life in a quartz pebble, but he understands that this isn't the time or place for him to know it; he needs to continue to experience life, to *keep walking*

RESPONSE STANCE: Please go back into one of these two poems—your choice—and write in your own words what you think the poem is saying about life.

BENEDICTION: What's your attitude toward life: how do you want to live it? As a poet, what's the *thing* you can use to symbolize your attitude? Beat out your own rhythm. And keep walking.

the drum

daddy says the world is
a drum tight and hard
and i told him
i'm gonna beat
out my own rhythm

—*nikki giovanni*

On the Road

By the toe of my boot,
a pebble of quartz,
one drop of the earth's milk,
dirty and cold.
I held it to the light
and could almost see through it
into the grand explanation.
Put it back, something told me,
put it back and keep walking.

—*Ted Kooser*

The Dream of Now

BY WILLIAM STAFFORD

SETTING THE STAGE: This is a beautiful, inspiring poem about the power that resides inside every person. The great William Stafford asks each of us to remember our energy, our strength, our purpose.

SOME FEATURES TO NOTICE:
- The metaphors and similes
- The second-person voice
- The strong theme of the importance of resolve

RESPONSE STANCE: Please go back into this generous, thoughtful poem and mark the words and lines you love.

BENEDICTION: The last stanza of "The Dream of Now" is so empowering that these are good words to know by heart. Tonight for homework, please take them into your head and heart; please memorize them.

The Dream of Now

When you wake to the dream of now
from night and its other dream,
you carry day out of the dark
like a flame.

When spring comes north and flowers
unfold from earth and its even sleep,
you lift summer on with your breath
lest it be lost ever so deep.

Your life you live by the light you find
and follow it on as well as you can,
carrying through darkness wherever you go
your one little fire that will start again.

—*William Stafford*

Aristotle

greatest thing

a master of m

he continued

thing that ca

from others.

Metaphor:
INTRODUCTION

Aristotle knew that "the greatest thing by far is to be a master of metaphor." But, he continued, "It is the one thing that cannot be learned from others." So while my kids read and love poems that view the world through the prism of *other*—via comparisons—I don't expect that every student will pick up this ball as a poet and run with it. As Aristotle observed, the imaginative leap of figurative language can't be taught. My role is to share examples that might intrigue and resonate for my kids, then to point them as poets toward accessible entrées to figurative language. In the case of middle school poets, that's personification.

When starting this selection of poems, it helps to ask the group to review "Reading Poetry as a Critic" and to touch again on the need for readers to consider individual words, lines, images, and metaphors in a poem in the context of its other words, lines, images, and metaphors. In other words, a critic can't build a successful theory of how or what a poem means based on one line, if his or her theory doesn't also fit the other lines of the poem.

I've also found it helpful to conduct the lesson on figurative language from *Lessons That Change Writers* ("Two Things at Once") before we read these poems; I've included it again on page 367. Definitions and examples will help students appreciate the differences between literal and figurative language before they take the plunge into metaphor.

PRESENTING THE POEM:

Metaphors

BY SYLVIA PLATH

SETTING THE STAGE: Sylvia Plath is one of my favorite American poets. Her imagery, wit, brutal honesty, passionate voice, and precision of language knock me out, but it's her play with figurative language—with *metaphor*—that has kept me coming back to her poems for forty years. Plath's life was brief and tragic: she died, a suicide, at the age of thirty-one. But she left behind hundreds of poems. "Metaphors" is one of my favorites.

When a poet speaks of one thing as if it's something else, in order to suggest or reveal a new perspective, this is called *figurative language* or *metaphor*. In this poem, Plath poses a riddle by speaking of one thing in terms of many something elses. Can you guess what the one topic of all these metaphors is?

SOME FEATURES TO NOTICE:

- How this poem about a pregnant woman plays with the number nine: the speaker is *a riddle in nine syllables;* the poem has nine lines; each line contains nine syllables
- How the choice of comparisons—the *tenor* of the metaphors—reveals the speaker's range of emotions about her pregnancy: she feels huge, heavy, ungainly, fertile, earthy, and ill; she carries something of great worth; she is reduced to a delivery system and an animal; she understands it's too late for her to change her mind

RESPONSE STANCE: Please go back into this poem on your own and try to figure out what real-life physical condition Plath is describing. Write a line about your theory at the bottom of the poem. Then we'll unpack it together.

BENEDICTION: Metaphor is the most creative writing act of all. In your poems, see if you can shed new, surprising light on your subjects by comparing them to something they're not. In other words, try to push beyond sensory descriptions into the world of tone. Try especially to use metaphors to help you capture your feelings. Some human emotions are impossible to describe—they can only be expressed indirectly, through the intense imagery of metaphor. See if metaphor can help you depict what's going on inside you.

Metaphors

I'm a riddle in nine syllables,
An elephant, a ponderous house,
A melon strolling on two tendrils.
O red fruit, ivory, fine timbers!
This loaf's big with its yeasty rising.
Money's new-minted in this fat purse.
I'm a means, a stage, a cow in calf.
I've eaten a bag of green apples,
Boarded the train there's no getting off.

—Sylvia Plath

PRESENTING THE POEM:

Poem

BY JULIA BARNES

SETTING THE STAGE: Julia had read and written enough poems by seventh grade to understand that the best way to express her strong feelings about poetry—about what it does in her life—is through metaphors.

SOME FEATURES TO NOTICE:
- How the poet speaks directly to a *you*; in this case, the poem
- How the subject of the poem appears only in its title and as the final word
- The range of emotions Julia conveys through her various metaphors
- The strength of the metaphors: the specific images they call up

RESPONSE STANCE: Please go back into Julia's poem on your own, consider what she did as a creator of metaphor, and underline your favorite metaphors.

BENEDICTION: The objects, ideas, and experiences of your life that elicit your strongest feelings are ripe to be expressed as metaphors. Something you might try, as a poet, is to list the objects and experiences you feel strongly about, then see if one of them invites you to view it with new eyes.

Poem

When the world gets too loud,
you are a grassy field
where the only sound is the wind
that whispers through trees.

When life is boring,
you are a circus,
you are a bull fight,
you are an airplane.
And I am the pilot.

When I am sad,
you are all the roses
any gardener could ever dream.
Your sweet, pungent smell
fills even the largest room.

But you are also the dank, dark streets
of some forlorn city.
And you are the bristly man
who wanders them,
hands rough with years
of too little love.

When I am lonely,
you are my friend
and I think
I can experience the whole world
right here, in my bedroom,
with you,
poem.

      —Julia Barnes

PRESENTING THE POEMS:

Dreams

&

Harlem (2)

BY LANGSTON HUGHES

SETTING THE STAGE: I think the success of a metaphor depends on two things. First, is it fresh? Surprising? There's a difference between a metaphor and a cliché. Think about phrases like *snow white* or *ice cold,* that you've heard a hundred times and that don't give rise to images. Secondly, a good metaphor conveys *tone:* it shows how the poet or speaker feels about a topic.

In these two poems, both about the role of dreams in life, Langston Hughes shows how he feels through the comparisons he chooses. The first poem uses metaphor to reveal a life without dreams; the second uses metaphor to answer the question, what happens when a dream is deferred—when others prevent its coming true?

SOME FEATURES TO NOTICE—"DREAMS":
- How the metaphors that describe a life *without* dreams suggest how essential dreams are
- Natural imagery—*bird* and *field*—that implies that dreams are natural to the human condition
- Short, packed lines and strong, simple nouns and verbs
- How the repetition of the first line emphasizes the importance of its meaning
- How easy this poem is to memorize

SOME FEATURES TO NOTICE—"HARLEM (2)":
- The tone and intensity of the metaphors: negative in the extreme, each conveying a different kind of destruction
- The strong, sensory verbs: *dry up, fester, run, stink, crust and sugar over, sag, explode*
- How the questions build momentum and power
- How the italics of the last line convey fury
- How easy this poem is to memorize

RESPONSE STANCE: Please go back into one of these poems—your choice—and write about the feelings or images you get from its metaphors.

BENEDICTION: Something else to think about as a poet is how the *vehicle* in a comparison can evoke specific feelings: that is, *what* you choose to compare something to in your poems will reveal your feelings about your subject. Successful metaphors have an *attitude.*

Dreams

Hold fast to dreams
For if dreams die
Life is a broken-winged bird
That cannot fly.

Hold fast to dreams
For when dreams go
Life is a barren field
Frozen with snow.

—*Langston Hughes*

Harlem (2)

What happens to a dream deferred?

Does it dry up
like a raisin in the sun?
Or fester like a sore—
And then run?
Does it stink like rotten meat?
Or crust and sugar over—
like a syrupy sweet?

Maybe it just sags
like a heavy load.

Or does it explode?

—*Langston Hughes*

PRESENTING THE POEMS:

Flowerless

&

Trinity

BY ALISON RITTERSHAUS

Skylight Man

BY NIALL JANNEY

&

Adirondack Chair

BY JACOB MILLER

&

Hypodermic

BY BENJAMIN F. WILLIAMS

SETTING THE STAGE: Personification is the easiest way I know for a poet to enter the world of metaphor. A personification treats an inanimate something as if it's alive and has human qualities, emotions, or behaviors.

Take a look at two versions of Alison's poem about clover, something she loves. In the earlier draft, with a working title of "Flowerless," she begins to experiment with personification in her choice of verbs: here, like a person, the clover *waits;* it *lies* dormant beneath ice; it *reaches* to the sun. Let's read it together . . .

As she revised, Alison pushed harder into the territory of personification and used it to strengthen and sharpen her vision. Read "Trinity" with me.

Do you notice how clover has a gender now? How each verb suggests that clover acts like a person and invites us to notice her?

Three boys in Alison's class tried their hands at personification. Read their poems along with me, and think about what we learn about their attitudes toward their subjects.

SOME FEATURES TO NOTICE:
- How in "Skylight Man" Niall discovers he has a symbiotic relationship with the skylight in his bedroom ceiling
- How in "Adirondack Chair" Jacob uses personification to express a positive attitude
- How in "Hypodermic" Ben uses personification to express a negative attitude

RESPONSE STANCE: Please choose one of these three poems to go back into on your own. Mark the lines you want to talk about, then write a word or two about the feeling or attitude you get from the poem.

BENEDICTION: Something you might try as a poet is to make a list of *objects, phenomena* (like wind or tides), and *ideas or feelings* (like anger or hunger) that you have an attitude about, or that you'd like to consider and figure out your attitude toward. These are potential topics for your personifications.

Flowerless

Clover, mint green
and fresh as cool water.
No fruit or floral adornment
to place it in a season.
It is always there,
an old stand-by substitute
patiently waiting for its day to rise,
lying dormant beneath the ice
or listlessly flat on the ground.
An unappreciated gem,
its three fronds gently
reach out to the sunlight.
The light illuminates a small flower,
mint green and fresh as cool water.

—Alison Rittershaus

Trinity

Clover wears mint green
as fresh as cool water.
No fruit or floral adornment
places her in a season.
She lies dormant beneath ice
or listless among brown blades
or expectant amidst bees
but she is always there,
the old stand-by,
patiently waiting
to be appreciated never.
Our unnoticed gem
spreads her three fronds—
mint green as fresh as cool water—
and catches the sun.

—Alison Rittershaus

Skylight Man

Forever watching,
forever staring,
forever he surveys the world
through his sun-tinted monocle.
Silent,
streaked with rain,
unmoved by wind,
he stands guard.
I see my face in him
as I wake and as I drift
to sleep.

I feel his solitude
seep down
into a cold gray puddle
around my feet.
He never smiles
nor does he blink.
I do those things for him
when the light
is just right.

   —Niall Janney

Adirondack Chair

The four-legged beast
squats, stationary.
Its back, arched toward heaven,
invites me.
I stalk it
then drop
into its rough, comforting embrace
and let myself be
taken.

   —Jacob Miller

Hypodermic

A devil
lies in wait
for its next sacrifice.
It spies one,
fills with poison,
and sends its puffy white assistant
to prepare the unwilling victim.
Then
this being of pure evil
roars up
and sinks its single fang
into the distressed prey,
pumps its poison into the bloodstream
until it has tortured sufficiently.
It retreats, fang glistening
with your blood.

   —Benjamin F. Williams

Personification is the easiest way I know for a poet to enter the world of metaphor.

PRESENTING THE POEM:

Litany

BY BILLY COLLINS

SETTING THE SCENE: Love poems are famous for their use of metaphors. There's a tradition in Western poetry that's hundreds of years old called a *blazon,* a poem in which the lover compares the loved one to lists of things that are beautiful or worthy or rare, to demonstrate the beauty, worth, and rarity of his or her love.

Billy Collins turns the convention of the *blazon* on its head in his poem "Litany." People use the word *litany* in everyday conversation to mean a long, monotonous list. Here, in his "litany," Collins lists ridiculous love metaphors.

He begins with an *epigraph:* that's a brief quote from someone else's writing, in this case, another poet's blazon. Then he borrows these first two lines of the other poet's poem and proceeds to rewrite the rest of it. It quickly becomes clear that Collins is poking twenty-first century fun—at the original poem, at metaphors that categorize the qualities of a loved one, and at this whole tradition of love poetry.

SOME FEATURES TO NOTICE:
- The humor
- The sarcastic attitude of the speaker
- The movement of the poem, from the stereotypical and flowery love imagery of the first stanza, to the shifts in tone to subtle sarcasm that are signaled by *however* at the beginning of the second stanza and *it might interest you to know* at the beginning of the fifth

- How the language *around* the metaphors is informal, conversational, and full of an attitude that isn't present in the metaphors
- The silliness of the individual images
- How, in the conclusion, Collins points out the improbability of the combination of metaphors in the epigraph borrowed first lines

RESPONSE STANCE: Please go back into this sarcastic poem and underline the lines and metaphors that crack you up—that you want to savor.

BENEDICTION: This poem, like so many by Billy Collins, was a joy to read aloud. Let's read it aloud together, with *attitude* . . .

I know how much you guys like sarcasm and parody. This is something you might try: to play with metaphor by going over the top, or by creating metaphors that either don't work or don't work the way they're "supposed" to.

Litany

You are the bread and the knife,
The crystal goblet and the wine . . .
—Jacques Crickillon

You are the bread and the knife,
the crystal goblet and the wine.
You are the dew on the morning grass
and the burning wheel of the sun.
You are the white apron of the baker
and the marsh birds suddenly in flight.

However, you are not the wind in the orchard,
the plums on the counter,
or the house of cards.
And you are certainly not the pine-scented air.
There is just no way you are the pine-scented air.

It is possible that you are the fish under the bridge,
maybe even the pigeon on the general's head,
but you are not even close
to being the field of cornflowers at dusk.

And a quick look in the mirror will show
that you are neither the boots in the corner
nor the boat asleep in its boathouse.

It might interest you to know,
speaking of the plentiful imagery of the world,
that I am the sound of rain on the roof.

I also happen to be a shooting star,
the evening paper blowing down an alley,
and the basket of chestnuts on the kitchen table.

I am also the moon in the trees
and the blind woman's tea cup.
But don't worry, I am not the bread and the knife.
You are still the bread and the knife.
You will always be the bread and the knife,
not to mention the crystal goblet and—somehow—the wine.
   —Billy Collins

How Can I Describe?

BY ZEPHYR WEATHERBEE

&

The Skirmish

BY NAT HERZ

&

Job Description

BY PHAELON O'DONNELL

SETTING THE STAGE: Zephyr, an eighth-grade poet, invented a new kind of poetic device, which he named a *decoded metaphor*. He was playing around with metaphor in a poem about ice skating and wrote a literal description of skating, alternating, in parentheses, with a metaphoric version of the same event. Read along with me . . .

Decoded metaphors caught on in Zephyr's class. Nat used a version of the technique to describe a soccer game, and Phaelon applied it to the effects of spring weather.

SOME FEATURES TO NOTICE:

- How Nat extends one metaphor—a soccer game as medieval warfare—throughout the poem, reverses Zephyr's approach, and sticks to simple, minimal language—nouns and verbs—in his parenthetical decodings
- How Phaelon's parenthetical decodings are sensory, specific, and crafted versions of her metaphors

RESPONSE STANCE: Please go back into "Job Description" and "The Skirmish" and mark your favorite decodings.

BENEDICTION: Here's a twist to writing with metaphor that might appeal to your playful side. What's a topic you'd like to write about twice in one poem?

How Can I Describe?

The ice
(black glass)
is covered in snow
(thick styrofoam),
and I can't see a thing
(I'm in a void)
because of the mist
(my cocoon).

I skate along
(float)
with my family
(above the crowd)

thinking
(not thinking at all).

    —Zephyr Weatherbee

Job Description

Spring delivers
the lushest lollipops
(blazing colors of flowers).
Spring showers
chitter chat on branches
(birds in pines, birches, poplars).
Spring shines sugarcake
(warmth from sun)
on everyone.

    —Phaelon O'Donnell

The Skirmish

I stride onto the field, prepared for battle (the game),
a warrior with an army (team) behind me.

The ambassadors (refs) check the generals (goalies),
and the skirmish (play) begins.

The opposing army makes the initial charge (kick),
but we counterattack (steal the ball).
Our archers (defense) put momentum (ball)
in the hands of our knights (offense).
We conquer their territory,

and suddenly there is nothing between me and their general.
I gallop (sprint) past him
and capture the castle (score).

I have drawn first blood.

    —Nat Herz

It might be that by virtue in rural Mau live close to r kids do deve to the woods

The Natural

World:

INTRODUCTION

It's easy to assume that by virtue of our location in rural New England, my students live close to nature. While some kids do develop strong ties to the woods, rivers, and shoreline of midcoast Maine, under the influence of parents whose work or interests take them outdoors, the majority of my students are as wrapped up as any adolescents anywhere in popular culture—celebrities, pro sports, movies, television series, MTV, Ipods, clothing brands, and video and computer games. I began teaching poetry about the natural world to get kids outside, to get them noticing what's out there, and to get them caring about preserving it.

An important incentive for my students to write nature poems is the annual River of Words poetry contest, co-sponsored by former U. S. Poet Laureate Robert Hass, the Library of Congress, and the International Rivers Network. Their website can be found at www.riverofwords.org. Many of the student poems included in this collection were winners or finalists in a River of Words competition.

Homemade Swimming Hole

BY MICHAEL STOLTZ

SETTING THE STAGE: Michael spent most of the summer before seventh grade in the pond behind his house—actually, not a pond, but a depression he and his dad dug and that rain filled with water. Michael's poem about his homemade swimming hole captures that summer for all time.

SOME FEATURES TO NOTICE:
- The strong, sensory diction: verbs, nouns, and adjectives
- The metaphor: *chocolate water*
- How Michael's line breaks mimic and support the action of the poem
- How the poem turns on the line *I am twelve* and becomes an elegy to a place and time in Michael's life

RESPONSE STANCE: Please go back into Michael's sensory poem on your own and note everything he did as a poet that puts you *there*, at his pond with him. Also notice his conclusion and what it does for the poem.

BENEDICTION: None of the nature poems we read over the next days will be about awe-inspiring encounters with raw and powerful nature: no avalanches, no typhoons, no white-water rafting expeditions. Rather, we'll visit moments and places where a person and the natural world intersected, and the individual noticed and transformed the experience as poetry. These are the best nature poems—when a poet brings together the landscape out there and the landscape within and makes his or her own meaning of it, as Michael did here. Start looking for and thinking about your moments, your places, where the outer and inner landscapes connect.

Homemade Swimming Hole

I clamber up the ladder,
its cold metal bars
slippery
from previous jumps.
I grab the soft white rope
high in hand,
pick up my feet,
and time stops
before I plunge
into chocolate water.

Seconds later
I resurface.
Moist evening air
surrounds me
as I float on my back,
bewitched
by a darkening sky.
I am twelve.
There is no better place
on Earth.

—*Michael Stoltz*

PRESENTING THE POEM:

As imperceptibly as Grief

BY EMILY DICKINSON

SETTING THE STAGE: Of all of America's poets, Emily Dickinson is best at bringing the events and language of natural phenomena to bear on the inner landscape of human feelings. Her poems were a diary of her insides, often described metaphorically through the language of science. For a woman of nineteenth century New England, she knew a lot about nature. Dickinson was a great botanist and geologist, and she studied astronomy. She viewed nature realistically. The ideas of science helped her as a poet to express the complexity of human existence.

Dickinson lived from 1830 to 1886, the last twenty-five of these years as a hermit on her father's property in Amherst, Massachusetts. She never married, and she published only eleven poems in her lifetime. After her death, her relatives found almost 1,800 poems in the drawers of her bedroom bureau, sewn into little packets. These were published, and their gemlike lyrics, startling metaphors, bold images, irregular rhymes, and wit were a major influence on the poets of the twentieth century.

My favorite quote from Emily Dickinson is, "My business is circumference." I think she meant that her job as a poet was to travel the boundaries of life through language and, with words, to create unity: to try to lasso the chaos through her poems.

Today's poem by Emily Dickinson is about the subtle changes in the natural world that signal the end of summer. It's difficult, but it's worth it.

SOME FEATURES TO NOTICE:
- Vocabulary:
  imperceptible means slight, gradual, or subtle;
  perfidy means disloyalty or treachery;
  distilled, here, means concentrated;
  sequestered means secluded or isolated;

harrowing, here, means deeply disturbing;
a **keel**, here, is a ship or boat
- The amazing, surprising diction and imagery
- How there is no title; Dickinson's poems are either numbered to keep track of them or referred to by their first line
- The odd use of dashes and capitals: this was Dickinson's style, and any edition of her work that doesn't reproduce it isn't authentic
- How Dickinson personifies summer as a guest who is ready to leave; as a female presence who makes a *light escape*
- How Dickinson compares the subtlety of summer's end to the way grief over someone's death gradually fades
- How the end of summer comes so gradually that its departure doesn't feel like an act of disloyalty
- The similes: how summer's end is like concentrated quiet; like a twilight that began a long time ago; like nature, also personified, spending an afternoon alone with herself
- How dusk comes earlier now and the morning light seems *foreign*—strange or remote
- How although summer doesn't leave rudely, its departure is still distressing to us
- How although summer departs like a physical presence, she doesn't have to fly like a bird or sail like a boat to make her escape
- How Dickinson proposes that summer's destination is *Into the Beautiful:* where else could something so wonderful alight?

RESPONSE STANCE: Please go back into this beautiful but difficult poem and mark all the words and lines that confuse you. We'll unpack this one together.

BENEDICTION: Dickinson is a poet whose words I say to myself often—not whole poems usually, but groups of lines that resonate. The day I understand that summer is truly gone and that fall is really here, I say the last four lines of this poem in my mind, and, somehow, it helps. Memorize them and see if they'll help you come September.

As imperceptibly as Grief
The Summer lapsed away—
Too imperceptible at last
To seem like Perfidy—

A Quietness distilled
As Twilight long begun,
Or Nature spending with herself
Sequestered Afternoon—
The Dusk drew earlier in—
The Morning foreign shone—
A courteous, yet harrowing Grace,
As Guest, that would be gone—
And thus, without a Wing
Or service of a Keel
Our Summer made her light escape
Into the Beautiful.

    —Emily Dickinson

PRESENTING THE POEM:

Out

BY BRENNA HAGEN

SETTING THE STAGE: Brenna, a seventh grader, also wrote a poem about the end of summer. Hers is filled with sensations—what she saw, felt, and heard; what she'll remember when winter comes, when it's too cold to go *out*.

SOME FEATURES TO NOTICE:

- How the poem is a list of the sensations Brenna remembers from a particular late-summer day
- How she decides to forgo punctuation and let the sensations of the day flow into one other
- The strong, sensory details
- The colloquial diction that strengthens the affect: *awesome; so cool*
- A concluding line that breaks the four-line stanza form and makes the poem personal
- A strong color word: *yellow*

RESPONSE STANCE: Please go back into Brenna's poem and mark everything here she did that you like and want to talk about.

BENEDICTION: Brenna wrote "Out" in December—closed her eyes and remembered August with all her senses. Think of a day in nature that you'd like to summon up. Sit quietly and see if the sights, sounds, and feelings that you loved lie waiting inside you, to be tapped as a poem.

Out

the yellow butterfly
against that awesome sky
the days those clouds
were so cool

the wind blowing t-shirts
and our hair as we felt
the breezes with all
our senses

the trees rocking
the grass blowing
the crickets humming
the last song of summer
calling my name

   —Brenna Hagen

PRESENTING THE POEMS:

When I was searching for a poem

BY ZOË MASON

&

Deeper

BY ROBERT LANGTON

SETTING THE STAGE: Zoë and Robert, two seventh graders, went looking for meaning in the natural world. Their experiences—with a fox and a bird—brought them different understandings than they had anticipated.

SOME FEATURES TO NOTICE—"WHEN I WAS SEARCHING FOR A POEM":

- How the title also functions as the first line of the poem
- How Zoë's use of repetition creates a cadence
- How her poem turns in the last stanza as she freeze-frames the image of herself and the fox with the one-word line *There.*
- How the conclusion draws a human and a wild being into the same universe and unites them with a feeling—*fear of the unknown*— and with the stone wall, which is half natural and half manmade.

SOME FEATURES TO NOTICE—"DEEPER":

- How each of the stanzas represents a point of view: the human's, then the bird's
- How Robert contrasts the human arrogance in the first stanza with the bird's dismissal of him in the second
- How the repetition of *deeper* and *a deeper meaning* creates a cadence

RESPONSE STANCE: Please go back into one of these two poems—your choice—and mark what seem to you to be its most important lines. Also, mark anything else the poet did that you like.

BENEDICTION: Searching for deep significance in the natural world, Zoë and Robert instead found particular connections that surprised them. As nature poets, you don't need a grand theme or an earth-shattering experience, just your own five senses and your own poet's mind, heart, and words to bring to bear on what you perceive.

When I was
searching for a poem

a fox stepped out of nowhere.
His long legs stretched across the stone wall.
He paused as we stared,
both wondering where the other was going,
although it was obvious each was wandering—
lost.
I paused as we stared,
both wondering why the other was here
on a stone wall
although it was obvious we were
using it for direction—
lost.
He wasn't a sly fox—
at least I didn't see it in his eyes.
He was frightened.
I'd never seen a fox before.
I was frightened, too.

There.
A living poem—
a girl, a fox
connected
only by a stone wall
and a fear of the unknown.

       —Zoë Mason

Deeper

A bird tapped at my window,
trying to crack open a sunflower seed.
I stared at it
in search of a deeper meaning
but found none.
Should I be surprised?
Can any creature but man have a purpose?

The bird stood up and looked me in the eye.
In that glint I saw
it searching for a deeper meaning.
Finding none, it turned
and flew away.

       —Robert Langton

The Lake

BY SOPHIE CABOT BLACK

SETTING THE STAGE: This is a mysterious, beautiful poem about, I think, an unlikely subject. Sophie Cabot Black personifies a lake, but not any lake. This one is high up and alone among mountains.

SOME FEATURES TO NOTICE:
- The series of images in this extended personification: *the lake dreams*; she has a *whole eye*, a *brow*, and a *cheek*; *she cannot help abundance*; etc.
- The specific visual imagery
- The surprising and beautiful diction
- The tone: one of isolation and loneliness
- How the final stanza compares the lake and the *abundance* of her *creeks* and *spill* to a woman whose children leave her

RESPONSE STANCE: Please go back into this poem and mark the words and lines that *personify* the lake—and any others that you like and want to talk about.

BENEDICTION: Again, let me invite you to think, as poets, about the technique of personification. I have a mental image of Sophie Cabot Black flying in a plane above mountains, spying a glacial lake below, and wondering how it "feels." Open your eyes and hearts. Look for the natural phenomena you'd like to empathize with and bring to life.

The Lake

Day and night, the lake dreams of sky.
A privacy as old as the mountains
And her up there, stuck among peaks. The whole eye

Fastened on hawk, gatherings of cloud or stars,
So little trespass. An airplane once
Crossed her brow; she searched but could not find

A face. Having lived with such strict beauty
She comes to know the sun is nothing
But itself and the path it throws; the moon

A riddled stone. If only a hand
Would tremble along her cheek, would disturb. Even the elk
Pass by, drawn to the spill of the creeks below—

How she cannot help abundance, even as it leaves
Her, as it sings all the way down the mountain.

    —*Sophie Cabot Black*

The Pond

BY MARNIE BRIGGS

SETTING THE STAGE: Marnie, an eighth grader, is lucky to have a pond behind her house—lucky, among other reasons, because a poem about it helped Marnie measure the cycles and seasons of her childhood.

SOME FEATURES TO NOTICE:
- The form: how each of the first four stanzas begins with a season
- The strong, evocative verbs: *trudge*, *perch*, *pull*, *glide*, etc., ending with *harbors*
- The sensory details that establish the mood
- How the poem turns in the last three lines, as Marnie draws personal meaning from the seasonal activities on the pond

RESPONSE STANCE: One of the strengths of this sensory poem is its verbs. First, would you mark the verbs you think are strongest—are most sensory? Then, would you please mark anything else Marnie did that you like? We'll also talk about the conclusion and what it does for the poem.

BENEDICTION: I didn't have a pond as a kid, but I did have a creek and field behind my house where I played and pretended, alone and alongside my dog, brother, sister, and neighborhood friends. The creek and field are the places in nature that framed my childhood; they're my poem about me back then, waiting to be written. What's your natural place?

The Pond

In winter
I trudge down to the pond.
Bundled up in winter protection,
I carry a bag stuffed with extra mittens and socks.
I perch on the icy dock that's halfway buried in snow,
pull on my skates,
and glide onto the clean cold glass.

In spring
I skip down to the pond,
my fishing rod swung over my back.
I try to catch minnows—use leaves as bait
and daydream under the new sun.

In summer
I scamper down to the pond
with a towel wrapped around my body.
I stand at the edge of the dock
and it kills me
not knowing what lurks in the mysterious waters.
But I take a running jump into the cold glaze anyway.
It shatters, sending ripples everywhere.

In fall
I wander down to the pond.
It's barren and deserted—
no skating, no swimming.
I gaze into the still water
and watch my pure reflection
as it changes from younger to older,

as the murky water harbors
the seasons of my childhood.

     —*Marnie Briggs*

©2006 by Nancie Atwell from *Naming the World: A Year of Poems and Lessons*
(Portsmouth, NH: Heinemann)

PRESENTING THE POEM:

Golden

BY SIOBHAN ANDERSON

SETTING THE STAGE: One—of many—things I like about today's nature poem is that it isn't set in nature. Here's the scene: Siobhan is inside her house. It's early morning, and she's on her way to the bathroom. The word *bathroom* does not appear in the poem; that's a bit of non-poetic information Siobhan revealed in a writing conference.

Anyway, she's stumbling down the hall and by chance glances out the window. And there it is: a golden moment and a poem waiting to be written.

SOME FEATURES TO NOTICE:
- How the whole poem is about a moment—a scene glimpsed and captured
- The form: four-line stanzas, with a two-line concluding stanza where the poem turns
- The color words that support the title and create a golden aura: *honey colored*, *amber*, *tawny*
- The alliteration: **s**unlight **s**treams through a **s**ingle window

RESPONSE STANCE: Please go back into "Golden" and mark the words and lines that help you see what Siobhan saw that morning.

BENEDICTION: Even when you're inside, the natural world is out there, waiting. Start glancing: what's the light doing? The sky? A bird? Find your own golden vision and capture it before the wind blows it away.

Golden

My eyes are still closed
as my feet find their way down the hall.
Sunlight streams through a single window.
I glance out, my eyes parallel to the horizon,

and the grass is a stunning emerald.
Out on the bay, peaked with gold,
ducks flock in honey colored beams.
Light sifts through amber feathers.

Each wears a tawny halo,
moves to the same rhythm,
a ballet so simple and fragile
a single breath of wind

could turn it all
into memory.

—Siobhan Anderson

©2006 by Nancie Atwell from *Naming the World: A Year of Poems and Lessons*
(Portsmouth, NH: Heinemann)

PRESENTING THE POEM:

There's a certain Slant of light

BY EMILY DICKINSON

SETTING THE STAGE: Today's poem by Emily Dickinson is one I've memorized in full. It describes a way that light sometimes appears on winter afternoons—not the cheerful light of full sun on snow, but what she calls a *slant* of light—a line of sun that comes down and hits the heart. There are afternoons in January and February when I see a slant of sun pierce the gray and I can name the somber feeling it gives me inside because of Emily Dickinson's poem.

SOME FEATURES TO NOTICE:
- Vocabulary:
  oppresses means weighs down or burdens
  heft means weight or heaviness
  seal, here, means a symbol of something
  imperial, here, means of a supreme ruler
  affliction means a state of misery or grief
  distance probably means coolness or aloofness, here—not familiar or friendly
  look, here, means appearance
- The surprising diction and imagery
- How the *Slant of light* doesn't hurt us physically—*we can find no scar*—but, rather, pains us inside

- How no one on earth can control or change it
- How it is the symbol of misery
- How the light reminds us—all living things, including the *landscape* and *shadows*—of death and our own mortality
- The similes: in the first stanza the slant of light weighs us down like heavy organ hymns in a cathedral; in the last, when the light disappears, it's as if we've seen the face of death

RESPONSE STANCE: Please go back into this amazing, difficult poem on your own and mark the hard words and lines, the ones that confuse you. Then we'll unpack the poem together.

BENEDICTION: You may want to take this poem into your life, too; it's a good one to know by heart. It's also good to know that nature poems don't have to be happy—aren't required to be joyful celebrations of the natural world. We can relate our inner landscape to the landscape *out there* in ways that reveal our confusion, grief, anger, or fear. Nature is a generous prism; she can absorb and reflect all of our moods as individuals who have feelings and write poems.

There's a certain Slant of light,
Winter Afternoons—
That oppresses, like the Heft
Of Cathedral Tunes—

Heavenly Hurt, it gives us—
We can find no scar,
But internal difference,
Where the Meanings, are—

None may teach it—Any—
'Tis the Seal Despair—
An imperial affliction
Sent us of the Air—

When it comes, the Landscape listens—
Shadows—hold their breath—
When it goes, 'tis like the Distance
On the look of Death—

    —Emily Dickinson

PRESENTING THE POEMS:

Through the Eyes of Morning
BY ANNE ATWELL-MCLEOD

&

Viewed
BY NIALL JANNEY

SETTING THE STAGE: Yesterday we talked about how nature poems don't have to be happy—how nature is a canvas that we can paint with dark moods and feelings, too. In seventh grade, Anne tried to find herself in a morning glimpse of a misty winter field, and Niall wondered if he had found his mood in the journey of a single snowflake.

SOME FEATURES TO NOTICE—"THROUGH THE EYES OF MORNING":
- How Anne slows down the poem and this moment with line breaks
- The strong, sensory diction: nouns, verbs, and adjectives
- The simile: the frozen fog as *lace* from the *intricate garments of a queen*
- How morning is personified
- The cadence created by the *yet/as* constructions
- How the poem turns and the tone changes in the last two stanzas, when Anne can't find her identity or lift her spirits in this wintry vision

SOME FEATURES TO NOTICE—"VIEWED":
- The strong, sensory diction: nouns, verbs, and adjectives
- The figurative language: *Dun grass sprouts/ like hair on a man's scalp;* the snow is *static* on *earth's TV screen*

- How the mood of the poem turns in the fourth stanza
- How the repetition of *Fooled* creates a cadence and emphasizes Niall's sense of unease about who he is
- How Niall invents a form—four-line stanzas— and how his title is part of the first line

RESPONSE STANCE: Please choose one of these two poems to go back into on your own. Mark where the poem turns—where its tone or mood changes. Would you also mark the words and lines you wish you had written?

BENEDICTION: The range of human emotion is wide and deep; so are the possibilities for poems that draw on earth's features for their imagery. Search in the natural habitat for metaphors for *all* your moods.

Through the Eyes of Morning

The long
complicated
elements of morning
drape themselves
across the dew touched meadow
as if they are
lace
from the intricate garments of a queen
who has chosen
this moment
to blow a frosty kiss to her people
through the fog—
so intensely ghost white
that if you look deep enough
you can see yourself.

And so I look.
Deep.
Hoping that if something as simple
yet intense,
as young
yet ancient,
as morning
knows who I am, maybe I will too.

But I only see the dew.
And the fog.

And who is anyone
through the distorted eyes
of morning?

          —*Anne Atwell-McLeod*

Viewed

from a window, the bitter wind
and torrent of snowflakes
seem a blessing. Dun grass sprouts
like hair on a man's scalp,

barely visible under the thin layer of snow.
I stare, transfixed by the static
of earth's TV screen.
Concentrating, I try

to follow a single snowflake to the ground
and succeed one, two, three times, then turn,
blinking. The feeling of a new beginning
swirls within me.

Yet, it's an end.
The snow falls silently to the grass—
a fatal conclusion to a plummeting journey.
Am I just another snowflake, tumbling

in joyful spirals? Fooled into believing
I'm climbing into crisp clean air?
Fooled into thinking my flight
will last forever? Fooled, until I hit the ground?

          —*Niall Janney*

PRESENTING THE POEM:

Traveling through the Dark

BY WILLIAM STAFFORD

SETTING THE STAGE: Poems about nature can also reveal our impact on nature—can draw notice to how people change or harm the natural world. William Stafford wrote one of the most subtle poems I know about the noxious effects of the Industrial Age.

SOME FEATURES TO NOTICE:

- How the word *swerve* in the first stanza refers to the speaker accepting what he must do, as well as preventing the possibility of another car and another accident; how the word *swerving* reappears in the final stanza to describe the speaker's moment of contemplation and regret
- How the first three stanzas tell a story and do so with strong visual imagery
- How the poem turns on the line *Beside that mountain road I hesitated* at the end of the third stanza
- How in the personification of the fourth stanza the speaker's car takes on the character of another living being in this landscape: it *aimed* its lights; its engine *purred*; its exhaust is *warm*
- How the man, the machine, the doe, and the fawn become a group—*our group*—observed by the wilderness around them, which wonders what the man will do
- How the man makes the only possible choice, although not before he *thought hard*—not without concern and regret that the machine age has brought this kind of devastation to the wilderness
- The form: four-line stanzas, with a two-line turn at the end

RESPONSE STANCE: Please go back into this thoughtful poem on your own and mark what you think are its most important lines.

BENEDICTION: In another of his poems, "Pretty Good Day," William Stafford wrote "All stories/ add up to where you are now." What's one of your stories about nature and you, or nature and other people, that adds up to how you feel about human encroachment on natural habitats?

Traveling through the Dark

Traveling through the dark I found a deer
dead on the edge of the Wilson River road.
It is usually best to roll them into the canyon:
that road is narrow; to swerve might make more dead.

By glow of the tail-light I stumbled back of the car
and stood by the heap, a doe, a recent killing;
she had stiffened already, almost cold.
I dragged her off; she was large in the belly.

My fingers touching her side brought me the reason—
her side was warm; her fawn lay there waiting,
alive, still, never to be born.
Beside that mountain road I hesitated.

The car aimed ahead its lowered parking lights;
under the hood purred the steady engine.
I stood in the glare of the warm exhaust turning red;
around our group I could hear the wilderness listen.

I thought hard for us all—my only swerving—
then pushed her over the edge into the river.
            —*William Stafford*

PRESENTING THE POEM:

Thoreau's Nightmare

BY ALISON RITTERSHAUS

SETTING THE STAGE: Here's Alison's story about how people are harming the natural world. It's set in Concord, Massachusetts, famous as the site of Walden Pond. That's where, back in the 1840's, the writer Henry David Thoreau lived all alone for two years in a sparsely furnished cabin.

Thoreau wrote, "I went to the woods because I wished to live deliberately, to front only the essential facts of life, and see if I could not learn what it had to teach, and not, when I came to die, discover that I had not lived." Thoreau got rid of most of his material possessions. In his cabin he read, wrote, and watched the seasons unfold. His observations, recorded in his book *Walden, or, Life in the Woods* (1854), are some of the most beautiful nature writing ever. Thoreau's overarching theme was that people should imitate the economy of nature: "Our life is frittered away by detail," he wrote. "Simplify, simplify."

Alison, a fan of Thoreau's writing, journeyed with her mother to Concord and Walden Pond a hundred and fifty years after he published *Walden*, and this is what she found.

SOME FEATURES TO NOTICE:
- The convincing sound effects
- The evocative figurative language: a *Starbucks . . . crouched in the elbow of an intersection; the sticky molasses of polluted air; the crying of the street; the tight fist/of chaos*
- The surprising diction: nouns, verbs, and adjectives

- The strong, specific imagery: readers can see, hear, and feel this scene
- How the repetition of *Don't* in the three questions that end the poem emphasizes Alison's anguish
- How Alison broke the words of the last stanza and italicized the last three lines to slow down and emphasize the meaning
- How she mentions *Thoreau* in the title and *Concordians* in the body of the poem and expects that a smart reader will unpack the setting and its significance

RESPONSE STANCE: Please go back into "Thoreau's Nightmare" and mark its tone: every word or line that reveals to you exactly what Alison was seeing, hearing, and feeling in twenty-first century Concord. You might as well start with the title.

RESPONSE TASK: Poems that protest can take lots of forms. Alison sharpened her powers of observation *and* her sense of sarcasm to vent about the poisoned atmosphere in a town that's famous world over for its celebration of wilderness. Her *particular* experience reveals a *universal* problem. What is a particular experience of yours related to pollution, litter, over-development, commercialization, loss of wilderness? Reveal and protest the universal issue of environmental devastation by crafting the specifics of your own story.

Thoreau's Nightmare

We pull out of Starbucks,
the coffee capitol
crouched in the elbow
of an intersection.
Cars impatiently honk—
Waaaank!—
and crisscross one another's path,
drivers cursing
through bared teeth.
Their angst makes the light
click green again,
and my mother's car slides forward
through the sticky molasses
of polluted air.

I crank my arm and roll open the window.
A low flying jet,
engine screaming,
rips through the air—
Vrrrriiiiiissssh!—
as the line of cars stops once again,
and a pedestrian scuttles along a crosswalk.
I crane my neck to watch the plane,
and the drivers accelerate—
Crrooooomeeeek!—
only to be jerked in their seats to another halt.

As the sub-woofers
of a hundred cars rush by
and around the bend—
ToomtoomWOOMtoomtoom!—
and careen out of sight,
two perfect Concordians,
crisp in white blouses
and black knee length skirts,
sidle up the road,
oblivious to the crying of the street.

Don't they see the distortion
of the history,
the beauty and the tranquility?
Don't they feel the tight fist
of chaos, of hurried crosswalks
and spilled coffee,
of stifling, poison air?

Don't they hear
all
this
noise?

—Alison Rittershaus

Madeleines:
INTRODUCTION

This collection began with a poem of my own. One April afternoon I was walking with my dog in the woods next to our house and something—some combination of the quality of the light and a rawness in the air—transported me to the field behind the house where I grew up and the fantasy lives I made-believe there for me and another dog, forty-five years before. The sensation became a poem.

Pioneer Dreams

In a green clearing
I clear my mind.
The air and the light
just right
reverse time.

I'm the girl
who escaped into green fields
with Lizzie the dog,
crashed through reeds,
whittled at sticks with a Girl Scout knife,
collected cockleburs,
and leapt the creek.
Heart brimful in love
with green,
solitude,
adventures I pretended with Rin Tin Tin,
Colin and Mary,
Annie Oakley,
and Francis Marion the Swamp Fox.
I was my own first romance.

Today in a green clearing,
the air and the light
just right,
I reclaim the green in me,
the daydream world,
and the lost girl.

I used the drafts of "Pioneer Dreams" to illustrate a lesson about revision and polishing, but my kids were more taken with the poem's subject than with my objective. There were lots of comments along the lines of, "Whenever I eat one of those round butterscotch candies, I'm back at my great-grandmother's house," or "When I see the first dandelions, I remember how I used to stage these dandelion battles in my backyard."

I told the kids the story of Proust's *madeleine*: the sugar cookie Marcel nibbles at the beginning of *Remembrance of Things Past* that summons up the first of many "privileged moments" of memory, and which allows him to live in the past and present and to glimpse the essence of both.

Some of the kids began to write their own "madeleines," and I began to notice and collect published poems that seemed, to me at least, Proustian.

On Turning Ten

BY BILLY COLLINS

SETTING THE SCENE: Grown-ups are excited for little kids when they turn ten: "Oh, you're growing up—you're double digits now." We forget that children don't always want to grow up— that as much as you gain, you lose. Billy Collins is a grown-up who does remember the downside of turning ten.

SOME FEATURES TO NOTICE:

- The apt figurative language in the first stanza: childhood diseases as metaphors for the child's emotion
- How the specific fantasies in the second stanza ring true and reveal what the boy will miss about childhood
- The visual imagery of the third stanza
- How the poem turns in the fourth stanza as the boy realizes that his new awareness of loss, his nostalgia for the time before ten, *is the beginning of sadness*
- The powerful concluding stanza that illuminates the difference between then and now

RESPONSE STANCE: Please go back into "On Turning Ten" on your own and mark every line that Collins *got right*—every point at which you recognize what he's talking about.

BENEDICTION: Again, grown-ups assume that kids don't feel nostalgic—that even at your age you're too young to look back at, remember, and *miss* your earlier incarnations. I think you guys know otherwise. I think there are times when something you see, hear, taste, even smell gives you a sudden glimpse of your childhood self. This week's poems, by kids and pros, are flashbacks to childhood. I hope they'll inspire flashback poems of your own.

On Turning Ten

The whole idea of it makes me feel
like I'm coming down with something,
something worse than any stomach ache
or the headaches I get from reading in bad light—
a kind of measles of the spirit,
a mumps of the psyche,
a disfiguring chicken pox of the soul.

You tell me it is too early to be looking back,
but that is because you have forgotten
the perfect simplicity of being one
and the beautiful complexity introduced by two.
But I can lie on my bed and remember every digit.
At four I was an Arabian wizard.
I could make myself invisible
by drinking a glass of milk a certain way.
At seven I was a soldier, at nine a prince.

But now I am mostly at the window
watching the late afternoon light.
Back then it never fell so solemnly
against the side of my tree house,
and my bicycle never leaned against the garage
as it does today,
all the dark blue speed drained out of it.

This is the beginning of sadness, I say to myself,
as I walk through the universe in my sneakers.
It is time to say good-bye to my imaginary friends,
time to turn the first big number.

It seems only yesterday I used to believe
there was nothing under my skin but light.
If you cut me I would shine.
But now when I fall upon the sidewalks of life,
I skin my knees. I bleed.

  —*Billy Collins*

Looking Back through My Telescope

BY EBEN COURT

SETTING THE STAGE: In a famous long novel by Marcel Proust titled *Remembrance of Things Past*, the narrator eats a sugar cookie called a *madeleine*, and the taste of it suddenly transports him back to his childhood. For Eben, a seventh-grade poet, his madeleine was a sailboat that's been sitting on his lawn for as long as he can remember. As a twelve-year-old he passed it every day without notice or a thought; then, one spring day, something in the air acted as Eben's madeleine.

SOME FEATURES TO NOTICE:

- How the first line and concluding stanza echo one another and create both a powerful lead and a poignant conclusion
- How the specific details of Eben's pirate fantasy bring it to life
- How the setting shifts between the second and third stanza, from past to present, with a signal from the word *Now*
- How, in the third stanza, the passage of time has transformed—reduced—the *golden telescope* into *a battered paper towel roll/ that someone long ago painted yellow:* a telling detail about the shift in Eben's perspective from childhood to adolescence

RESPONSE STANCE: Please go back into Eben's poem, read it, and write a sentence or two about the feelings you get from it. Then mark the lines and words that summon up those feelings.

BENEDICTION: What's your version of the *Old Crow?* Is it a treehouse? A wooded place near your house or the school? Your bedroom closet? Your basement rec room? Your swing-set? Your old dress-up clothes? The collection of toys your grandmother kept at her house for you and your cousins to play with? See if you can summon up the feelings and details of your place of fantasy play.

Looking Back through
My Telescope

All hands on deck I yell
as I stand on the bow of the *Old Crow*,
the abandoned sailboat
propped in our backyard
and now my very own red and black pirate ship.
All that summer I explore the seven seas
with my first and second mates,
Jerry and Joe.

Land ho I yell
as I check the lines
and peer through my golden telescope.
I spot another ship—
it flies the skull and crossbones, too.
We come up beside it.
Fire the cannons I scream
as I board her,
then fight off the pirates
and steal their chests of treasure.

Now I look back at the *Old Crow*
through a battered paper towel roll
that someone long ago painted yellow.
The boat's still red and black
but Joe and Jerry made their escape,
for good I suppose,
and it's almost as if my ship
has disappeared
or I can't see it anymore.

All hands on deck.
All things must change.
 —*Eben Court*

©2006 by Nancie Atwell from *Naming the World: A Year of Poems and Lessons*
(Portsmouth, NH: Heinemann)

PRESENTING THE POEM:

Wax Lips

BY CYNTHIA RYLANT

SETTING THE STAGE: For me, penny candy is a major madeleine. I understand that these days no candy still costs a penny, but you recognize the kind I'm thinking of: Atomic fireballs, Bazooka, Smarties, Nik'l'Nips. Just saying the names makes me feel ten again. This poem by Cynthia Rylant evokes the sensation of one of the best penny candies ever.

SOME FEATURES TO NOTICE:
- The particular, sensory details that bring Todd's Hardware and the experience of wearing wax lips to life
- The visual color words: *red*, *purple*, *white*
- The conclusion that measures the distance between a child biting hard on sugared wax and the day she'll have *lips worth kissing*

RESPONSE STANCE: Please go back into this sensory poem and mark the lines you can see, feel, and taste.

BENEDICTION: What's your candy? What's *the one* that acts as your madeleine and brings it all back for you?

Wax Lips

Todd's Hardware was dust and a monkey—
a real one, on the second floor—
and Mrs. Todd there behind the glass cases.
We stepped over buckets of nails and lawnmowers
to get to the candy counter in the back,
and pointed at the red wax lips,
and Mary Janes,
and straws full of purple sugar.
Said goodbye to Mrs. Todd, she white-faced and silent,
and walked the streets of Beaver,
our teeth sunk hard in the wax,
and big red lips worth kissing.

— *Cynthia Rylant*

PRESENTING THE POEM:

Digging for China

BY RICHARD WILBUR

SETTING THE STAGE: I don't know if there's a child in America who hasn't been told that if you dig down far enough into the earth, you'll wind up in China. Some children even try it. In today's poem, Richard Wilbur remembers that day and reveals what he found.

SOME FEATURES TO NOTICE:
- Vocabulary:
  a **coolie** is a cheaply-employed, unskilled, day laborer in China or India; the word is a borrowing from Hindi, one of the main languages of India; today coolie is regarded as an offensive term in English usage
  pall, here, means a square cloth used to cover the chalice of wine during the celebration of Holy Communion in a Catholic mass
  a **paten** is the round metal plate on which the bread is placed during Holy Communion
- How the first stanza establishes the digging-to-China legend, as well as its attraction for a bored child: *it's nothing like New Jersey . . . much, much different. Nothing looks the same.*
- How the details of the second stanza bring the scene to life
- The aptness of the simile: *sweated like a coolie*, i.e., an unskilled Chinese laborer
- How, in the second stanza, Wilbur introduces a religious theme: *a sort/ Of praying, I suspect*
- How, in the third stanza, the boy experiences something akin to a religious epiphany: when he stands up, the sunlight and the rush of blood from his head make him dizzy. The world seems to spin, and he perceives something vastly different in his surroundings: a vision of brightness and beauty, with round and square shapes of light and leaves that resemble round and square objects used in celebrating Holy Communion

- How *China, China, China* in the last line echoes *Sanctus, Sanctus, Sanctus* or *Holy, Holy, Holy*, the words sung in a mass just before communion: the boy has experienced something like the presence of God

RESPONSE STANCE: Please go back into this poem and annotate it in two ways: mark every line in which you understand what's happening with an *X*, and mark any line where you're not sure about what's going on, or you have a question, with an *O*. Then we'll unpack it together.

BENEDICTION: Do you remember when you tried to do something impossible as a child—tried to build, make, or create something, from a fort to a sled jump to a lemonade stand, when the act of building, making, or creating was the point, not an adult-like finished product? Think about your stories of all-consuming adventures. These are also poems that can reveal your childhood.

Digging for China

"Far enough down is China," somebody said.
"Dig deep enough and you might see the sky
As clear as at the bottom of a well.
Except it would be real—a different sky.
Then you could burrow down until you came
To China! Oh, it's nothing like New Jersey.
There's people, trees, and houses, and all that,
But much, much different. Nothing looks the same."

I went and got the trowel out of the shed
And sweated like a coolie all that morning,
Digging a hole beside the lilac-bush,
Down on my hands and knees. It was a sort
Of praying, I suspect. I watched my hand
Dig deep and darker, and I tried and tried
To dream a place where nothing was the same.
The trowel never did break through to blue.

Before the dream could weary of itself
My eyes were tired of looking into darkness,
My sunbaked head of hanging down a hole.
I stood up in a place I had forgotten,
Blinking and staggering while the earth went round
And showed me silver barns, the fields dozing
In palls of brightness, patens growing and gone
In the tides of leaves, and the whole sky china blue.
Until I got my balance back again
All that I saw was China, China, China.

　　　—Richard Wilbur

PRESENTING THE POEMS:

Almost Hollywood
BY MARLEY WITHAM

&

Dandelion Wars
BY LIAM ANDERSON

&

Whenever I See Field of Corn
BY TESS MCKECHNIE

SETTING THE STAGE: In the first of today's poems, Marley, a seventh grader, remembers her favorite, longest running childhood fantasy: imaginary cameras were trained on her at all times as she enacted the movie of her life. In the next poem, Liam, an eighth grader, remembers his valiant efforts as a young soldier serving in the dandelion wars. And in the last, another eighth grader, Tess, recalls one of her earliest memories, exploring a cornfield with a beloved toy in tow.

SOME FEATURES TO NOTICE—"ALMOST HOLLYWOOD":
- The humor
- How the particulars of Marley's childhood movie fantasy bring it to life
- The sensory verbs
- How Marley uses italics and a shift in verb tense to separate the second stanza, about the impact of her first Oscars broadcast

SOME FEATURES TO NOTICE—"DANDELION WARS":
- The humor
- How the particulars of Liam's childhood battle fantasy bring it to life
- The sensory verbs
- How Liam signals the shift from past to present with the one-word line *Now*
- The strong conclusion

SOME FEATURES TO NOTICE—"WHENEVER I SEE A FIELD OF CORN":
- The choice of present tense
- The simple, childlike diction and sentence structures that suggest Tess's age at the time of this memory
- The sensory verbs and descriptions
- The effective repetition of *we love it*

RESPONSE STANCE: Please go back into one of these three madeleines on your own—your choice—and mark the words and lines that help you see and feel Marley's or Liam's fantasy life, or Tess's three-year-old memory.

BENEDICTION: What was one of your childhood-make-believe identities—who or what did you pretend to be? I think a poem about that fantasy could be not only funny but fun to write, too. And so could a poem about your earliest memories, in which you become again who you were then and speak in your little boy or girl voice.

Almost Hollywood

I twirl before the cameras
before walking outside,
making sure every-step-is-perfect.
I whisper my lines to myself.
Each word,
though soft,
drips with expression.
I love this movie,
the never-ending film of me.
It's my job to make the imaginary audience
sense the sensations, feel my feelings, live my life.
There's no plot
and the other actors are unreliable,
so most of the time
I act for them, too.

Then
I saw the Oscars for the first time.
That night in dreams
I sauntered down the red carpet.
My film won.
My acceptance speech was long
and sprinkled with crocodile tears.
They were my prize.

I wake up happier than ever.
The movie continues.
Now, in my backyard Hollywood,
I am *a star.*

  —*Marley Witham*

©2006 by Nancie Atwell from *Naming the World: A Year of Poems and Lessons*
(Portsmouth, NH: Heinemann)

Dandelion Wars

I gaze upon the army:
hundreds of yellow heads.
Although they stand just three inches tall,
I know they are deadly.
I draw my sword from my sheath.
I, King Lord Sir Mr. Al Bob, take no prisoners

As the head pops off the first man,
I smile a mean smile, then glare at my next target.
After a wild battle scream,
head number two sails through the air.
I'm on a roll.
I throw my sword high in the air to show off my skills,
only to have it land on my foot.

I lie on the lawn, pretending to be dead.
"They'll never guess this," I whisper with a grin.
Then I jump up, grab my sword,
and put on my best pose.
I can tell they're shaking in their shoes.
I begin to hum my war song,
emphasizing a note whenever a head flies.
I, King Lord Sir Mr. Al Bob, take no prisoners.

Finally, the battle is over.
I give the falling bodies my signature look—
frightening frown, eyes narrowed, ears back—
accompanied by a short grunt as I exit on my steed.
I, King Lord Sir Mr. Al Bob, take no prisoners.

Now
I watch my little brother kill dandelions
with Mother's broom,
hum Wishbone's theme song,
and ride away on a tree branch.
I shake my head and think,
"What the heck are you doing?"
But then I remember the dandelion wars,
how I thought I was tough
when I popped off the head of a weed.

And I miss it.

So I throw on a jacket
and some shoes,
grab a broom,
and head outside to join Eoin for a taste of my childhood.
I, King Lord Sir Mr. Al Bob, still take no prisoners.

—*Liam Anderson*

Whenever I See a Field of Corn

My fat fingers clasp
his fuzzy paw.
He is Dandelion.
My lion.
My rattle.
My partner in crime.

Together
we follow my mother
to the cornfield.
He hangs limply
by my side
or bounces lightly
against my legs.
I run.
He rattles.
We are ready to explore.
We love it.

In the cornfield
we trot
the mud filled paths.
On either side
brittle cornstalks
tower over us.
We could get lost here.
We love it.

My yellow rubber boots
hop
from puddle
to puddle.
Each splash
sprays more brown water.
It dries on us
and leaves us speckled
and dirty.
But we don't care.
We love it.

To us
nothing else matters.
We are happy
together
in a cornfield,
stuck
in my memory
forever
we love it.

—Tess McKechnie

PRESENTING THE POEM:

Revelations in the Key of K

BY MARY KARR

SETTING THE STAGE: Here's a great madeleine poem by Mary Karr, a poet and memoirist—she's the author of *Liar's Club*, which I know some of you have read. I *love* this poem. It's a flashback to kindergarten and the moment Karr's real life began, beneath an arrangement of three lines drawn in chalk above a blackboard.

SOME FEATURES TO NOTICE:

- How the rich particulars of Karr's memories of elementary school bring this classroom to life
- The specific and visual imagery
- The strong and sensory verbs, nouns, and adjectives
- The humor
- How Karr moves from the past—from the time of her initiation into literacy—to the present with the single word *Then* at the end of the eighth stanza, combined with the metaphor of the ninth, in which time's passage is *smeared* like a *charcoal sketch*
- How *all/ to zip* in the tenth stanza suggests the letters of the alphabet, A-Z
- How the lines *And when I blunder in the valley/ of the shadow of blank* are an allusion to Psalm 23 from the Old Testament of the Bible: *Yea, though I walk through the valley of the shadow of death, I will fear no evil: for thou art with me; thy rod and thy staff, they comfort me.*
- How Karr derives her spiritual comfort, when she *blunders*, from letters and words, from her literacy: *my being leans against my spinal K,/ which props me up*

- The powerful concluding line, stanza, and metaphor: she is a *crypt of meat*, a creature of flesh that is dying/will die, leaning on a *strong bone*: her faith in the power of words
- How Karr invents a form—three-line stanzas—and departs from it only to strengthen and emphasize her conclusion

RESPONSE STANCE: Please go back into this amazing poem on your own and mark every line you want to talk about, either because it confuses you or you love it.

BENEDICTION: Your own early memories of writing, reading, and drawing may be among your most powerful, too. What can you recall about your initial experiences with the letters of the alphabet? With books? With poems? With putting your words or visions on paper? And what line can you draw between who you were then and who you are now? These will be powerful poems.

Revelations in the Key of K

I came awake in kindergarten,
under the letter K chalked neat
on a field-green placard leaned

on the blackboard's top edge. They'd caged me
in a metal *desk*—the dull word writ
to show K's sound. But K meant *kick* and *kill*

when a boy I'd kissed drew me
as a whiskered troll in art. On my sheet,
the puffy clouds I made to keep rain in

let torrents dagger loose. "Screw those
who color in the lines," my mom had preached,
words I shared that landed me on a short chair

facing the corner's empty, sheetrock page. Craning up,
I found my K high above.
You'll have to grow to here, its silence said.

And in the surrounding alphabet, my whole life hid—
names of my beloveds, sacred vows I'd break.
With my pencil stub applied to wall,

I moved around the loops and vectors,
Z to A, learning how to mean, how
in the mean world to be.

But while I worked the room around me
began to smudge—like a charcoal sketch my mom
was rubbing with her thumb. Then

the instant went, the month, and every season
smeared, till with a wrenching arm tug
I was here, grown, but still bent

to set down words before the black eraser
swipes our moment into cloud, dispersing all
to zip. And when I blunder in the valley

of the shadow of blank about to break
in half, my being leans against my spinal K,
which props me up, broomstick straight,

a strong bone in the crypt of meat I am.

    —*Mary Karr*

Trouble with Math in a One-Room Country School

BY JANE KENYON

SETTING THE STAGE: In yesterday's poem, Mary Karr drew a line between herself in a kindergarten class, at the moment she joined the literacy club forever, and her self today, a woman who derives strength and comfort from her faith in the power of the alphabet. In today's poem, Jane Kenyon also draws a line between an elementary school classroom and the woman she became. This line is straight, strong, and still angry.

SOME FEATURES TO NOTICE:

- How the rich particulars of Kenyon's descriptions bring to life her classmate Ann, this classroom, and the cloakroom
- The strong and sensory verbs, nouns, and adjectives
- The sensory details and imagery: we can see this poem, smell it, hear it
- How the poem turns in the last four lines, after the extra pause created with the ellipsis, and points its theme: the injustice of the teacher's punishment changes Kenyon into someone who won't trust or bend to authority

RESPONSE STANCE: Please go back into this sensory poem on your own and mark all the words and lines you can see, smell, and hear. Then, mark what seem to you to be its most important lines.

BENEDICTION: Your memories of teachers or other adults in positions of authority may not be entirely positive. I can feel my own face flame when I recall my third-grade teacher and the day she made me write "I am a rude person" five hundred times because Charles Thompson, who sat behind me, asked me how to spell a word, and I . . .

Okay, okay, you don't need to hear my sad story. But I need to think about it—to write it as a poem and, I hope, discover what there is to learn from it. What are your stories of injustice and authority? What are the lines you might draw between a moment of shame and the person you are or the one you're becoming?

Trouble with Math in a One-Room Country School

The others bent their heads and started in.
Confused, I asked my neighbor
to explain—a sturdy, bright-cheeked girl
who brought raw milk to school from her family's
herd of Holsteins. Ann had a blue bookmark,
and on it Christ revealed his bleeding heart,
holding the flesh back with His wounded hand.
Ann understood division. . . .

Miss Moran sprang from her monumental desk
and led me roughly through the class
without a word. My shame was radical
as she propelled me past the cloakroom
to the furnace closet, where only the boys
were put, only the older ones at that.
The door swung briskly shut.

The warmth, the gloom, the smell
of sweeping compound clinging to the broom
soothed me. I found a bucket, turned it
upside down, and sat, hugging my knees.
I hummed a theme from Haydn that I knew
from my piano lessons . . .
and hardened my heart against authority.
And then I heard her steps, her fingers
on the latch. She led me, blinking
and changed, back to the class.

—*Jane Kenyon*

PRESENTING THE POEM:

Proustian

BY EDWARD HIRSCH

SETTING THE STAGE: Edward Hirsch, whom you already know as the author of "Execution," the poem about his high school football coach who was dying of cancer, doesn't fool around in the title of today's poem. He calls it "Proustian," so we know right from the get-go that this will be Hirsch's version of a madeleine. It is lovely: a perfect poem to weave together all the threads of the Proustian poetry of the last few days.

SOME FEATURES TO NOTICE:
- The vivid visual description
- The rich, sensory diction: verbs, nouns, and adjectives
- How the particulars of Hirsch's memories bring his childhood—and his experience of remembering it—to life
- The effective repetition—and accuracy—in the lines *Like memories that we imagine we imagined* in the third stanza and *There was once a time before we knew about time* in the final stanza
- The thoughtful concluding stanza, about the power and importance of both childhood *and* memory
- How Hirsch invents a form: stanzas of three lines

RESPONSE STANCE: Please go back into "Proustian" and mark the lines that got you thinking and remembering and that you'd like to talk about. Notice the conclusion, too: it's a good one.

BENEDICTION: What Edward Hirsch did in this poem makes me think of something William Carlos Williams wrote: "That is the poet's business. Not to talk in vague categories but to write particularly, as a physician works with a patient, upon the thing before him, in the particular to discover the universal."

Hirsch could have written a poem in which he *tells* his theory about the power of remembering childhood. Instead he *shows* us what he derives through remembering the particulars of his childhood and, thereby, evokes our own childhood memories *and* our awareness of their importance to our lives.

It's a universal lesson about good poetry that we can take away from all of the particular madeleines we've read. Your poems about the specifics of your personal experiences will come alive, will resonate, for readers whose personal experiences are different from yours, in ways that a generalized statement, say, about *childhood* or *memory,* never could. Discover your own madeleines, reveal them to us, and reveal us to ourselves.

Proustian

At times it seems lucky and unexpected, the past,
And who we were then, and what the mind brings
Back on an overcast day in late September,

The dense, evanescent clouds shifting overhead,
The wind fingering the branches in the live oaks,
The little chunks of our childhood selves

Floating to the surface after all these years
Like memories that we imagine we imagined,
Or tiny bits of metal constellating on magnets.

One moment we are drinking coffee at the window
On a wet day falling around us, the next moment
We are putting our heads down on our desks

For story-time, or cleaning our lockers,
Or filing into the schoolyard for a fire drill.
Soon we are pulling on sleek yellow slickers

And splashing home in the rain to our parents
And grandparents. I see a boy throwing his arms
Around his grandmother's neck and hugging her.

He eats sugar cookies that he dunks in milk,
And plays in his room by himself now, happily,
In a fort that he has built next to his bed…

Sometimes it is enough just to remember
There was once a time before we knew about time
When the self and the world fit snugly together.

    —Edward Hirsch

I found th
by one over
cherished ea
Seventh and
have a hard
what it mean

Gender:
INTRODUCTION

I found these poems one by one over the years and cherished each discovery. Seventh and eighth graders have a hard time talking about what it means in our culture to be a boy or a girl and what it will mean to become a man or a woman. They're self-conscious—and that's okay. But I also know that my kids think about questions related to gender, and I've learned they sometimes worry that there's something "wrong" with them. These poems put words to gender-related feelings in ways that bring comfort and perspective.

`I need to add one caveat: discussions of this group of poems are the quietest of the school year, I think because kids are reluctant to go on the record about role-related anxieties in front of peers. But at the end of the trimester, when I poll them about favorite poetry, the poems about gender are prominent at the tops of their lists.

PRESENTING THE POEMS:

Boy's Life

BY NAT HERZ

&

The Tyranny of Nice or Suburban Girl

BY SARAH J. LIEBMAN

SETTING THE STAGE: This week's poems, some by kids and some by pros, are considerations of what it means to be male or female in our culture: how boys and girls are "supposed" to act, and how societal expectations and stereotypes can affect their sense of themselves. Today, two students, Nat and Sarah, take on two of the worst gender stereotypes: boys are supposed to be macho and tough, and girls are supposed to be passive and nice.

SOME FEATURES TO NOTICE—"BOY'S LIFE":
- How in each of the first three stanzas Nat gives us a different, specific image to suggest a "manly" boy's rep
- How he decided to forego caps and punctuation
- How he created a form of five-line stanzas
- The strong, sarcastic conclusion

SOME FEATURES TO NOTICE—"THE TYRANNY OF NICE OR SUBURBAN GIRL":
- How in each of the five stanzas the poet gives us a different, specific image to suggest the profile of a "nice" girl
- The use of parenthetical phrases to suggest what's hidden behind a façade of pleasant submission
- The strong, sarcastic conclusion

RESPONSE STANCE: Please go back into both of these poems on your own and mark the lines that give you a strong feeling or idea.

BENEDICTION: What are boys supposed to be like? How are girls supposed to act? Have you felt those pressures? As a poet, do you have a voice to raise about this issue, a story to tell about a time when you felt stereotyped or limited by gender?

Boy's Life

somewhere out there
is a boy
who can bench one-fifty without effort
but as far as i'm concerned
it will never be me

showing no emotion
he's the captain
of the football team
who won't leave the field
til he's blinded by his own blood

cheering mindlessly
he's the number one fan
of TV wrestlers
who love to hear
the loudest crunch

one day
he'll encounter the real world
and realize what it means
for a man to be
strong

—*Nat Herz*

The Tyranny of Nice or Suburban Girl

Leave your nice house each morning
and walk nicely down your well-landscaped street.
Wait patiently for the nice yellow bus.
(face behind makeup)

When you arrive at your nice school
you talk nicely with your equally nice friends.
You laugh because you are all wearing the same nice outfit.
(cares behind chitchat)

Then you sit nicely in class,
listening—but not saying much
and taking notes in your nice handwriting.
"Nice job" reads the red ink on the paper
your nice teacher returned today.
(ideas behind silence)

After school you go to practice.
Whether you win or lose, you're nice about it.
You get a ride from a nice friend
who drops you off at your nice house
and waves goodbye nicely.
(assertiveness behind a smile)

You sit down to a nice family dinner.
"Did you have a nice day?" they ask.
You nod and everyone talks nicely
but nobody really says anything.
Nicely, you help clean up the kitchen
and then do your homework.
(anything that isn't nice behind anything that is)

"How nice," people say of you.

—*Sarah J. Liebman*

When My Dad, Gordon, Cried

BY MICHAEL G. NERN

SETTING THE STAGE: I found this poem in a collection of Ohio teachers' poetry, and it knocked me out. Michael Nern's dad and mine come from the same generation: Men Who Never Cry. But a stroke can have odd effects. After his second stroke, Nern's father became a man who cries.

SOME FEATURES TO NOTICE:

- The colloquial but evocative diction: *emotion-ally screwed; he'd get weepy; a bony little hand*
- The specifics in the second stanza that describe what made Gordon cry and what the list shows about him
- The handful of sensory details that gives us just enough imagery to visualize Gordon
- How at the end the poet, taking deep breaths, is another man trying not to cry

RESPONSE STANCE: Please go back into this poem on your own and mark the words and lines that surprise you. Then notice the end of the poem: what do you think is about to happen?

BENEDICTION: Have you seen your dad or grandfather cry? Is there a story there, to tell as a poem?

When My Dad, Gordon, Cried

Gordon was the typical man
who did not cry. I had only
seen him cry once until he had
his second stroke, which left
him emotionally screwed for
what was left of his life.

These things could make him cry:
Gary Cooper dropping a villain with a
right to the jaw, Neill O'Donnell to
Yancey Thigpen for a Steeler touchdown,
The Star Spangled Banner, my dog Jane
when I left her with him for company
and she would perk up her ears and
run to the door whenever she heard
a car. "She was looking for you,"
he'd tell me, as he cried.

When he'd come to visit me in
Zanesville after Mom died, he'd
be okay for two days. On the third
day, he'd get weepy. He'd turn his
head away from me and put his hand
over his mouth and cry. Then he'd
ask me to take him home the next day.
and I would. At his house we'd smoke
on the front porch and when I said I had
to go, he'd say have another cigarette.
and I would, but I'd still have to leave.

He'd stand in the driveway and watch
me and by the time I was in the street
a bony little hand would move to cover
the quivering lip and the last thing I would
see was my dad crying and waving with his
other hand and I would think about him
going back into the house to watch
Gary Cooper on American Movie Classics
and I'd take a deep breath, and another.

—*Michael G. Nern*

Eye of the Beholder

BY MARK VINZ

SETTING THE STAGE: Today's poem begins with a droll epigraph from the poet Paul Zimmer: "I've often wondered what it would be like to be beautiful. I've never had the problem." In America today, physical beauty seems to be our culture's most valued attribute, right up there with wealth. It's sad, and it's shallow. Mark Vinz, father of a daughter, speaks about our obsession with appearance in his poem "Eye of the Beholder." By the way, the title's an allusion to a famous, anonymous saying. Can anyone complete the quote? What does it mean?

SOME FEATURES TO NOTICE:
- How the title quotes the adage, "Beauty is in the eye of the beholder."
- The visual image or scene that's conveyed in the second and third stanzas
- How the concluding stanza contains the most important lines in the poem and states its theme
- How Vinz invents a form: stanzas of five lines

RESPONSE STANCE: Mark what feel to you like the most important lines in the poem; then, mark any others you'd like to talk about.

BENEDICTION: What is beauty? How would you define it? And what's the effect in our culture on girls who are made to feel unbeautiful? What you say to yourself about yourself when you look in the mirror is a poem, too.

Eye of the Beholder

for Sarah

"I've often wondered what it would be like to be beautiful.
I've never had the problem." —Paul Zimmer

We're always reminded, aren't we—
on every screen, on every page
we turn. Perhaps somehow we too
might find a way to measure up,
the secret of each serene gaze...

Today we go shopping, my fine
tall daughter and I—who looms
above the others in the store
that pause in aisles to gape
at what they think they see.

She smiles and looks at me
as if to say it doesn't matter,
even if we both know
there are times and ways it does.
But what we also know is this:

Beautiful is understanding what you
cannot ask from those who stare—
more than their eyes, more than ours.
And beautiful is finally judged
by all the reasons that you're missed.

—Mark Vinz

Bones in an African Cave

BY PETER MEINKE

SETTING THE STAGE: You'll remember Peter Meinke as the author of the haunting and beautiful "Elegy for a Diver." In today's poem, he considers the nature of a man's inhumanity toward other men: what is the source of a male's inclination to violence and brutality? Meinke discovers an answer in an archaeologist's find in a cave in Africa.

SOME FEATURES TO NOTICE:
- The subtle rhyme scheme—ABAB, CDCD, etc.—that gives meaning priority over rhyme
- The allusion to the Old Testament tale of Cain and Abel: the history of male brutality is as old as the story of one son of Adam killing the other
- How Meinke, as a man and the father of a boy, not only acknowledges the male's heritage of *fierce blood / that won't die out*, but determines to celebrate it; he urges his son to become what nature intends: *tall and wild,/ strong-voiced and loud; proud of the fierce blood / that won't die out.*

RESPONSE STANCE: Please go back into this poem and try to unpack it: make notes next to each stanza about what you think it's about, then write in your own words, at the end, what you think the whole poem is saying.

BENEDICTION: So, do you agree with Meinke? Is violence part of a male's nature—is it in his blood and therefore unstoppable? Is there no hope for peace on earth? And is there a poem in you about your opinion or feelings?

Bones in an African Cave

Bones in an African cave
gave the show away:
they went violent to their grave
like us today.

Skulls scattered on the ground
broke to the brain;
the missing link is found
pointing to Cain.

Children in the street
pry up the cobblestones.
Old instincts repeat
in slender bones.

To my violent son,
beautiful and strong,
caps in his polished gun,
I hymn this song.

Grow tall and wild,
strong-voiced and loud;
be proud of the fierce blood
that won't die out.

All things repeat
after the floods and flames:
new boys play in the streets
their ancient games.

     —Peter Meinke

Why I'm in Favor of a Nuclear Freeze

BY CHRISTOPHER BUCKLEY

SETTING THE STAGE: In yesterday's poem, Peter Meinke explored the inherent nature of violence: his feeling that it is inevitable that men will kill. Today another American male poet, Christopher Buckley, says *wait a minute.*

SOME FEATURES TO NOTICE:

- How this is a *prose poem:* a cross between poetry and prose that mostly looks like prose, but reads, in its diction and imagery, like poetry
- How, until the last stanza, the poem is a flashback
- The revealing and specific details and imagery in the story of the day spent hunting
- The revealing dialogue as the two boys, *thinking* they *were someone* after they kill the doves, talk as they believe men might
- How in the last stanza, set in the present, the poem turns: the poet appreciates other kinds of experiences now: *lizards/ daring the road I run along; yellow meadowlarks . . .*
- How the last two-and-a-half lines establish the poem's theme—the boys killed because their weapons gave them the option and the power to kill—and how the concluding lines circle back to the meaning of the title

RESPONSE STANCE: Please go back into "Why I'm in Favor of a Nuclear Freeze" and mark the lines throughout that you think are its most important.

BENEDICTION: We've talked about how a poem can *turn*, as this one does in its final stanza. Sometimes our attitudes can *turn*, too, from not caring about something to caring deeply, from not thinking about or getting something to suddenly understanding. I had a lot of personal and ethical *turns* when I was a teenager. What have your experiences been so far, in terms of values and perspectives that have changed? Is there a poem waiting here?

Why I'm in Favor of a Nuclear Freeze

Because we were 18 and still wonderful in our bodies,
because Harry's father owned a ranch and we had
nothing better to do one Saturday, we went hunting
doves among the high oaks and almost wholly quiet air . . .
Traipsing the hill and deer paths for an hour,
we were ready when the first ones swooped—
and we took them down in smoke much like the planes
in the war films of our regimented youth.
                    Some were dead
and some knocked cold, and because he knew how
and I just couldn't, Harry went to each of them and,
with thumb and forefinger, almost tenderly, squeezed
the last air out of their slight necks.
                    Our jackets grew
heavy with birds and for a while we sat in the shade
thinking we were someone, talking a bit of girls—
who would "go," who wouldn't, how love would probably
always be beyond our reach . . . We even talked of the nuns
who terrified us with God and damnation. We both recalled
that first prize in art, the one pinned to the cork board
in front of class, was a sweet blond girl's drawing
of the fire and coals, the tortured souls of Purgatory.
Harry said he feared eternity until he was 17, and,
if he ever had kids, the last place they would go would be
a parochial school.
                    On our way to the car, having forgotten
which way the safety was off or on, I accidentally discharged
my borrowed 12 gauge, twice actually—one would have been Harry's
head if he were behind me, the other my foot, inches to the right.
We were almost back when something moved in the raw, dry grass,
and without thinking, and on the first twitch of two tall ears,
we together blew the ever-loving Jesus out of a jack rabbit
until we couldn't tell fur from dust from blood . . .
                    Harry has
a family, two children as lovely as any ever will be—
he hasn't hunted in years . . . and that once was enough for me.
Anymore, a good day offers a moment's praise for the lizards
daring the road I run along, or it offers a dusk in which
yellow meadowlarks scrounge fields in the gray autumn light . . .
Harry and I are friends now almost 30 years, and the last time
we had dinner, I thought about that rabbit, not the doves
which we swore we would cook and eat, but that rabbit—
why the hell had we killed it so cold-heartedly? And I saw
that it was simply because we had the guns, because we could.

—*Christopher Buckley*

PRESENTING THE POEM:

What's that smell in the kitchen?

BY MARGE PIERCY

SETTING THE STAGE: A pre-feminist-era adage about the proper role of women in society declared that "a woman's place is in the kitchen." In this poem, Marge Piercy, a feminist poet and novelist, visits kitchens all over America to see what's going on behind the kitchen door. She finds a nation of women who have *had enough*.

SOME FEATURES TO NOTICE:

- The vivid metaphors, similes, and imagery that reveal what life behind the kitchen door feels like: *calico smile; platters glittering like wax; Anger sputters in her brainpan, confined / but spewing out missiles of hot fat;* etc.

- How the tone is one of anger and despair, yet the poem is also humorous

- After the general statement of the first line, the references to specific dinner entrées that are being burned by women in particular cities across the U.S.

- How the last line sums up and resonates, almost like a manifesto

RESPONSE STANCE: This poem is loaded with great metaphors, similes, and images that convey what a kitchen-bound woman's life is like. Please go back in on your own and mark your favorites.

BENEDICTION: Figurative language is a great way to uncover or reveal a situation and show your feelings about it. When people stereotype you, as an adolescent male or female, what does it feel *like?*

What's that smell in the kitchen?

All over America women are burning dinners.
It's lambchops in Peoria; it's haddock
in Providence; it's steak in Chicago
tofu delight in Big Sur; red
rice and beans in Dallas.
All over America women are burning
food they're supposed to bring with calico
smile on platters glittering like wax.
Anger sputters in her brainpan, confined
but spewing out missiles of hot fat.
Carbonized despair presses like a clinker
from a barbecue against the back of her eyes.
If she wants to grill anything, it's
her husband spitted over a slow fire.
If she wants to serve him anything,
it's a dead rat with a bomb in its belly
ticking like the heart of an insomniac.
Her life is cooked and digested,
nothing but leftovers in Tupperware.
Look, she says, once I was roast duck
on your platter with parsley but now I am Spam.
Burning dinner is not incompetence but war.

—*Marge Piercy*

PRESENTING THE POEM:

uncurled

BY ALEXIS KELLNER BECKER

SETTING THE STAGE: In this poem, Alexis, a seventh grader, started to think about the girl—or, as she put it, *girly girl*—she used to be and to wonder: so who am I now? And what have I lost?

SOME FEATURES TO NOTICE:

- The strong figurative language: *dawn of time; dusk of time; like a doll in the window; no recollection of what I bought with it*
- The specific visual imagery: *lace and pigtails; mud-caked and stained; bubbly shiny;* etc.
- The tone: mournful and nostalgic
- How the concluding stanza suggests Alexis' sense of loss: her feet are on the ground as she mourns the loss of her girlhood angel
- How the stanzas divide both the poem's action and the poet's emotions
- How Alexis decided to forgo capital letters, commas, and end-stop punctuation

RESPONSE STANCE: Please go back into "uncurled" and mark the lines and words you can see, as well as those that give you a strong feeling. Then, write a few words: how does this poem make you feel?

BENEDICTION: The act of leaving behind little girlhood or boyhood can be a mixed blessing. Yes, you're moving closer to adulthood and autonomy, but you're also losing access to that other world. Alexis named, and got some interesting perspective on, her sense of loss by writing "uncurled." I think your own version of this transformation is waiting to be written.

uncurled

at the dawn of time I was girly girl in lace and pigtails
morally aghast at the thought of wearing pants—
came home mud-caked and stained
at the dawn of time the world was bubbly shiny
I was fully aware of tragedy fully aware of pain
(neither could touch me)

now it's the dusk of time
I can't stand and look like a doll in the window
the blonde curls and I went our separate ways long ago
fortunately I was able to return them for a refund
not store credit
and here I am with no recollection of what I bought with it

the rain is a freak accident
I wish the snow would come
then we could be angels

    —Alexis Kellner Becker

PRESENTING THE POEM:

First Practice

BY GARY GILDNER

SETTING THE STAGE: Today's poem comes full circle and brings us back to Nat's "Boy's Life." There, Nat showed that he understood and rejected what boys are "supposed" to be like. In "First Practice," Gary Gildner gives us a word portrait of a high school football coach, a man who makes it his business to ensure that boys act like men are "supposed" to act.

SOME FEATURES TO NOTICE:

- How Gildner captures the voice and attitude of the coach and, through the dialogue, reveals his character
- How the poet decides to forgo quotation marks to set off the dialogue, and how effective this is
- The simple, colloquial diction: guy talk
- How the end resonates and leaves us, as readers, writing in our heads, continuing the action of the poem

RESPONSE STANCE: Please go back into "First Practice" and mark the words and lines that show you what this coach is like. Then, would you also notice the ending: what is about to happen here?

BENEDICTION: Grownups aren't always right. We don't always know, do, or advise what's best—this comes as no surprise to you, I'm sure. And sometimes we impose our needs and perspectives on you. I think this often happens in organized sports, classrooms, and other group activities where there's an adult in charge. You may have your own version of "First Practice" to explore, in which an adult man or woman tried to impose his or her vision of masculinity or femininity on you.

First Practice

After the doctor checked to see
we weren't ruptured,
the man with the short cigar took us
under the grade school,
where we went in case of attack
or storm, and said
he was Clifford Hill, he was
a man who believed dogs
ate dogs, he had once killed
for his country, and if
there were any girls present
for them to leave now.
                                No one
left. OK, he said, he said I take
that to mean you are hungry
men who hate to lose as much
as I do. OK. Then
he made two lines of us
facing each other,
and across the way, he said,
is the man you hate most
in the world,
and if we are to win
that title I want to see how.
But I don't want to see
any marks when you're dressed,
he said. He said, *Now.*

   —Gary Gildner

By spring
are ready, as
writers of po
fresh challe
Poetic form
else is possi

Some Forms:
INTRODUCTION

By spring, my students are ready, as readers and writers of poems, to experience fresh challenges and satisfactions. Poetic forms show them what else is possible for poets. They teach kids the pleasures of complexity and the potential of effects, beyond those created by line and stanza breaks, to support and emphasize meaning.

Some of the forms I've illustrated here are official poetic genres: the haiku, pantoum, tritina, sestina, and Elizabethan sonnet. Others are forms that published poets invented in the twentieth century: Pablo Neruda's irregular odes, Wallace Stevens' thirteen ways, and Robert Pack's rounding-it-out. And still others are forms my kids created, like Nora Bradford's parallel stanza format or the quintina, invented by Alison Rittershaus. Each of the forms I've included here is one that inspired my student poets to give it a try.

PRESENTING THE POEMS:

Two crows

BY BAILEY IRVING

&

The Old Fence

BY NORA BRADFORD

&

Swimming Haiku

BY NIALL JANNEY

&

reading on a wet day

BY WYATT RAY

&

Iris Sins

BY BELLA PROVAN

SETTING THE STAGE: Haiku is a form of poetry that originated in Japan over seven hundred years ago. Haiku are *meditative nuggets:* brief, three-line descriptions or observations of nature or people. Sometimes they do follow the syllable rule I know you've been taught but is *not* a requirement of haiku: five syllables in the first line, then seven, then five. Really, the essence of a haiku lies more in its tone and the way its three lines connect to our senses, and less in the number of syllables. Let's take a look at some poems written by seventh graders and try to tease out what makes these haiku.

SOME FEATURES TO NOTICE:
- Three lines
- Present-tense verbs
- No rhyme

- Every word counts; every word is necessary
- Strong, simple diction
- Concrete details
- A focus on the world of the senses: what can be seen, heard, felt

RESPONSE STANCE: What do you notice about these poems? Please go back in and jot some notes about what you can discover from these poems about the features of a haiku. Then we'll create a group definition.

BENEDICTION: Haiku are fun to write: a tight, sensory challenge. Spend some time this afternoon or evening observing the natural world—earth and sky—or your own activity. Look for moments that strike your senses. See if one of them begs to be written as a haiku.

Two crows

glide and circle
to earth and alight between
gray sky and gray snow.

—Bailey Irving

The Old Fence

rots away
as the new
snow falls.

—Nora Bradford

Swimming Haiku

1.
I anticipate
pain, intensity, exhaustion.
Clench my teeth: *win.*

2.
Screams of the crowd melt away.
As I surge, my world transforms
into a shimmering battleground.

3.
It's over.
Last touch, stop of the clock, rapid heartbeat.
The liquid world drips off me: *I'll be back.*

—Niall Janney

---

reading on a wet day

T.S. Eliot
and Douglas Adams may meet—
on a cold rainy afternoon

—Wyatt Ray

Iris Sins

Sloth
She will sleep,
recalling summer's festive rains
until the last snow.

Envy
Atop tall stems
she scowls, covered in shadows
of her own hatred.

Pride
On a snowy day
away from bright city lights
the *iris* glows.

Lust
Center of attention:
the iris *is* the lighthouse.
Light is what she *needs.*

Greed
Perfected purple
melts the winter with her touch
and steals its color.

Gluttony
Withering vibrance,
she swallows nutrients
by the dose, through the root.

Wrath
She will sleep . . .
all the anger inside
is no match for ice.

—Bella Provan

PRESENTING THE POEMS:

Starry Night Tritina
BY MOLLY JORDAN

&

Gardening with Mom
BY ROSE BEVERLY

&

Christmas Tritina for Marshall
BY BAILEY IRVING

SETTING THE STAGE: I learned about tritinas from a profile of the poet Marie Ponsot that appeared in the *New York Times*. I loved her tritinas, and I loved the form. It depends on *three* and *repetition*—how three words repeated in a particular order at particular junctures create a cadence and emphasize a meaning, but without the poet saying the same thing over and over again.

Let's look at a poem Molly wrote in seventh grade, called "Starry Night Tritina," and see if we can figure out the tritina form together . . .

SOME FEATURES TO NOTICE:
- The three lines of each of the first three stanzas end in one of three words, repeated in the order below. The last stanza, or *envoy*, is one line that contains all three words.
- Stanza 1:   1
                2
                3
- Stanza 2:   3
                1
                2
- Stanza 3:   2
                3
                1
- Stanza 4 (Envoy): one line in which all three words appear

MORE SETTING THE STAGE: Now, let's check out tritinas that seventh graders Rose and Bailey composed as gifts of writing. Rose gave hers to her mom; Bailey's little brother Marshall received his as a Christmas present.

RESPONSE STANCE: Please go back into all three tritinas now and choose a favorite. Then, mark up your favorite: what did the poet do with the form, and otherwise, that makes her tritina the one that appeals to you most?

BENEDICTION: This is an immensely satisfying form—and one that's doable, too. If you decide to attempt a tritina, my advice is to choose a subject you have strong feelings about and to select end words that are versatile, that have a lot to offer. For example, Molly used the word *cold* as both a noun and an adjective, as Bailey did with *dark*. Words like *ring*, *light*, *talk*, and *wonder* can function as both nouns and verbs, and *you*, *me*, and *it* are versatile pronouns. Play with this form—it's a satisfying challenge.

Starry Night Tritina

Riding along under a night sky,
my family huddles together
under blankets to elude the African cold.

We stop and stare through the cold
darkness at the star-soaked sky.
We gasp together

then whisper together
about how bright and plentiful these stars are. Cold
fingers and noses are forgotten. We are in awe of the sky.

Cold doesn't exist: my family is together under a luminous African sky.

—*Molly Jordan*

Gardening with Mom

You put on the straw hat
that screens your face from sun.
You are ready to plant in the rich, spring dirt.

But first: much turning over of dirt.
You adjust the hat
to shield your eyes from the new-burning sun.

The sun
heats my bare head, but I ignore it and join you, hands in the dirt.
I can live without a hat

but not without you: I am content—hatless, dirty, and by your side
under a May sun.

—*Rose Beverly*

Christmas Tritina
for Marshall

I open my eyes to the dark
of 4:30 a.m. I slip into your room to shake you awake,
but you're already sitting up, silent, waiting.

Wordlessly I join you in the seasonal waiting,
jumping into the dark
lump that is your bed. We pray for Mom and Dad to awake.

Finally they are out of bed, though only half awake.
You and I scamper to the top of the stairs, waiting,
yet again, for Dad and his camera. We can't peek downstairs: it's too dark.

I will remember, forever, waiting in the dark for the others to awake and
whispering my dreams to you.

—*Bailey Irving*

PRESENTING THE POEM:

Car Ride: A Sestina

BY MARLEY WITHAM

SETTING THE STAGE: If a tritina is a challenge, what can I say about a sestina? It's another repetitive poetic form, this time based on six, that was invented by the troubadour poet Arnaut Daniel. Let's take a look at Marley's "Car Ride," a kind of lullaby about a late-night ride home, in the back seat of the family car, and see if we can unpack the form.

SOME FEATURES TO NOTICE:
- The six lines of each of the first six stanzas end in one of six words, repeated in the order below. The seventh stanza, the *envoy*, has three lines, each of which includes two of the six words.
- Stanza 1:
  1
  2
  3
  4
  5
  6
- Stanza 2:
  6
  1
  5
  2
  4
  3
- Stanza 3:
  3
  6
  4
  1
  2
  5
- Stanza 4:
  5
  3
  2
  6
  1
  4
- Stanza 5:
  4
  5
  1
  3
  6
  2
- Stanza 6:
  2
  4
  6
  5
  3
  1
- Stanza 7 (Envoy): 1–2
  3–4
  5–6

RESPONSE STANCE: Now that we've unpacked the form, please go back into "Car Ride" and notice what Marley did to rise to the challenge of the form's demands: what did she do as a poet *and* a sestina-er that's effective?

BENEDICTION: This is a form that will set your hair on fire, it's so hard to say something new each time one of the six words rolls around. But talk about *satisfying*. My advice is the same as for a tritina: choose a subject you *really* care about, one that interests you deeply, because you'll spend so much time and so many lines considering it. And try to select end words that have the potential to do more than one thing. For example, the words *CD* or *rug* won't hold much promise for long, but *promise* and *long* can function as different parts of speech and express different meanings.

Car Ride: A Sestina

I press my hand against the cold glass.
A ring of frost appears, framing rain
that pours endlessly into dark.
My eyes threaten sleep
as I stare into the never-
ending yellow lights

that are too bright, lights
that flicker against the water on the glass.
I can barely hold my head up. Home will never
come. But as I close my eyes and listen to the rain
and its vibrations, I am not sure I want it to. Sleep
is coming instead. Now dark

is all around me. Dark
conceals the pinpricks of lights.
When I am almost asleep
and the cold outside the glass
melts away, the sound of rain
hitting the roof grows louder. I never

want to leave this shelter, never
want to dash out into dark
through rain.
I want the lights
that shatter the black glass
to keep shining. I want to sleep . . .

Sleep.
Soft colors blur behind eyelids so heavy they'll never
open. My head falls against glass.
Cold dark is trapped outside the window, and inside the dark
of dreams welcomes me. The lights
that approach are no more than a comfort now, like the rain.

Rain
beats out the song of my sleep.
My whole body feels light,
elevated by the movement of the car. We will never
reach home: I want to stay in the soothing dark.
I want to stay where glass

separates me from cold, where glass shields me from rain.
But the dark womb of sleep
vanishes. The home that seemed never to come, does: my house shines
      its own warm lights.
     —*Marley Witham*

PRESENTING THE POEM:

Quintina: Night

BY ALISON RITTERSHAUS

SETTING THE STAGE: Alison, an eighth grader, met the challenges of a tritina and a sestina. Then she took the repetitive-end-word format an obsessive step further. She invented a new poetic form, the quintina, based, of course, on five. Listen to and read along with her exquisite creation, "Quintina: Night."

SOME FEATURES TO NOTICE:

- The five lines of each of the first five stanzas end in one of five words, repeated in the order below. The sixth stanza, or envoy, has two lines: the first contains words one and two, the second words three, four, and five.

- Stanza 1:
  - 1
  - 2
  - 3
  - 4
  - 5

- Stanza 1:
  - 5
  - 3
  - 1
  - 2
  - 4

- Stanza 3:
  - 4
  - 5
  - 2
  - 1
  - 3

- Stanza 4:
  - 3
  - 1
  - 4
  - 5
  - 2

- Stanza 5:
  - 2
  - 4
  - 5
  - 3
  - 1

- Stanza 6 (Envoy): 1–2
  - 3–4–5

RESPONSE STANCE: This time, see if you can unpack the form on your own: how does Alison's quintina work?

BENEDICTION: Here's another form for you to try—a bridge, difficulty-wise, between a tritina and a sestina. And maybe it's an inspiration form-invention-wise, too. So far as I know, no one has yet invented a repetitive-end form based on four.

Quintina: Night

The sky fades to pink and I
retreat into the quiet
of my room. I let the radio whisper
until dark,
when I silence

it with one push of a button. My room is filled by a silence
so impenetrable, I feel the need to whisper
a few words, so I
know this quiet
is not permanent. I turn out the light. My room is enveloped in dark.

Out the window the trees are dark
silhouettes, smothering all light from the silence
of a full moon. Wind shakes my window and I think, *Quiet,*
wind, don't disturb the perfection of near sleep. I
turn away. The sheets whisper

protestations, whisper
and grind their threadbare teeth. I
love the dark,
cherish the silence,
and in this deep quiet,

poetry floats as freely as a lily on quiet
waters. Night transforms everything into dark
shapes, changes my perspective and my idea of silence,
banishes fear until it is but a whisper
of its true self. I

always knew that night brought dreams, but now I see it brings travel to those who
must stay home and a quiet
whisper to the lonely, and I understand that the dark brings silence to those who are never alone.

—Alison Rittershaus

PRESENTING THE POEM:

The Summer We Didn't Die

BY WILLIAM STAFFORD

SETTING THE STAGE: A pantoum is a great verse form to play with. It started out in Malaysia, in Southeast Asia, in the 1400's. The number of lines and stanzas is indefinite—a pantoum can go on forever. The trick is that the second and fourth lines of one stanza become the first and third lines of the next stanza. And the very last stanza takes, as its second and fourth lines, the third and first lines of the very first. *Whew*.

So the deal is, every line in a pantoum is used twice. The pleasure comes from the way that recurring lines meander in and out of the text and do different things with each appearance. Let's read "The Summer We Didn't Die" by William Stafford, about a childhood memory, and feel the pleasures of a pantoum.

SOME FEATURES TO NOTICE:

- The straightforward diction, typical of Stafford
- How each line in the pantoum is strong; how each line bears repeating
- How the repetition creates an almost primitive cadence and builds a mood

RESPONSE STANCE: Please go back into Stafford's pantoum and see how it works: number the lines in the first stanza and follow what happens next. Also, note the lines and language you love.

BENEDICTION: I think this is a tempting form. The rhythm and the feeling created by the repetition of whole lines are pleasing but also mysterious. It's not an especially easy form to write, but the results are worth it. My advice to potential pantoumers: *every line* needs to bear repeating, so polish each one until it shines.

The Summer We Didn't Die

That year, that summer, that vacation
we played out there in the cottonwood—
we were young; we had to be brave.
Far out on those limbs above air,

we played out there in the cottonwood
above grown-ups who shouted, "Come down!"
Far out on those limbs above air
we were brave in that summer that year.

Above grown-ups who shouted, "Come down,
you'll be killed!" we were scared but held on.
We were brave in that summer that year.
No one could make us come down.

"You'll be killed!" We were scared, but we held on.
That year, that summer, that vacation,
no one could make us come down.
We were young. We had to be brave.

  —*William Stafford*

"The Summer We Didn't Die," ©1991 by William Stafford.

A Pantoum for Blue

BY BAILEY IRVING

SETTING THE STAGE: Yesterday we enjoyed a pantoum by William Stafford; today our pantoumer is Bailey, a seventh grader. She varies the structure of her pantoum in the final stanza. Is this okay? *Yes.* Poets sometimes modify forms to help achieve the effects they seek.

SOME FEATURES TO NOTICE:
- How Bailey chose to modify the conventions of the pantoum form in her final stanza
- Her sensory images and verbs
- How every line is strong and bears repeating
- How the repetition creates a cadence and builds a mood

RESPONSE STANCE: Please go back into Bailey's pantoum and mark what you think are its strongest lines—it's okay if there are many.

BENEDICTION: Again, I hope you'll decide to play with this form. It's perfect for a subject that evokes your feelings, or a topic you can see in your mind's eye, because the repetition of the form will emphasize emotions and descriptions. Craft one gorgeous, stand-alone line upon another, and see if you can add them up as a pantoum.

A Pantoum for Blue

I gaze into blue.
I taste salt in my mouth:
my hand meets bottomless ocean indigo as it douses
my greedy fingers.

I taste salt in my mouth
as I suckle
my greedy fingers.
I live in colors

as I suckle
the blue from this moment.
I live in colors,
as I wrap myself in blue:

the blue from this moment.
The sky blazes the brightest cobalt.
I wrap myself in blue.
I live in colors.

The sky blazes the brightest cobalt:
so blue it hurts to look.
I wrap myself in blue,
and I imagine your eyes:

so blue, it hurts to look.
And I imagine your eyes,
deep as the salty-sweet ocean:
I gaze into blue.

— *Bailey Irving*

PRESENTING THE POEM:

Sonnet 18

BY WILLIAM SHAKESPEARE

SETTING THE STAGE: Sonnets began in Italy around eight hundred years ago. Contemporary poets are still playing with—and changing—the conventions of the form. Some basics do hold true. A sonnet has fourteen lines. The first eight, or the *octave*, establish a scene or situation. In either the next six lines (the *sestet*) or the last two, the poet reaches a conclusion. The poet Ron Padgett says "if you want to write in the sonnet form, it's good to understand the concept of 'therefore,'" because in the last lines of a sonnet, the poet is saying, "Therefore, this is the way I feel."

In Shakespeare's time, at the turn of the seventeenth century, the sonnet's form was strict, and its purpose was usually to flatter or praise someone: lovers, but also friends or people in positions of power. The rhyme scheme followed an *abab cdcd efef gg* pattern; that is, four *quatrains* and a *couplet*. There was also a set rhythm, called *iambic pentameter*, which means five stressed beats or syllables in each line alternating with unaccented syllables. Finally, each line had ten syllables, occasionally eleven.

Let's try one of Shakespeare's sonnets to understand the structure. This one was written around 1609 to honor and praise a "fair young man," as were many of Shakespeare's 154 sonnets. Literary scholars have guesses about who the fair young man might have been and what position of power he might have held in Elizabethan society, but no one knows for sure. The language that Shakespeare uses is the English of his time.

SOME FEATURES TO NOTICE:
- The fourteen lines paraphrase as:
  Should I compare you to a day in summer?
  You're more beautiful and even-tempered than that.

In May, strong winds can damage lovely blossoms,
And summer only stays for a short time (so that comparison won't work).
Sometimes in summer the sun is too hot;
Other times it's covered by clouds;
And all beautiful things on earth will lose their beauty eventually,
Either by accident or through the passage of time (and I can't compare you to things that don't last).
But your loveliness will never fade.
You'll never lose the beauty you own.
Nor will death ever cast its shadow on your beauty
because I've written about it here.
Therefore, for as long as civilization exists, this poem will survive and so will the memory of your beauty (because future generations will read these words I've written about you).

RESPONSE STANCE: Please go back into this flattering sonnet on your own and find the fourteen words that make up the *abab cdcd efef gg* rhyme scheme. Next, see if you can figure out what Shakespeare is saying here in this poem of praise. Write a couple of sentences: your best guess about what he wants the fair young man to understand. Don't worry—we'll unpack the meaning together.

BENEDICTION: If you want to try more of Shakespeare's sonnets, please borrow one of my copies of the collected sonnets. They are wonderful. If you want to try to write a sonnet, would you please hold off for a day? I have two to show you, written by seventh graders, that I think will help and inspire your own sonnets.

Sonnet 18

Shall I compare thee to a summer's day?
Thou art more lovely and more temperate:
Rough winds do shake the darling buds of May,
And summer's lease hath all too short a date:
Sometimes too hot the eye of heaven shines,
And often is his gold complexion dimm'd;
And every fair from fair sometimes declines,
By chance or nature's changing course untrimm'd;
But thy eternal summer shall not fade
Nor lose possession of that fair thou owest,
Nor shall Death brag thou wander'st in his shade,
When in eternal lines to time thou grow'st:
So long as men can breathe or eyes can see,
So long lives this and this gives life to thee.

—*William Shakespeare*

PRESENTING THE POEMS:

Arizona Sunset

BY LINCOLN BLISS

&

Concord Sonnet

BY ALISON RITTERSHAUS

SETTING THE STAGE: As I promised yesterday, here are two Shakespearean-style sonnets written by seventh graders. The language is modern English, but the structure—fourteen lines in an *abab cdcd efef gg* pattern—is the same, and so is the purpose. Lincoln *praises* an amazing sunset he saw once, when he stayed with his grandmother in Arizona, and Alison *praises* the power and beauty of a certain wooden bridge in Concord, Massachusetts, site of the "shot heard round the world" and the opening salvos of our War for Independence.

SOME FEATURES TO NOTICE:
- How each sonnet conforms to an *abab cdcd efef gg* rhyme scheme
- How each line contains ten syllables
- How Lincoln and Alison did *not* attempt iambic pentameter: the rhyme scheme and syllable count just about did them in
- How each poet creates sensory images; uses beautiful, precise diction; and makes a personal connection, in the final couplet, to his or her own topic as a "therefore" statement

RESPONSE STANCE: Please go back into one of these two sonnets—your choice—and note how it does or doesn't conform to the conventions of a Shakespearean sonnet. Then, mark the language—the words, phrases, and lines—you love.

BENEDICTION: If you want to try a sonnet, go for it. It may help you to know that Lincoln and Alison began with their *topics*—a gorgeous, inspiring, Arizona sunset that Lincoln observed and remembered and Alison's moving, inspiring, return visit to Concord with her mom. They started with topics that invited praise. I'll invite you to do the same: who and what are the people, animals (remember Ben's sonnet for his kitten Shoelace?), natural phenomena, places that leave you awestruck?

I'll also invite you to consult a rhyming dictionary, if you decide to become a sonneteer. A good rhyming dictionary will offer you tons of choices for the word you need to rhyme. More importantly, it will help you maintain a focus on your intended meaning, instead of settling for the rhyming words you can come up with on your own.

Arizona Sunset

The sun sets over the farthest mountain.
Silky darkness envelops the landscape
and casts shadows over the knotted plain.
Ghostly cacti rise before me, their shape
like rotted moors of a forgotten pier.
The stones of the patio are littered
with pale light and violet sunbeams, clear.
The fields reach out, shining and undeterred;
they glow, a faint light, high above the rest.
The wind is chiseled, tight, and soaked with dew,
the grass a ceaseless wave—softly caressed.
The land is laid out before me in blue.
Under soft evening light that surrounds me,
that subtracts my emotions, I am free.

—*Lincoln Bliss*

Concord Sonnet

From here the bridge looks like a fading dream.
The river's current sweeps unseen beneath.
A mist rises from deep within the stream.
Its pilings break the flow with grinning teeth.
The tangled gardens where we walk are old:
an Eden overgrown by ghostly hands.
The spider's silk here is tainted with gold
where sunlight glints and spreads above the lands.
Together we wish we were here that day,
when soldiers marched along the bridge's arc,
when many ancient ties unfurled from fray,
when fire burst forth from barrels long and dark.
Towards the resolute structure we two peer,
linked through history, hand in hand, each year.

—*Alison Rittershaus*

PRESENTING THE POEM:

Ode to the Apple

BY PABLO NERUDA

SETTING THE STAGE: And now we come to the first of some of my favorite made-up forms. Pablo Neruda, a Chilean poet, political activist, and diplomat, won the Nobel Prize in Literature in 1971. He's regarded as the greatest Latin American poet ever. *And* he invented the irregular ode.

Regular odes were invented in ancient Greece around 500 B.C. by the poet Pindar. Back then, odes followed a set, intricate pattern of stanzas. They were serious, dignified, choral songs that were performed to celebrate great victories.

In the twentieth century, Neruda retrofitted the ode. He abandoned serious topics, discarded the rules about stanzas and meter, and wrote odes that sang the praises of everyday life and ordinary objects: a pair of socks, onions, a tomato, ironing, a spoon, French fries, a bar of soap, a storm, laziness. Many of these are collected in his book *Odes to Common Things*.

I love Neruda's "Ode to the Apple." Not only does he explore *appleness*, he also creates a political manifesto calling for a world united by apples.

SOME FEATURES TO NOTICE:
- The first-person presence and voice, which directly addresses the subject: the apple
- The sensory imagery
- The exaggeration of the apple's admirable qualities
- The specificity of the descriptions
- The short lines
- The humor that results from Neruda's boundless enthusiasm
- The strong conclusion

RESPONSE STANCE: Please go back into Neruda's version of an ode and mark the lines you love and want to talk about—also any line that makes you feel like eating an apple *right now*.

BENEDICTION: Neruda-esque odes are a joy to write. You get to expound without limits about something you love. My advice, if you decide to try one, is to pick an object you *adore*, a word I don't use lightly. You almost can't be too extreme in your praise when it comes to an ode. It's also important to stay true to the spirit of Neruda's odes: part of the fun lies in choosing an everyday object. Tomorrow we'll read odes by two girls who rose to the challenge.

Ode to the Apple

You, apple,
are the object
of my praise.
I want to fill
my mouth
with your name.
I want to eat you whole.

You are always
fresh, like nothing
and nobody.
You have always
just fallen
from Paradise:
dawn's
rosy cheek
full
and perfect!

Compared
to you
the fruits of the earth
are
so awkward:
bunchy grapes,
muted
mangos,
bony
plums, and submerged
figs.
You are pure balm,
fragrant bread,
the cheese
of all that flowers.

When we bite into
your round innocence
we too regress
for a moment
to the state
of the newborn:
there's still some apple in us all.

I want
total abundance,
your family
multiplied.
I want
a city,
a republic,
a Mississippi River
of apples,
and I want to see
gathered on its banks
the world's
entire
population
united and reunited
in the simplest act we know:
I want us to bite into an apple.

—*Pablo Neruda*

"Ode to the Apple," ©1994 by Pablo Neruda and Fundacion Pablo Neruda
(Odes Spanish); ©1994 by Ken Krabbenhoft (Odes English Translation)

PRESENTING THE POEMS:

Ode to a Star

BY NORA BRADFORD

&

Ode to Subway

BY HAYLEY BRIGHT

SETTING THE STAGE: Nora was a star-gazer: she couldn't name any of the heavenly bodies, but she loved the night sky. Hayley was a lover of Subway turkey sandwiches. Each poet sang the praises of something she adored in an ode inspired by Pablo Neruda.

SOME FEATURES TO NOTICE:
- The first-person voice and presence
- The sensory imagery
- The exaggeration
- The metaphors
- The humor
- The strong conclusions
- The differences in stylistic choices: Hayley's longer lines and centered format vs. Nora's short lines and list format

RESPONSE STANCE: Please choose one of these two odes that you'd like to read again and unpack. Then, go back in and mark your favorite descriptions and metaphors.

BENEDICTION: Again, the happiest way to enter the act of ode making is with a short list of common objects that you appreciate, enjoy, *adore*. Choose one, and create a planning sheet: list everything you notice, feel, taste, smell, hear, think, and wonder about your topic. Then, craft your ode with the help of the ideas in your notes, which is what Nora and Hayley did.

Ode to a Star

O, star in heaven,
do you relax during the day
with Zeus
in his palace?
Are you shiny
from being waxed
at the drive-thru
car wash?
Or were you once an albino fly
that climbed high,
high until you hit
indigo flypaper,
and now you're stuck,
squirming to be free?
Are you a diamond
that fell off
my charm bracelet,
and you're searching
the midnight sky
for the lonely chain?
Are you the ornament
I decorated
last Christmas,
the one the cat
knocked off our tree?
I gaze
into the cobalt sky
and wish
this was the night
I might name one,
just one, constellation
(other than the Big Dipper,
of course).
But no.
Once again I fail
as an astronomer.
I know that I will never
join a star-gazing club
to tally the arrival of you
and your sisters and brothers.

O, star,
your mother's brother's daughter's aunt
would be my favorite constellation
if I were ever accepted
into the astronomers association.
Until then I will lie
on the snow,
sing your praises,
and discover my own
constellations.

—Nora Bradford

Ode to Subway

Ahhhhh…perfection.
The right amount of everything.
I watch as they
fold each piece of cold, fresh turkey—
one, two, three, four, five, six.
Inside I am twitching.
I can't wait to stuff
this little piece of heaven
in my mouth.
They wrap up my sandwich—
in its blankie, so it doesn't get cold—
and hand me the holy bread.

In the car I peel back each corner
to reveal pure beauty.
I can almost hear the saints and angels
singing.
I take the first bite….
Ahhhhhhh,
perfection.

—Hayley Bright

Thirteen Ways of Looking at a Blackbird

BY WALLACE STEVENS

SETTING THE STAGE: The first time I read this poem my jaw dropped, it was so rich, funny, and mysterious. I read it again, then again, and finally I began to catch glimmers of what Stevens was up to. "Thirteen Ways of Looking at a Blackbird" is a poem about Western civilization.

SOME FEATURES TO NOTICE:

- How Stevens packs this poem, seemingly about a mere blackbird, with literary, cultural, and scholarly references to aspects of Western civilization:

Stanza I	The blackbird is a tiny detail in a vast, still landscape, but it is the only thing that's alive, that perceives, that matters
Stanza II	A simile, in which the blackbird suggests the speaker's frame of mind
Stanza III	The world is a stage set; the blackbird is one of many players
Stanza IV	A metaphorical math problem about male-female relationships
Stanza V	A philosophical proposition or meditation on personal preference
Stanza VI	A mystery story out of Poe, starring the blackbird
Stanza VII	A sermon or Bible quotation
Stanza VIII	The blackbird as the salt of the earth: human intelligence and culture grounded by nature
Stanza IX	A metaphysical geometry problem; perhaps a reference to the falcon in Yeats's "Second Coming," with many circles instead of the one *widening gyre* of Christianity
Stanza X	A legend or myth
Stanza XI	A fairy tale
Stanza XII	A pearl of folk wisdom from the *Farmer's Almanac*
Stanza XIII	Once again the blackbird is a tiny detail in a vast landscape, but this time we seem to be viewing him at something like the end of the world

RESPONSE STANCE: See what I mean by rich, funny, and mysterious? Would you please get together in pairs? Then, would each pair take one of the thirteen *ways* and try to unpack it? What aspect of human culture is Stevens suggesting in your stanza? I'll come around among you and offer any help I can, based on my own, *not* definitive reading of the poem. Then we'll come back together and try to unpack the whole poem.

BENEDICTION: Now that we've made a stab at laying bare what Wallace Stevens was up to, may I invite you to try a *ways* poem of your own? It doesn't have to be thirteen, but now that you have a sense of how Stevens developed this theory and form, I think you'd be surprised at what a pleasure it is to write. We'll read some student *ways* poems tomorrow, so you can see what I mean.

Thirteen Ways of Looking at a Blackbird

I

Among twenty snowy mountains,
The only moving thing
Was the eye of the blackbird.

II

I was of three minds,
Like a tree
In which there are three blackbirds.

III

The blackbird whirled in the autumn winds.
It was a small part of the pantomime.

IV

A man and a woman
Are one.
A man and a woman and a blackbird
Are one.

V

I do not know which to prefer,
The beauty of inflections
Or the beauty of innuendoes,
The blackbird whistling
Or just after.

VI

Icicles filled the long window
With barbaric glass.
The shadow of the blackbird
Crossed it, to and fro.
The mood
Traced in the shadow
An indecipherable cause.

VII

O thin men of Haddam,
Why do you imagine golden birds?
Do you not see how the blackbird
Walks around the feet
Of the women about you?

VIII

I know noble accents
And lucid, inescapable rhythms;
But I know, too,
That the blackbird is involved
In what I know.

IX

When the blackbird flew out of sight,
It marked the edge
Of one of many circles.

X

At the sight of blackbirds
Flying in green light,
Even the bawds of euphony
Would cry out sharply.

XI

He rode over Connecticut
In a glass coach.
Once, a fear pierced him,
In that he mistook
The shadow of his equipage
For blackbirds.

XII

The river is moving.
The blackbird must be flying.

XIII

It was evening all afternoon.
It was snowing
And it was going to snow.
The blackbird sat
In the cedar-limbs.

—Wallace Stevens

PRESENTING THE POEMS:

Nine Ways to Look at a Hammer
BY MICHAEL STOLTZ

&

Seven Ways of Looking at a Cup of Espresso
BY SIOBHAN ANDERSON

&

Eleven Ways of Looking at Paper
BY JAMES MORRILL

SETTING THE STAGE: After a summer spent helping his father with various "projects" around the house, Michael knew right away what the subject of his Wallace Stevens-inspired ways poem would be. Here's Michael's "Nine Ways to Look at a Hammer."

SOME FEATURES TO NOTICE:
- The humor
- How the format and the tone mimic Stevens
- The choices Michael made of which approaches to borrow and parody from among the original thirteen

RESPONSE STANCE: Take out your marked-up copy of Wallace Stevens' "Thirteen Ways of Looking at a Blackbird," and let's compare Michael Stoltz's parody to the original. Mark up Michael's "Nine Ways to Look at a Hammer" in terms of what he did that you appreciate in this goof on Stevens.

BENEDICTION: Here are two more student *ways* poems for you to read tonight for homework and enjoy, about a cup of espresso and a piece of paper. I know that if they were here, Siobhan and Jim would tell you they had fun writing these. If you're inspired, start brainstorming potential topics, choose one that most strikes your writer's imagination, and start to play.

Nine Ways to
Look at a Hammer

1.
Among a thousand items on the hardware store shelves,
the only one purchased
was the hammer.

2.
A hammer and a nail
aren't much;
a hammer, a nail, and some wood—
well, they're a house.

3.
The bang of the hammer
createth carpentry,
and whenith the threshold is completeth,
thou resteth upon thy hammer.

4.
Rome wasn't built in a day,
especially without a hammer.

5.
When the house was complete,
the hammer clanked
to the bottom
of one of many tool boxes.

6.
I don't know which to prefer,
the sound of hammer against nail
or the silence when the job is done.

7.
The nail's in the wood.
It must be hammer time.

8.
Noah didn't make the ark himself, you know.
The hammer helped out, too.

9.
It was evening all afternoon.
The nail gun nailed and it was going to nail.
The hammer lay untouched in the tool shed.

> —*Michael Stoltz*

©2006 by Nancie Atwell from *Naming the World: A Year of Poems and Lessons*
(Portsmouth, NH: Heinemann)

Seven Ways of Looking
at a Cup of Espresso

1.
Amidst the twelve Green Mountains
the only moving thing
was steam,
smoking from the frothy surface
of the espresso.

2.
And God said to the weary traveler:
Take and drink of this cup
and you shall be healed.

3.
The Starbucks is open.
The espresso must be flowing.

4.
Somewhere in the countryside
a man jumped from the jolt of an electric fence.
Several miles away
another man drank espresso.

5.
Laughter and energy are one.
Laughter and energy and espresso
are *one.*

6.
The mighty prince slew the dragon
and entered the cave of treasures.
All that lay inside was a cup of espresso.
He drank and saw diamonds.

7.
Across the earth snow fell,
covering all
but a patch of green
where spring stayed,
heated by the warmth of espresso.

  —*Siobhan Anderson*

Eleven Ways of Looking at Paper

1.
Among the desks,
the notebooks and pens,
the white lined paper held authority.

2.
The dishes must be put away,
the room cleaned.
The paper lay untouched,
the assignment stalled.

3.
The paper staggered in the midst of chaos.
It fell with Macbeth into the rubbish bin.
The writer surrendered.

4.
A creative mind and ink
are two.
A creative mind, ink, and paper
are one.

5.
I am torn:
the new book in hand
or the old one on the shelf?
The passion of writing on paper
or the crisp satisfaction of the computer?

6.
The girl ripped the pink floral paper out of her diary.
Her thoughts screamed at the sound
of heart-filled entries severed.
Her foolish crush would be remembered
nevermore.

7.
Exodus 34:28
Moses was upon the mountain with the Lord
for forty days and forty nights.
In all that time he neither ate nor drank.
God wrote the terms of the covenant
—the Ten Commandments—
on stone tablets.
Not paper.

8.
If I were smashed into pulp,
rolled paper thin,
would all my imperfections show,
or would I have lines instead?

9.
The unsubstantial thought
sank on a paper airplane
down to the coffin below.

10.
She clutched the invitation
written on scented paper.
Her glass shoes winked
in the moonlight.

11.
A ball of paper meets a trash can;
an aged tree must be falling.

—*James Morrill*

©2006 by Nancie Atwell from *Naming the World: A Year of Poems and Lessons*
(Portsmouth, NH: Heinemann)

Mom,

&

I Once Knew a Girl

BY NORA BRADFORD

SETTING THE STAGE: You've met Nora Bradford already, as the author of "Watermelon," "The Old Fence," and "Ode to a Star." As a seventh-grade poet, Nora enjoyed experimenting with other poets' forms and styles. As an eighth-grade poet, Nora invented her own form and style. Let's read two of her poems; then see if you can describe what Nora did here.

SOME FEATURES TO NOTICE:

- How in each of the poems, two stanzas *parallel* one other, line to corresponding line; Nora called her form *parallel stanzas*
- How she varied the form in "I Once Knew a Girl" by setting off the first and last lines as separate stanzas
- How parallel stanzas allow a poet to create strong contrasts and imply strong themes

RESPONSE STANCE: Please go back into Nora's two poems and figure out her form. Then, mark anything else she did as a poet—words, lines, or ideas—that struck you.

BENEDICTION: I think these are powerful poems. Their power derives from the direct, sharp contrast that Nora establishes between *then* and *now*. I know your life is filled with *then* and *now* experiences and understandings, as the ground beneath you shifts faster than it ever will again. Consider a parallel-stanzas poem as a way to illustrate the distance between you *then* and you *now*.

Mom,

I remember last year—
that whole week I was in a bad mood.
The only words I said were *yes* and *no*.
I believed the world was against me.
You offered to buy me
chocolate milk and a whoopie pie.
But since I was supposed to hate you,
I said no—
or maybe I didn't even answer.
Either way,
while I sulked in the van
listening to the music you hate,
you stood in the checkout
and spent $2.49 on snacks
I didn't want.
I know you did it because you love me,
and I knew you wouldn't like it
if I didn't eat them,
but I only took one sip.

And I remember last Tuesday—
this whole month I was in a good mood.
All I wanted to do was talk,
and I thought the world believed in me.
You offered to buy me a treat,
and since it's so easy to love you,
I said *yes*.
You wanted to stay in the car
and listen to the news I hate,
but I convinced you to come in.
You spent $1.40 on the whoopie pie
I wanted.
I know you did it because you love me,
and I knew you would like it
if I ate it,
so I gave you one bite
and devoured the rest.

      —Nora Bradford

I Once Knew a Girl

I once knew a girl who

ran through the green fields barefoot,
played tag on weekends,
and woke with the sun at six.
She loved school
and never brushed her hair.
She slept with Teddy
and went to bed with the night light on.

Now
she paints her toenails green,
reads upstairs on weekends,
and dozes till eleven.
She finds school a bore
and spends hours in the bathroom.
Teddy is under her bed,
and she sleeps in darkness.

That girl is gone.

      —Nora Bradford

©2006 by Nancie Atwell from *Naming the World: A Year of Poems and Lessons* (Portsmouth, NH: Heinemann)

Aubade

BY ROBERT PACK

&

January Thaw

BY BRENNA HAGEN

SETTING THE STAGE: The poet Robert Pack invented today's form, which he called *rounding it out*. His collection of poems that are written in this form opens with a morning song, an *aubade*, in praise of sunlight.

SOME FEATURES TO NOTICE:
- The form, a cross between a sonnet and a villanelle, which repeats its opening line several times
- Sixteen lines, with two of these repeating
- The first line returns as the last line
- The second line returns somewhere in the middle of the poem, sometimes with a variation
- A rhyme scheme of *abab, cbcb, dede, aaca*

RESPONSE STANCE: Can you determine the form of a *rounding-it-out* from this one example of Robert Pack's? Please go back in and give it your best shot.

SETTING THE STAGE (2): Here's another example of rounding it out, this time by Brenna, a seventh grader. Let's see if the form is more apparent now, as we put the two poems side by side.

BENEDICTION: Like the sonnet, this is a difficult form but a beautiful one. It's musical, in the way it both rhymes and repeats. Consider rounding it out as a way to comment on and think about one of your experiences or observations. And if you decide to rise to the challenge, be sure to keep a rhyming dictionary by your side.

Aubade

Our sun has left just half its life to spill—
About five billion years before it must
Explode, collapse upon itself, and will
Back to the universe its final thrust
Of heat we creatures have long counted on.
Waking warm here in bed, we trust
This light to help imagine when light will be gone
About five billion years from now; it must
Experience diminishment,
As we must too, as must we all.
Observers, we can find our last content
In comprehension that the fall
Of yellow petals on our window sill,
Like little suns, is what we have to will,
A melody to whistle in the dawn:
Our sun has left just half its life to spill.

   —Robert Pack

January Thaw

Cold winter took a vacation,
and today has an odd spring essence.
The birds show a form of elation,
and the sun finally presents
itself as a radiating globe.
It is hard to find any evidence
of cold December in my wardrobe.
Today has an odd spring essence,
and I plan to take advantage
of the sunshine by going for a walk
and exploring the age
of time and rock,
discovering inspiration
and loving the sensation
of warmth as I probe.
Cold winter took a vacation.

   —Brenna Hagen

©2006 by Nancie Atwell from *Naming the World: A Year of Poems and Lessons* (Portsmouth, NH: Heinemann)

It's natural development, as they say— and pre-ado... absorbed. I... is everything

The *Larger* World:

INTRODUCTION

It's natural—developmentally appropriate, as they say—for adolescents and pre-adolescents to be self-absorbed. Personal identity is everything to kids aged twelve to eighteen. The poems that comprise the bulk of this anthology plumb the deepening waters of change and self and what it means to be human.

But adolescence is also a time for students to begin to consider the social, political, and ethical implications of what it means to be *a* human living on a planet among billions of others. Poetry can become a source of insight for kids into such big ideas as justice, mercy, truth, courage, fairness, compassion, equality, and freedom. And poetry can help adolescents begin to look outward, beyond their selves, to connect with the larger world and become inspired to take action. Sometimes their actions take the form of new poems of passion and protest.

Lawrence Ferlinghetti once wrote a poem in which he pitted "the little airplanes of the heart/ with their brave little propellers" against "the winds of darkness." The poems in this section helped my students discover "their brave little propellers" and launch themselves into the larger world.

PRESENTING THE POEM:

Patriotics

BY DAVID BAKER

SETTING THE STAGE: The poet Walt Whitman wrote, in the middle of the nineteenth century, about the promise of America and democracy. In the middle of the twentieth century, the poet Allen Ginsberg wrote about America's broken promise. In this poem by David Baker, written near the turn of the twenty-first century, listen for the echoes of Whitman and Ginsberg.

SOME FEATURES TO NOTICE:

- The sensory diction: verbs, nouns, and adjectives
- The powerful imagery: visual and auditory
- The voice: a first person *I* speaking to *America*
- The tone: sarcastic and despairing
- The alliteration
- The powerful and ironic concluding image: Americans who've lost sight of what America means, standing with their mouths open in wonder at the sight of fireworks on the Fourth of July
- The form: four-line stanzas, with lines two and four indented, except for the concluding stanza

RESPONSE STANCE: Please go back into "Patriotics" on your own and discover what has happened, *is* happening, literally, in the America of this poem. Write one or two sentences. Then, mark what you think are its most important lines, plus any others you'd like to talk about.

BENEDICTION: The poems of the next couple of weeks will ask you to focus beyond yourself and your immediate environment. Like "Patriotics," this poetry expresses anger, despair, and dissatisfaction about the larger world, as well as hope, courage, and solidarity. We'll read it not to become angry or depressed about the state of the world, but to see how expressing anger and angst—and hope—in poetry can touch hearts when minds may already be closed. We'll see how poets' visions of the larger world can become sources of new insights, can give us courage, and can inspire us to take action.

In today's poem, David Baker set his vision of America at a small-town Fourth of July celebration. As poets, where would you set your vision of our country? Where do you find your America?

Patriotics

Yesterday a little girl got slapped to death by her daddy,
    out of work, alcoholic, and estranged two towns down river.
America, it's hard to get your attention politely.
    America, the beautiful night is about to blow up

and the cop who brought the man down with a shot to the chops
    is shaking hands, dribbling chaw across his sweaty shirt,
and pointing cars across the courthouse grass to park.
    It's the Big One one more time, July the 4th,

our country's perfect holiday, so directly a metaphor for war
    we shoot off bombs, launch rockets from Drano cans,
spray the streets and neighbors' yards with the machine-gun crack
    of fireworks, with rebel yells and beer. In short, we celebrate.

It's hard to believe. But so help the soul of Thomas Paine,
    the entire country must be here—the acned faces of neglect,
the halter-tops and ties, the bellies, badges, beehives,
    jacked-up cowboy boots, yes, the back-up singers of democracy

all gathered to brighten in unambiguous delight
    when we attack the calm and pointless sky. With terrifying vigor
the whistle-stop across the river will lob its smaller arsenal
    halfway back again. Some may be moved to tears.

We'll clean up fast, drive home slow, and tomorrow
    get back to work, those of us with jobs, convicting the others
in the back rooms of our courts and malls—yet what
    will be left of that one poor child, veteran of no war

but her family's own? The comfort of a welfare plot,
    a stalk of wilting prayers? Our father's dreams come true as nightmare.
So the first bomb blasts and echoes through the streets and shrubs:
    red, white, and blue sparks shower down, a plague

of patriotic bugs. Our thousand eyeballs burn aglow like punks.
    America, I'd swear I don't believe in you, but here I am,
and here you are, and here we stand again, agape.
    —David Baker

At the Cancer Clinic

BY TED KOOSER

SETTING THE STAGE: Ted Kooser, U.S. poet laureate, glimpsed a vision of another America in a waiting room at a cancer clinic. This is a poem of hope. A word you should know the meaning of is *grace*: in this poem, it means the spirit of God—of love and beauty—showing itself in humans.

SOME FEATURES TO NOTICE:
- The strong visual imagery
- The sensory verbs
- The metaphors
- The quiet, contemplative, powerful conclusion, as the speaker and the other patients in the waiting room witness—and participate in—a moment of grace

RESPONSE STANCE: Please go back into Ted Kooser's vision and mark the lines you can see, too. Then, mark what you find to be the most important lines in this poem.

BENEDICTION: Again, where will you set your vision of America? Start thinking; start looking around you.

At the Cancer Clinic

She is being helped toward the open door
that leads to the examining rooms
by two young women I take to be her sisters.
Each bends to the weight of an arm
and steps with the straight, tough bearing
of courage. At what must seem to be
a great distance, a nurse holds the door,
smiling and calling encouragement.
How patient she is in the crisp white sails
of her clothes. The sick woman
peers from under her funny knit cap
to watch each foot swing scuffing forward
and take its turn under her weight.
There is no restlessness or impatience
or anger anywhere in sight. Grace
fills the clean mold of this moment
and all the shuffling magazines grow still.

—*Ted Kooser*

PRESENTING THE POEM:

We the People

BY ALEXIS KELLNER BECKER

SETTING THE STAGE: Alexis, an eighth grader, found her vision of America in the flickering images of her TV screen.

SOME FEATURES TO NOTICE:
- How the title quotes the opening of the Preamble to the U.S. Constitution
- How the poem is one long sentence
- The allusion to Greek mythology in *Achilles heel*
- The lively diction and rhythm
- The metaphors
- The ironic conclusion
- Alexis' theme of how difficult it is for an American teen to resist being defined and controlled by peer pressure and mass culture

RESPONSE STANCE: Please go back into Alexis' poem on your own, unpack it, and write one or two sentences: why do you think she might have written this poem?

BENEDICTION: So far we've witnessed three different examples of contemporary poets' visions of America. Keep thinking: what is yours? *Where* will you ground it?

We the People

the so called MTV generation
is locked in a box
by the constant barrage of should and ought
by the undertow of popularity
of conformity of density and intensity
by the need to choose whether
to expose the Achilles heel that is your reality
or to wear boots
by the blur of the line between *want* and *need*
by the ease of staring at what they say you should be
what you don't want to be
by the mass generalization
the labels that society embroiders on your sweaters
by the box you have to fit into
the box that becomes your reality
which is a tragedy, really

he says as he flips on the TV

  —Alexis Kellner Becker

Richard Cory

BY EDWIN ARLINGTON ROBINSON

SETTING THE STAGE: In poems he wrote almost a hundred years ago, Edwin Arlington Robinson set his vision of America in an imaginary village he named "Tilbury Town." He based it on Gardiner, Maine, where he grew up as a member of a family and a society whose main goals were social position and money.

Most of Robinson's poems about Tilbury Town are narratives: stories or psychological portraits based on real people he knew—tramps, a butcher, a store clerk, and various dreamers and drunks, all wrecks of a society driven by greed. Robinson helped his readers understand the lonely, the discarded, and the dispossessed. The best known of his characters, perhaps the saddest, is Richard Cory. Robinson based him on a banker he knew who *seemed* to have everything.

SOME FEATURES TO NOTICE:
- Vocabulary:
  clean favored means having a pleasing appearance
  imperially, here, means regally or like an emperor
  arrayed, here, means attired or dressed
  in fine means in conclusion
- The theme that wealth is an empty value that cannot guarantee happiness or a sense of self-worth

RESPONSE STANCE: Please go back into "Richard Cory" on your own and consider two questions: Who is the speaker? Who are *we people on the pavement*? And what do you think they don't grasp that Robinson understood and wants us to understand, too? Write a sentence or two.

BENEDICTION: So here's another way to explore and express your vision about what you perceive is wrong and right in our society. You can combine poetry and fiction: develop characters based on the people you think we need to notice and understand. Let characters tell their stories and animate your vision.

Richard Cory

Whenever Richard Cory went down town,
We people on the pavement looked at him:
He was a gentleman from sole to crown,
Clean favored, and imperially slim.

And he was always quietly arrayed,
And he was always human when he talked;
But still he fluttered pulses when he said,
"Good-morning," and he glittered when he walked.

And he was rich—yes, richer than a king—
And admirably schooled in every grace:
In fine, we thought that he was everything
To make us wish that we were in his place.

So on we worked and waited for the light,
And went without the meat, and cursed the bread;
And Richard Cory, one calm summer night,
Went home and put a bullet through his head.

    —*Edwin Arlington Robinson*

PRESENTING THE POEM:

To an Old Black Woman, Homeless and Indistinct

BY GWENDOLYN BROOKS

SETTING THE STAGE: Gwendolyn Brooks is one of the great American poets of the twentieth century. In 1950, she was the first African American to receive the Pulitzer Prize for poetry. Her subject is the dreams and struggles of Blacks living in the urban North, especially Chicago, where she grew up and still lives. The poem of hers that's most frequently anthologized is "We Real Cool," about a group of young, doomed, inner city pool players, but the poem kids have liked best over the years is this one. Gwendolyn Brooks helped them to *pay attention.*

SOME FEATURES TO NOTICE:
- *Bacchanal* means a drunken celebration; it's used here ironically
- How Brooks has selected isolated but significant nouns to capitalize: *The People, Rich Girl, Home, Plan, Review*
- Her use of repetition to create cadence and emphasis
- The tone: one of no-nonsense, even caustic, observation
- The specific portrait Brooks creates of the life of the *Rich Girl*, a distinct individual who is defined by her possessions, in contrast with the *indistinct* image we have of the *old Black woman*, who people either don't see or don't want to see
- The sad irony of the last four lines—how distinctive the old woman once was; how individual and unmistakable; how loved, admired, talented, and full of promise

RESPONSE STANCE: Please go back into this poem and compare the portrait Brooks paints of the *Rich Girl* against what we learn about the homeless woman. What do you think Brooks is up to as a poet: why these particular details?

BENEDICTION: It's painful to contemplate poverty and despair. It's easier to pass it by, to not meet eyes, to allow the people in our society who are suffering to stay indistinct and separate from us. Or we can determine to pay attention. We can give people their humanity, understand that everyone matters, and ask what we can do so that no one is poor, homeless, *indistinct.*

To an Old Black Woman, Homeless and Indistinct

I.
Your every day is a pilgrimage.
A blue hubbub.
Your days are collected bacchanals of fear and self-troubling,

And your nights! Your nights.
When you put you down in an alley or cardboard or viaduct,
your lovers are rats, finding your secret places.

II.
When you rise in another morning,
you hit the street, your incessant enemy.

See? Here you are, in the so-busy world.
You walk. You walk.
You pass The People.
No. The People pass you.

Here's a Rich Girl marching briskly to her charms.
She is suede and scarf and belting and perfume.
She sees you not, she sees you very well.
At five in the afternoon Miss Rich Girl will go Home
to brooms and vacuum cleaner and carpeting,
two cats, two marble-top tables, two telephones,
shiny green peppers, flowers in impudent vases,
visitors.
Before all that there's luncheon to be known.
Lasagna, lobster salad, sandwiches.
All day there's coffee to be loved.
There are luxuries
of minor dissatisfaction, luxuries of Plan.

III.
That's *her* story.
You're going to vanish, not necessarily nicely, fairly soon.
Although essentially dignity itself a death
is not necessarily tidy, modest, or discreet.
When they find you
your legs may not be tidy nor aligned.
Your mouth may be all crooked or destroyed.

Black old woman, homeless, indistinct—
Your last and least adventure is Review.
Folks used to celebrate your birthday!
Folks used to say "She's such a pretty little thing!"
Folks used to say "She draws such handsome horses, cows, and houses."
Folks used to say "That child is going far."

 —*Gwendolyn Brooks*

PRESENTING THE POEM:

Lucky

BY TESS MCKECHNIE

SETTING THE STAGE: Tess, a seventh grader, paid attention. She was on a trip with her grandparents to Ecuador, in Central America. From a high window in an expensive, air-conditioned, hotel room, she looked down. She continued to look. And then she started thinking.

SOME FEATURES TO NOTICE:

- How Tess structures the poem so it mimics her experience: first noticing, then understanding what she's seeing, then realizing that only the luck of her birth separates her from the homeless kids of Guayaquil
- The effective repetition of *somehow* at the conclusion, which creates cadence and emphasizes Tess's theme

RESPONSE STANCE: Please go back into Tess's poem on your own, then write a brief response: what do you think she understands about life—her life and others'—at the end of this poem?

BENEDICTION: Do you have a poem in you like Tess's, about a moment when you felt the distance between your life, with all its guarantees, and another's? Someone you glimpsed, and suddenly you *understood*?

Lucky

I stare out a hotel window
at the city of Guayaquil.
Below me
miniature citizens rush along sidewalks.
I watch a group of kids
who look like they're my age.
They cluster in the barren part of the city—
the place where houses were knocked down,
leaving only sorrowful walls
standing alone.
From high above
I study those walls.
Tiny structures
made of cardboard and sheets of metal
are nestled in the corners.
They look fragile—
as if they could tumble
with the touch of a breeze.
I find myself glued to the sight.
And I realize the small buildings
are actually houses.
And some of those kids
must live in them.
Questions flood my mind:
What would that be like?
What would it be like to *live there*?
To sit,
melting, in the ninety-degree sunlight?
And then I realize:
I could be one of them.
But somehow, I'm not.
Somehow, I was lucky.
And somehow,
they weren't.

—*Tess McKechnie*

From the Preface to the First Edition of Leaves of Grass

BY WALT WHITMAN

SETTING THE STAGE: This isn't actually a poem. It's part of the prose preface to the first edition of Walt Whitman's collection of poems entitled *Leaves of Grass*, first published in 1855. In this introduction, which I've taken the liberty of breaking as lines of a poem, Whitman explains what someone who wishes to be a great poet must do. It is my favorite prose poem of all time: words that inspire not just great poetry, but a life that's worthwhile, too.

SOME FEATURES TO NOTICE:

- *these leaves* are the poems in *Leaves of Grass*

RESPONSE STANCE: Please go back into Whitman's preface to *Leaves of Grass*. Which of his pieces of advice, which words of inspiration, mean the most to you and your life?

BENEDICTION: Here's a poem to tape to your bedroom wall or inside your locker and to take into your heart: the instructions for how your life might become *a great poem*. Thank you, Walt, for inventing free-verse poetry, for championing democracy and equality, and for counsel that inspires the best in us.

From the Preface to the First Edition of *Leaves of Grass*

Love the earth and sun and the animals,
despise riches, give alms to everyone that asks,
stand up for the stupid and crazy,
devote your income and labor to others,
hate tyrants,
argue not concerning God,
have patience and indulgence toward the people,
take off your hat to nothing known or unknown
or to any man or number of men,
go freely with powerful uneducated persons
and with the young and the mothers of families,
read these leaves in the open air
every season of every year of your life,
re-examine all you have been told
at school or church or in any book,
dismiss whatever insults your own soul
and your very flesh shall be a great poem.

—*Walt Whitman*

Dulce et Decorum Est

BY WILFRED OWEN

SETTING THE STAGE: Today, all over Europe, there are memorials to the Great War. World War I lasted from 1914 to 1918. It killed— *slaughtered*, is a better word—ten million, a lost generation of young men. And it was senseless: it started for no good reason; it was fought horribly, with poison gas and artillery in trenches and mud; and it settled nothing, ending as a virtual stalemate.

When the war began in August, 1914, the immediate cause was the assassination of Archduke Francis Ferdinand of Austria-Hungary by a Serbian nationalist. But the real cause was the rivalries among Europe's major powers and a disease called *nationalism*.

Austria-Hungary, supported by Germany, declared war on Serbia. Then, convinced that France was about to attack, Germany declared war on France, too. When the Germans marched through Belgium, a neutral country, it gave England an excuse for entering the war. In the following weeks, Montenegro and Japan joined England, France, Russia, Serbia, and Belgium as the Allies. Later Portugal, Rumania, and Greece also sided with the Allies. In 1917, after Germany announced a new tactic of submarine warfare, the United States entered the war. The Allies' foe, the Central Powers, consisted of Germany, Austria-Hungary, Turkey, and Bulgaria.

In England, at the beginning of the Great War, everyone was gung-ho. Young men swarmed to enlist and join the adventure, a sort of military soccer match that everyone was convinced would be over in a matter of months. That year Rudyard Kipling, a poet you know best as the author of *The Jungle Book*, wrote a long call to arms that begins:

> For all we have and are,
> For all our children's fate,
> Stand up and meet the war.
> The Hun is at the gate!

It ends:

> There is but one task for all—
> For each one life to give.
> Who stands if Freedom fall?
> Who dies if England live?

A year later, after it became clear that no one's freedom was at stake in a brutal, senseless war, after his son John became one of the slaughtered, Kipling wrote a very different kind of poem, this time in the voice of a soldier, two lines that say it all:

> If any question why we died,
> Tell them, because our fathers lied.

I mentioned the monuments, plaques, and cemeteries you can see throughout Europe today that memorialize the ten million who died in the Great War and the twenty million who were wounded. But there's another, more powerful legacy of the war: the poetry it gave birth to. Soldiers in the trenches began to describe the horrors of war. Siegfried Sassoon, Robert Graves, Saki, Rupert Brooke, Isaac Rosenberg, and others became soldier-poets. With outrage and compassion, they raised their voices and stung the consciences of their readers.

Wilfred Owen was one of the soldier-poets. After he was shell-shocked in the trenches in 1915, Owen was sent to a hospital in Scotland to recover. There he met Siegfried Sassoon, also a patient, who encouraged him to express his rage about the politicians who perpetuated the war and his pity for his fellow soldiers as poetry. When Owen recovered his health, he was sent back to the front. He was killed on November 4, 1918, a week before the Armistice was declared. In 1920, his friend Sassoon published *The Poems of Wilfred Owen*. It includes Owen's most famous anti-war poem, "Dulce et Decorum Est," a description of a poison gas attack.

The title is meant to be sarcastic. It's the beginning of a Latin phrase from the Roman poet Horace that every British schoolboy read and memorized: *Dulce et decorum est pro patria mori*. It translates as *It is sweet and honorable to die for one's country*.

SOME FEATURES TO NOTICE:
- The remarkable metaphors and similes
- The vivid visual images
- The subtle rhythm and rhyming
- The tone: one of both pity and bitterness

RESPONSE STANCE: Please go back into this powerful anti-war poem and mark the lines that strike you and that you want to talk about.

BENEDICTION: The First World War was known as "the war to end all wars." It didn't, of course. But the poetry that came out of it provides a lasting testament to the men who sacrificed themselves to its senseless horrors. And the poems remain as burning questions: Where is the glory in war? When, if ever, is a war justified?

Dulce et Decorum Est

Bent double, like old beggars under sacks,
Knocked-kneed, coughing like hags, we cursed through sludge,
Till on the haunting flares we turned our backs
And towards our distant rest began to trudge.
Men marched asleep. Many had lost their boots
But limped on, blood-shod. All went lame; all blind;
Drunk with fatigue; deaf even to the hoots
Of tired, outstripped Five-Nines that dropped behind.

Gas! Gas! Quick, boys!—An ecstasy of fumbling,
Fitting the clumsy helmets just in time;
But someone still was yelling out and stumbling
And flound'ring like a man in fire or lime . . .
Dim, through the misty panes and thick green light,
As under a green sea, I saw him drowning.
In all my dreams, before my helpless sight,
He plunges at me, guttering, choking, drowning.

If in some smothering dreams you too could pace
Behind the wagon that we flung him in,
And watch the white eyes writhing in his face,
His hanging face, like a devil's sick of sin;
If you could hear, at every jolt, the blood
Come gargling from the froth-corrupted lungs,
Obscene as cancer, bitter as the cud
Of vile, incurable sores on innocent tongues,—
My friend, you would not tell with such high zest
To children ardent for some desperate glory,
The old Lie: Dulce et decorum est
Pro patria mori.

   —Wilfred Owen

And the poems remain
as burning questions:
where is the glory in war?

Naming of Parts

BY HENRY REED

SETTING THE STAGE: Today I want to help you to understand a bit about World War II, then appreciate perhaps the greatest poem that came out of that conflict, "Naming of Parts" by Henry Reed.

The Second World War began in 1939 when Germany, under Hitler, invaded and conquered Poland. It was the last straw for England and France, which had watched Germany take over Austria, then Czechoslovakia. They declared war on Germany. Then France was conquered by Germany in 1940. Germany by then was part of the Axis Powers, along with Italy and Japan. But, in 1941, England gained two new allies: first, the Soviet Union and then, after the Japanese bombed our military base at Pearl Harbor, the United States.

This was a popular war, meaning that the majority of our soldiers and the civilian population knew and supported the reasons for the conflict: to stop the militaristic, totalitarian dictatorships of Germany, Italy, and Japan from expanding to take over other countries. World War II was fought on two fronts—in Europe, and in the Pacific and East Asia. The suffering, once again, was beyond comprehension, but this time it was regular people, not just soldiers, who bore the brunt of it.

For the first time in a war, civilians were bombed. Entire cities were wiped out. Famine and epidemics were widespread. War crimes were rampant. Apart from its war effort, Germany attempted to exterminate whole racial groups and murdered millions—Jews, homosexuals, gypsies. And nuclear weapons entered the picture.

World War II ended in Europe on May 8, 1945, when Germany surrendered to the Allies. It ended in the Pacific on August 14, 1945, after the United States dropped the first atomic bomb ever on the Japanese city of Hiroshima on August 6, followed by a second bomb on Nagasaki on August 9.

Henry Reed was a soldier in World War II—he was conscripted into the British Army in 1941. "Naming of Parts," about his war experience, is the only poem Reed is known or remembered for. But it's also, as the critic Ian Hamilton observed, "*the* poem of the Second World War," perfectly capturing "the strange mix of tedium and fear" for soldiers during those six long, horrific years.

SOME FEATURES TO NOTICE:

- How there are two distinct voices speaking in each stanza but the last: first we get three and a half lines from a military instructor, who barks piecemeal lessons about the parts of a rifle; then, after a *caesura* (or natural pause) in the fourth line, the voice of a recruit takes over
- How the instructor's dialogue is coarse, unimaginative, repetitious, boring, and absurd
- How the recruit, distracted by a nearby garden, thinks in language that's alive, sensuous, and flowing
- How each stanza ends with the recruit picking up one phrase—one *part*—of the lesson, as an ironic comment that links the two voices
- How the word *spring* has a double meaning: a part of a lethal weapon and the renewing season of life
- How Reed contrasts life in the garden—like Eden, a place of peace, beauty, abundance, and innocence—with the sterility and brutality of life in the military, where a man's purpose is to *ease* the spring on an instrument used to destroy life
- How Reed contrasts the recruit's thoughts about spring, pollination, and the renewal of life with what human existence becomes during a time of war: a lesson in how to destroy

RESPONSE STANCE: Please go back into "Naming of Parts" on your own and listen for its voices: there are two. See if you can tell where one voice stops and the other begins. Then, make your best guesses about *who* each of the speakers might be.

BENEDICTION: Unlike Wilfred Owen's "Dulce et Decorum Est," Henry Reed isn't protesting the politics of a particular war. Instead, he reveals how modern warfare turns men into sterile, technically-trained brutes, skilled in the arts of death.

Let's end by reading "Naming of Parts" aloud together, as a poem for two voices—half of you as the instructor, and the other half as the recruit.

Naming of Parts

Today we have naming of parts. Yesterday,
We had daily cleaning. And tomorrow morning,
We shall have what to do after firing. But today,
Today we have naming of parts. Japonica
Glistens like coral in all of the neighbouring gardens,
     And today we have naming of parts.

This is the lower sling swivel. And this
Is the upper sling swivel, whose use you will see,
When you are given your slings. And this is the piling swivel,
Which in your case you have not got. The branches
Hold in the gardens their silent, eloquent gestures,
     Which in our case we have not got.

This is the safety-catch, which is always released
With an easy flick of the thumb. And please do not let me
See anyone using his finger. You can do it quite easy
If you have any strength in your thumb. The blossoms
Are fragile and motionless, never letting anyone see
     Any of them using their finger.

And this you can see is the bolt. The purpose of this
Is to open the breech, as you see. We can slide it
Rapidly backwards and forwards: we call this
Easing the spring. And rapidly backwards and forwards
The early bees are assaulting and fumbling the flowers:
     They call it easing the Spring.

They call it easing the Spring: it is perfectly easy
If you have any strength in your thumb: like the bolt,
And the breech, and the cocking-piece, and the point of balance,
Which in our case we have not got; and the almond-blossom
Silent in all of the gardens and the bees going backwards and forwards,
     For today we have naming of parts.

—Henry Reed

Spring has a double meaning:
a part of a lethal weapon
and the renewing season of life.

PRESENTING THE POEM:

A Bummer

BY MICHAEL CASEY

SETTING THE SCENE: America's involvement in Vietnam lasted from 1960 to 1973, but the war there raged from 1954 to 1975. It started as a civil war, like our own, between North and South. But soon North Vietnam was receiving weapons from two Communist powers, China and the former Soviet Union, and the U.S. was training, then supporting, then arming, then fighting alongside, the South Vietnamese. At the height of the war, in 1969, there were more than half a million U.S. soldiers in Vietnam. In spite of massive U.S. military aid, horrific numbers of civilian casualties, and unprecedented bombing (the U.S. dropped on tiny Vietnam three times the explosives used in all the theaters of World War II, including the atomic bombs at Hiroshima and Nagasaki), the U.S. and South Vietnam couldn't defeat the North Vietnamese and Viet Cong forces.

Meanwhile, at home, for the first time ever, Americans viewed war on their television screens. Vietnam became "the living room war." The high U.S. casualties, our attacks on civilians, the revelations of war crimes against civilians by U.S. soldiers, the effects of the military draft, the length of the conflict, and the lack of any clear or compelling reasons for U.S. involvement in Vietnam in the first place, all helped to turn many Americans against the war. An anti-war movement, with huge public demonstrations, began. The division in the U.S., over support for the war, was the most severe since our own civil war.

In the end, a peace agreement was reached in Paris in 1973, calling for the withdrawal of U.S. troops and the end of hostilities. But the fighting continued between North and South after we left. When North Vietnamese troops marched into and occupied Saigon, the capital of South Vietnam, Vietnam was formally reunified as one country in July, 1976, under Communist rule.

By then, more than 58,000 U.S. soldiers were dead. So were approximately 400,000 South Vietnamese and 900,000 North Vietnamese. It was America's worst foreign policy defeat ever, and the longest war in U.S. history.

The answer to the question, "Why did the U.S. fight in Vietnam?" is still controversial. A central concern in the era after World War II was the "containment" of Communism. Some American political leaders believed that if North Vietnam won the civil war and Vietnam became a communist state, then other countries in Southeast Asia—Cambodia, Thailand, Laos—would also fall, like a row of dominoes, under the control of China and the U.S.S.R. This never happened.

What did happen was that Americans learned that they can—that they must—challenge their government's authority and the words and decisions of their leaders when they believe that politicians are wrong or not telling the truth.

Many songwriters and poets raised their voices alongside those who demonstrated against the war. Michael Casey served in Vietnam at the height of the war as a gate guard at the Chu Lai air base. His job brought him into contact with Vietnamese civilians; he made friends, and he studied their language. And he wrote poems that tell stories, in the voices of soldiers and officers, that reveal what the U.S. did in Vietnam. In 1972, Michael Casey's book of war poetry, *Obscenities*, won the Yale Younger Poet Award. His best known poem is "A Bummer."

SOME FEATURES TO NOTICE:

- How the simple, monosyllabic diction, the lack of punctuation, and the short lines create a convincing, inarticulate soldier's voice
- How although the speaker is a G.I., the reader identifies with the Vietnamese farmer
- The aggressive, crude, American-culture names given to the tracked vehicles
- The contrast between a farmer's rake and the power of seven tracked military vehicles: the senseless overkill
- The concluding stanza, which almost sounds like a play on an old joke

RESPONSE STANCE: Please go back into "A Bummer" on your own. What do you notice about the form and the language? Why do you think Casey wrote the poem this way?

BENEDICTION: Michael Casey made poetry that's a kind of anti-poetry. His book *Obscenities* is filled with exactly what the title suggests. His soldier's voice was an important one to join the chorus against the war in Vietnam because it spoke the crude, awful truth of what the war was like.

A Bummer

We were going single file
Through his rice paddies
And the farmer
Started hitting the lead track
With a rake
He wouldn't stop
The TC went to talk to him
And the farmer
Tried to hit him too
So the tracks went sideways
Side by side
Through the guy's fields
Instead of single file
Hard One, Proud Mary
Bummer, Wallace, Rosemary's Baby
The Rutgers Road Runner
And
Go Get Em—Done Got Em
Went side by side
Through the fields
    If you have a farm in Vietnam
And a house in hell
Sell the farm
And go home

   —*Michael Casey*

track: tracked vehicle
TC: track commander

And poets raised their voices, alongside those who demonstrated against the war

PRESENTING THE POEM:

What Were They Like?

BY DENISE LEVERTOV

SETTING THE STAGE: The best known—and the most effective, I think—poem about the U.S. involvement in Vietnam is by a woman, Denise Levertov. Often, and beautifully, Levertov's poems address contemporary political and social issues. "What Were They Like?" is potent, mysterious, and unforgettable.

SOME FEATURES TO NOTICE:

- How the poem is structured as a Q and A: a dialogue in which two Western voices discuss the Vietnamese as archaeologists might, as a vanished race
- How Levertov focuses on the effects of the war on ordinary Vietnamese people—peasants, farmers, families
- How the language is both conversational and poetic
- The contrast: how the device of a Q and A mimics the distance that ordinary Americans experienced from the lives of ordinary Vietnamese, yet how the imagery and language bring the people of Vietnam and their culture to life

RESPONSE STANCE: Please go back into "What Were They Like?" on your own. Of the questions and answers, which, to you, are the most powerful and telling?

BENEDICTION: We're seeing that there are many approaches to poems that question wars. Each poet is trying to find the most effective way to bypass people's intellects and to reach their hearts—not to tell us that a war is wrong, but to show us what the war is doing to the people caught up in it. As Donald Murray put it, "Poets remind us not to preach, but merely to reveal."

What Were They Like?

1) Did the people of Viet Nam
   use lanterns of stone?
2) Did they hold ceremonies
   to reverence the opening of buds?
3) Were they inclined to quiet laughter?
4) Did they use bone and ivory,
   jade and silver, for ornament?
5) Had they an epic poem?
6) Did they distinguish between speech and singing?

1) Sir, their light hearts turned to stone.
   It is not remembered whether in gardens
   stone lanterns illumined pleasant ways.
2) Perhaps they gathered once to delight in blossom,
   but after the children were killed
   there were no more buds.
3) Sir, laughter is bitter to the burned mouth.
4) A dream ago, perhaps. Ornament is for joy.
   All the bones were charred.
5) It is not remembered. Remember,
   most were peasants; their life
   was in rice and bamboo.
   When peaceful clouds were reflected in the paddies
   and the water buffalo stepped surely along terraces,
   maybe fathers told their sons old tales.
   When bombs smashed those mirrors
   there was time only to scream.
6) There is an echo yet
   of their speech which was like a song.
   It was reported that their singing resembled
   the flight of moths in moonlight.
   Who can say? It is silent now.

   —Denise Levertov

PRESENTING THE POEM:

Stained

BY MARLEY WITHAM

SETTING THE STAGE: As a seventh grader during the late winter of 2003, Marley was distraught that her country, the United States, was about to invade another country, Iraq. She asked her parents and her older sister *why*, but they had no answers either. Our president said the leader of Iraq, Saddam Hussein, was developing nuclear weapons; that he wanted to attack our country with these and other weapons of mass destruction; that he was working in cooperation with the terrorists who had attacked us on 9/11; that the citizens of Iraq would welcome an invading army with flowers and open arms.

But in Marley's view, the evidence for each of these claims was shaky. It seemed to her that the U.S. was about to drop bombs on families halfway around the world for no good reason. She was upset and angry. She was also a poet.

SOME FEATURES TO NOTICE:
- The strong visual imagery
- Until the penultimate stanza, the mystery of the identity of the *you*
- How the title functions as a metaphor for the stain on Marley's conscience, as a citizen of one country about to invade another; how, after her act of protest, her hands feel *lifeless but no longer stained*

- The contrast between the mood created by the last stanza, when Marley reveals what she and her sister are doing, vs. the natural imagery of the rest of the poem
- The sense of power Marley derived from this small act of protest

RESPONSE STANCE: Please go back into Marley's poem and mark what feel to you like its most important lines.

BENEDICTION: Can people your age feel strongly about political issues, about government policies? Yes, absolutely, stronger than some adults give you credit for. You don't have to be a policy wonk who reads the *New York Times* front to back every day to have a sense of what's right and wrong, to raise your voice, to have a *say*.

Stained

To be with one another—
but also to escape the depression
that leaks into our house from the news on the radio—
we skip down the path,
enjoying the way sunlight
glazes the trees in mock-summer light.
I haven't been down this way for months.
I welcome the familiar roots and rocks under my feet.
We turn the bend
and spy the sparkling water.
I don't know how many times it will take before
I see this sight and do not gasp.
The way the light reflects into the pond,
the distorted trees, the green depths—
they enchant me always.

You step onto well-worn rocks.
I breathe in clear air and lower myself.
Green moss rolls over the ground
and creates emerald silk.
I spot the fallen tree leaning, its base upright,
and charcoal from fires of the past.
You grab a piece of the black wood
and draw a line in the granite.
I join you.

Your eyes skim the landscape.
Then, fixing them, you smile when you
find the stretching bald rock.
Reading your mind I scamper
to where your gaze leads.
We each pick our utensil.
The charcoal is cold and damp.
We smudge it on the rock.
As we begin to form the P,
we laugh and talk.
Today the pond is ours.

We finish,
stand back, and grin.
I poke my finger into the water,
testing for non-existent warmth,
then plunge my hand into the iciness
and wipe it clean on the moss.
My fingers are lifeless but no longer stained.

You fantasize about someone seeing our work—
someone high above being touched by the letters,
someone powerful enough to make change,
to end the madness.
I laugh, grab your hand, my sister, and look back.

PEACE.

　　—*Marley Witham*

*She was
upset and angry.
She was also a poet.*

MAYA
ANGELOU

PRESENTING THE POEM:

It Is Dangerous to Read Newspapers

BY MARGARET ATWOOD

SETTING THE STAGE: There's one more anti-war poem I think we should read together. I know this is a depressing topic, but we need to give Margaret Atwood the final word. I'm not a general, and you're not soldiers; on the face of it, none of us should feel guilty about the atrocities of wars we're not fighting, right? But, at some level, does our *knowledge* make us complicit?

SOME FEATURES TO NOTICE:

- How Atwood, born in 1939, was a child during World War II; the first two stanzas refer to the Holocaust and the nuclear attacks on Hiroshima and Nagasaki, when she was too young to know what was going on
- How the innocent child of the opening stanzas plays and is oblivious to war, to evil, in contrast with the newspaper-reading adult, who has lost her innocence
- How the danger of newspapers—of literacy— is the exposure to the evils of war and the sense of responsibility and feeling of helplessness that come with knowledge
- The metaphors and similes: how her educated, literate self and knowledge become weapons

RESPONSE STANCE: This is a difficult but worthwhile poem. Please go back inside it independently. *Circle* the lines and stanzas you understand, and *underline* those that confuse you. Then we'll try to unpack it together.

BENEDICTION: We're taught that knowledge is power. But in this poem knowledge is a horrific burden—the understanding that we are a self-destructive species and there seems to be nothing we can do about it. Is this true? To use Marley's metaphor, are we stained? Or do you disagree? Is there a poem in you that responds to Atwood?

It Is Dangerous to Read Newspapers

While I was building neat
castles in the sandbox,
the hasty pits were
filling with bulldozed corpses

and as I walked to school
washed and combed, my feet
stepping on the cracks in the cement
detonated red bombs.

Now I am grownup
and literate, and I sit in my chair
as quietly as a fuse

and the jungles are flaming, the under-
brush is charged with soldiers,
the names on the difficult
maps go up in smoke.

I am the cause, I am a stockpile of chemical
toys, my body
is a deadly gadget,
I reach out in love, my hands are guns,
my good intentions are completely lethal.

Even my
passive eyes transmute
everything I look at to the pocked
black and white of a war photo,
how
can I stop myself.

It is dangerous to read newspapers.

Each time I hit a key
on my electric typewriter,
speaking of peaceful trees,

another village explodes.

   —Margaret Atwood

A Prayer for the Twenty-First Century

BY JOHN MARSDEN

SETTING THE STAGE: John Marsden is a young-adult novelist. Some of you are familiar with him as the author of the amazing series that begins with *Tomorrow When the War Began*. It's dystopian sci-fi, set in Australia. While a group of teenaged friends is off camping in the outback, their country is invaded. They return to civilization to discover that almost everyone they know and love has vanished. So they transform themselves into guerilla fighters who take on the invaders, and the main character/leader is a smart, powerful girl. Talk about action-packed and thought-provoking.

Here's another side of John Marsden: the poet. And, after the despairing stances of our last handful of poets, here's an opportunity for uplift and inspiration.

SOME FEATURES TO NOTICE:
- How, thematically, the poem covers all the bases of the conditions for a fair, safe, balanced, healthy, and equitable world
- How this isn't the typical prayer of salvation and protection—for oneself—but for all the people, creatures, and natural environments of our planet
- How Marsden uses both rhyme and repetition to create rhythm and cadence

RESPONSE STANCE: Please go back into this remarkable prayer and mark your favorite lines—the ones that mean the most, personally, to you.

BENEDICTION: So many of the traditional prayers of organized religions sound and flow as poetry, it seems like the most natural thing in the world to write a poem that's a prayer. What would you pray for, in a poem about your vision for the world?

A Prayer for the
Twenty-First Century

May the road be free for the journey,
May it lead where it promised it would,
May the stars that gave ancient bearings
Be seen, still be understood.
May every aircraft fly safely,
May every traveler be found,
May sailors in crossing the ocean
Not hear the cries of the drowned.

May gardens be wild, like jungles,
May nature never be tamed,
May dangers create of us heroes,
May fears always have names.
May the mountains stand to remind us
Of what it means to be young,
May we be outlived by our daughters,
May we be outlived by our sons.

May the bombs rust away in the bunkers,
And the doomsday clock not be rewound,
May the solitary scientist, working,
Remember the holes in the ground.
May the knife remain in the holder,
May the bullet stay in the gun,
May those who live in the shadows
Be seen by those in the sun.

    —*John Marsden*

I Care and I'm Willing to Serve

BY MARIAN WRIGHT EDELEMAN

SETTING THE STAGE: Marian Wright Edelman is the founder and chief executive officer of the Children's Defense Fund, an organization dedicated to feeding, educating, and protecting all of America's children. My favorite quote of hers is "Service is the rent you pay for living;" in other words, all of us alive and surviving on the planet have an obligation to help one another.

In today's poem, another prayer, we hear Edelman despair that she doesn't have the talents of some of the great individuals who have changed our world for the better, BUT she *cares* and she's *willing to serve*. And that's a *but* that all by itself changes the world for the better.

SOME FEATURES TO NOTICE:

- How, line by line, Edelman *names* the great fighters for peace, freedom, justice, and equality of modern times: writers, activists, politicians, feminists, civil rights leaders, humanitarians, labor leaders, religious leaders
- How the repetition of *But I care, and I'm willing to serve* builds cadence and emphasizes the power and potential of one compassionate, willing individual
- How the final stanza is the original—and meaningful—context for the phrase *no child left behind*

RESPONSE STANCE: Please go back into this poem on your own and do two things: circle the names of Edelman's heroes whom you'd like to know more about, then write a line or two about why you think she wrote this poem.

BENEDICTION: I'm not well-known or influential like Marian Wright Edelman, but I care, and I'm willing to serve. It's why I'm here today. I can help you learn to read and write. I can feed you literature that may help you become both tough-minded and compassionate. I can invite you to write so that you might have power and a voice. And I can be inspired every day by your passion and brilliance.

I know you already care. I can't wait to see how you decide to serve.

I Care and I'm Willing to Serve

These are our talents.

Even though we can't preach like Dr. Martin Luther King, or turn a poetic phrase
like Pablo Neruda or Maya Angelou,

I care and I'm willing to serve.

I don't have Fred Shuttlesworth's courage, or Harriet Tubman's spirit, or Andy
Young's political skills,

But I care, and I'm willing to serve.

I can't sing like Fannie Lou Hamer as much as I wish, or organize like Ella Baker
and Bayard Rustin,

But I care, and I'm willing to serve.

I'm not holy like Archbishop Tutu, or forgiving like Nelson Mandela, or
disciplined like Gandhi,

But I care, and I'm willing to serve and do whatever I have to do to end hunger
and protect children.

I'm not brilliant like Elizabeth Cady Stanton, or eloquent like Sojourner Truth or
Booker T. Washington,

But I care, and I'm willing to serve in the struggle until justice reigns.

I have not Mother Theresa's saintliness, or Dorothy Day's love, or Cesar Chavez's
gentle tough spirit,

But I care, and I'm willing to serve.

God, it's not as easy as the Sixties to frame an issue and forge a solution,

But I care, and I'm willing to serve and try new things to build a movement.

My mind and my body are not as swift as in youth and my energy comes in spurts,

But I care, and I'm willing to serve.

I'm so young, nobody will listen, I'm not so sure what to say or to do,

But I care, and I'm willing to serve.

I can't see or hear well, speak good English, stutter sometimes, and get real scared
if I have to stand up before others,

But I care, and I'm willing to serve.

Use me as thou will, today and tomorrow, to build a nation and a world where
no child is left behind and every child is fed and loved and protected and safe.

—*Marian Wright Edelman*

The Negro Speaks of Rivers
&
American Heartbreak

BY LANGSTON HUGHES

SETTING THE STAGE: James Langston Hughes was born in Joplin, Missouri, in 1902. He worked as a truck farmer, a waiter, a mess boy on a ship, and, finally, as a writer. When he died in 1967 in New York City, he was celebrated as the poet laureate of Harlem—the most versatile, prolific writer of the movement known as the Harlem Renaissance, a period when African-American writers, singers, artists, actors, and dancers emerged as a vital part of American culture: Black life from the perspective of Black artists.

Langston Hughes wrote poems, novels, short stories, and plays about the experience of African-American life. His poems combined Black bitterness and energy—in blues and jazz rhythms, he depicted the working lives, hopes, heartaches, humor, stories, struggles, and dreams of his people. Before there was a Civil Rights movement in America, there was the voice of Langston Hughes. And when the Civil Rights movement needed voices to inspire true democracy in America, there were the poems and essays of Langston Hughes. He was a political poet.

Julian Bond, today chairman of the Board of Directors of the NAACP, once said, "I first met Langston Hughes when he visited my college on one of his many speaking tours. He was like his poetry: sly, humorous, deeply connected to his roots and race, kind and thoughtful, a fierce enemy of injustice, and a keen observer of his time, place, and fellow human beings. He—and his poetry—are very much alive today."

And very much aware of yesterday, of the whole history of African Americans. Let's look at two of Hughes's best known poems.

SOME FEATURES TO NOTICE—"THE NEGRO SPEAKS OF RIVERS":
- The references to times and places throughout history where Blacks lived, prospered, and achieved—how Hughes lays claim to and celebrates their identity, cultural heritage, and accomplishments
- The use of repetition to create a cadence
- The sensory diction

SOME FEATURES TO NOTICE—"AMERICAN HEARTBREAK":
- The economy of the language: not one extra word
- The metaphors and the personification
- The historical reference to—and addendum to textbook entries about—Jamestown: the much celebrated first colony that began the great democratic experiment of America was also the place where the importation and exploitation of African slaves began, in 1619

RESPONSE STANCE: Please go back into these two poems by Langston Hughes and mark the lines you want to talk about or ask about.

BENEDICTION: The poetry of Langston Hughes also comments on the current events of his time—on what was happening to twentieth-century African Americans in the Jim Crow South and the urban ghettoes of the North. Tomorrow we'll read another of his poems and hear another of his voices as a poet.

The Negro Speaks of Rivers

I've known rivers:
I've known rivers ancient as the world and older than the
    flow of human blood in human veins.

My soul has grown deep like the rivers.

I bathed in the Euphrates when dawns were young.
I built my hut near the Congo and it lulled me to sleep.
I looked upon the Nile and raised the pyramids above it.
I heard the singing of the Mississippi when Abe Lincoln
    went down to New Orleans, and I've seen its muddy
    bosom turn all golden in the sunset.

I've known rivers:
Ancient, dusky rivers.

My soul has grown deep like the rivers.

    —Langston Hughes

American Heartbreak

I am the American heartbreak—
Rock on which Freedom
Stumps its toe—
The great mistake
That Jamestown
Made long ago.

    —Langston Hughes

PRESENTING THE POEM:

The Bitter River

BY LANGSTON HUGHES

SETTING THE STAGE: The Langston Hughes that children encounter in textbooks and anthologies isn't the whole man or poet. Kids seldom see the funny poems, the sassy, sexy ones, the brilliant translations of other poets, or the angry poems about race and class oppression. "The Bitter River" is a bitter poem—also a blues lament, a polemic, and a weary cry from the heart.

It begins with a dedication . . .

Charlie Lang and Ernest Green, two black boys just about your age, were playmates with a thirteen-year-old white girl. One day a white man drove past just as the two boys were chasing the girl out from under a bridge. The boys were arrested, charged with attempted rape, and jailed. A white mob came to the jail, took the boys to the bridge, and lynched them.

Lynching means hanging, or otherwise murdering, a person through the actions of a mob. In the Jim Crow South, between 1882 and 1968, at least 3,500 Black men and women were lynched by white mobs. This was a terror tactic to intimidate Blacks—to keep them from voting and seeking other civil and social rights. Blacks were lynched for being vocal or for other "offenses." Local governments in the South did nothing to stop the lynchings; that took the Civil Rights movement of the 1960's.

Notice in this poem how Langston Hughes, through his metaphors, transforms racism, the class struggle, and the terror of lynching into a poisonous, *bitter river/ Flowing through the South.*

SOME FEATURES TO NOTICE:

- How Hughes extends the *bitter river* metaphor: its *gall* and *the blood of the lynched boys* poison him; it drowns the hopes of Blacks and strangles their dreams; it doesn't reflect the sky, but *only the glint of steel bars* that confine innocent people, condemned because of their skin color (*dark bitter faces*); discriminatory judicial practices (*the Scottsboro boys*); their poverty (*the voteless share-cropper*); their activism (*the labor leader*); their power, which is perceived as a threat (*the soldier*); their petty crimes of hunger (*the 15-cent mugger*); their history and heritage as slaves (*my grandfather's back with its ladder of scars*)
- How, in the fourth stanza, Hughes castigates as useless the advice of those who urge patience, and the voices of capitalism as those of liars
- How the overall tone is one of impatience, weariness, and bitterness, yet the poem is moving and inspiring
- How "The Bitter River" is a *dirge:* a poem of lament for the deaths of the two boys

RESPONSE STANCE: Please go back into "The Bitter River" and mark the lines that strike you, that move you, that you want to talk about.

BENEDICTION: Langston Hughes was a complex writer and one of America's greatest. It's important to know that in addition to the lovely poems of childhood, like "Dreams" and "April Rain Song," he was on fire as a poet against injustices that sprang from race and class. He also loved and observed the bawdy side of life and the eclectic characters who peopled Harlem, wrote gospel songs, told jokes, and used the vernacular like a jazz musician—gave Black working class people a literature of their own. Please check out *The Collected Works of Langston Hughes* and meet more sides of this amazing poet.

The Bitter River

(Dedicated to the memory of Charlie Lang and Ernest Green, each fourteen years old when lynched together beneath the Shubuta Bridge over the Chickasawhay River in Mississippi, October 12th, 1942.)

There is a bitter river
Flowing through the South.
Too long has the taste of its water
Been in my mouth.
There is a bitter river
Dark with filth and mud.
Too long has its evil poison
Poisoned my blood.

I've drunk of the bitter river
And its gall coats the red of my tongue,
Mixed with the blood of the lynched boys
From its iron bridge hung,
Mixed with the hopes that are drowned there
In the snake-like hiss of its stream
Where I drank of the bitter river
That strangled my dream:
The book studied—but useless,
Tool handled—but unused,
Knowledge acquired but thrown away,
Ambition battered and bruised.
Oh, water of the bitter river
With your taste of blood and clay,
You reflect no stars by night,
No sun by day.

The bitter river reflects no stars—
It gives back only the glint of steel bars
And dark bitter faces behind steel bars:
The Scottsboro boys behind steel bars,
Lewis Jones behind steel bars,
The voteless share-cropper behind steel bars,
The labor leader behind steel bars,
The soldier thrown from a Jim Crow bus behind steel bars,
The 15¢ mugger behind steel bars,
The girl who sells her body behind steel bars,
And my grandfather's back with its ladder of scars,
Long ago, long ago—the whip and steel bars—
The bitter river reflects no stars.

"Wait, be patient," you say.
"Your folks will have a better day."
But the swirl of the bitter river
Takes your words away.
"Work, education, patience
Will bring a better day."
The swirl of the bitter river
Carries your "patience" away.
"Disrupter! Agitator!
Trouble maker!" you say.
The swirl of the bitter river
Sweeps your lies away.
I did not ask for this river
Nor the taste of its bitter brew.
I was given its water
As a gift from you.
Yours has been the power
To force my back to the wall
And make me drink of the bitter cup
Mixed with blood and gall.

You have lynched my comrades
Where the iron bridge crosses the stream,
Underpaid me for my labor,
And spit in the face of my dream.
You forced me to the bitter river
With the hiss of its snake-like song—
Now your words no longer have meaning—
I have drunk at the river too long:
Dreamer of dreams to be broken,
Builder of hopes to be smashed,
Loser from an empty pocket
Of my meagre cash,
Bitter bearer of burdens
And singer of weary song,
I've drunk at the bitter river
With its filth and its mud too long.
Tired now of the bitter river,
Tired now of the pat on the back,
Tired now of the steel bars
Because my face is black,
I'm tired of segregation,
Tired of filth and mud,
I've drunk of the bitter river
And it's turned to steel in my blood.

Oh, tragic bitter river
Where the lynched boys hung,
The gall of your bitter water
Coats my tongue.
The blood of your bitter water
For me gives back no stars.
I'm tired of the bitter river!
Tired of the bars!

—*Langston Hughes*

The Langston Hughes that children encounter in textbooks isn't the whole man or poet.

PRESENTING THE POEM:

Langston's Time

BY HENRY WORKMAN

SETTING THE STAGE: Henry, an eighth grader, *got* Langston Hughes. As a white kid living in the second whitest state in the nation, he loved the passion, the politics, and the poetics of the poet laureate of Harlem.

SOME FEATURES TO NOTICE:
- The straightforward voice and diction
- The allusions to elements from Hughes's poems
- The heartfelt conclusion

RESPONSE STANCE: Please go back into Henry's paean to Langston Hughes and mark the lines you can identify with—that mirror your feelings about Hughes's poems and themes.

BENEDICTION: Empathy isn't a response I can teach you. The ability to put yourself in someone else's shoes and imagine his or her life comes with time, desire, and experience. Here, Henry's experience, as a boy from Maine, was vicarious instead of firsthand; reading Langston Hughes allowed him to enter another time and place, to experience skin of a different color, and to dream.

Langston's Time

I wasn't alive when Langston Hughes wrote poetry,
so I don't know what America was like then.
I've never known a world
without computers, cellphones,
and other so-called necessities—
without civil rights—
so I couldn't know
what it was like in Langston's time.

Yet somehow, when I read his poems,
I can picture exactly how it must have been.
I can hear a time when the blues was popular
because it was a way of both celebrating
good times and despairing.
I can feel a time when memories of slavery
still haunted African-Americans.
Young black boys were drowned and lynched,
and Hughes was there to speak against it.

Hughes wrote about everything
from the joys
of a Saturday night
to the deep anger
he felt toward America.
I wasn't alive when Langston Hughes wrote poetry,
but he taught me about the way things were
and the way they ought to be.

> —*Henry Workman*

©2006 by Nancie Atwell from *Naming the World: A Year of Poems and Lessons*
(Portsmouth, NH: Heinemann)

PRESENTING THE POEM:

The low road

BY MARGE PIERCY

SETTING THE STAGE: There's no other way to say it: Marge Piercy is an inspiration. Her poems inspire me to act—to work, write, think, care, and fight, and to join hands with others who want to do good. "The low road" is a poem I taped to the wall above my desk. It reminds me to have hope, to keep working for change—and to laugh.

SOME FEATURES TO NOTICE:

- One meaning of the expression *high road* is an easy or certain course; Piercy coins the phrase *low road* to describe a difficult, uncharted journey
- How the tone of the first stanza is one of despair and terror
- How the feeling begins to change in the second stanza, from one of powerlessness to one of strength, with the addition of a comrade
- How the poem and its attitude open up in the third stanza—it includes humor and becomes more rhythmic, as others join the cause and create a movement
- How the final stanza states the poem's theme
- The way repetition creates a cadence and moves the poem

RESPONSE STANCE: Please go back into this strong poem on your own and mark the lines that strike or inspire you.

BENEDICTION: I'd call this poem a rallying cry. Piercy doesn't sugarcoat how hard it is to speak up and try to change the world, but she shows how it's possible: if you can act, even when others say not to, and if you can reach out to others to join you, there's the beginning.

What are the injustices you notice in the world? In our country and state? In your community? In our school? On the playground? In this classroom? What acts of intolerance, inequality, cruelty, racial or ethnic prejudice, gender stereotyping, homophobia, exploitation, or pollution of our environment need your voice and efforts to call attention to them, to correct them? Not just on a national or global scale but right here and right now? *It starts when you care to act.* Writing—your poems, your letters to editors and decision-makers—is one way to *act*.

The low road

What can they do
to you? Whatever they want.
They can set you up, they can
bust you, they can break
your fingers, they can
burn your brain with electricity,
blur you with drugs till you
can't walk, can't remember, they can
take your child, wall up
your lover. They can do anything
you can't stop them
from doing. How can you stop
them? Alone you can fight,
you can refuse, you can
take what revenge you can
but they roll over you.

But two people fighting
back to back can cut through
a mob, a snake-dancing file
can break a cordon, an army
can meet an army.

Two people can keep each other
sane, can give support, conviction,
love, massage, hope, sex.
Three people are a delegation,
a committee, a wedge. With four
you can play bridge and start
an organization. With six
you can rent a whole house,
eat pie for dinner with no
seconds, and hold a fund raising party.
A dozen can make a demonstration.
A hundred fill a hall.
A thousand have solidarity and your own newsletter;
ten thousand, power and your own paper;
a hundred thousand, your own media;
ten million, your own country.

It goes on one at a time,
it starts when you care
to act, it starts when you do
it again after they said no,
it starts when you say *We*
and you know who you mean, and each
day you mean one more.

  —Marge Piercy

These are r
poems of all.
that poets de
they create u
acts of litera
the core. Th

Reading & Writing:

INTRODUCTION

These are my favorite poems of all. The insights that poets develop and images they create when contemplating acts of literacy thrill me to the core. They express, in a handful of lines, what I couldn't in several books' worth of prose about what writing and reading do for my life.

Almost nothing has made me happier than reading. Almost nothing has changed and enriched my life more than writing. Almost nothing has made me feel as human, as alive, as unsettled, as hopeful, as powerful. These are feelings I want my kids to know. This collection of poems invites students to imagine reading and writing through the minds and hearts of poets who are on fire with words.

PRESENTING THE POEM:

Reading Myself to Sleep

BY BILLY COLLINS

SETTING THE STAGE: How many of you read yourself to sleep on a regular basis . . . ? Is there a better—more effective but also more *satisfying*—sleeping pill? I love to read until my eyelids get heavy, then slip out of consciousness through the tunnel of a great character or story. Billy Collins has written the best description ever of the sensation of reading into sleep.

SOME FEATURES TO NOTICE:

- The vivid and sensory imagery
- The many metaphors and similes that summon up the sensations of solitary, late-night reading
- How the central metaphor—of drifting to sleep as slipping underwater—leads to the humorous conclusion: in the morning, the cast-off book is *wet and streaked with daylight*
- How Collins invented a form: three-line stanzas

RESPONSE STANCE: Please go back into this perfect poem and mark all the lines you can see and feel. Then we'll talk about *why*—about what Billy Collins did to give us these sensations.

BENEDICTION: The next group of poems explores two of the best experiences available to the human race: reading and writing. I know it shouldn't be surprising that people who work with words for a living might write about it— for example, that poets will write poems about poems. But as I began to come across poems about writing and reading, they knocked me out because the poets were describing *my* feelings and experiences as a writer and reader. I identified with these poems more strongly than any others. I hope they'll resonate for you, too.

Reading Myself to Sleep

The house is all in darkness except for this corner bedroom
where the lighthouse of a table lamp is guiding
my eyes through the narrow channels of print,

and the only movement in the night is the slight
swirl of curtains, the easy lift and fall of my breathing,
and the flap of pages as they turn in the wind of my hand.

Is there a more gentle way to go into the night
than to follow an endless rope of sentences
and then to slip drowsily under the surface of a page

into the first tentative flicker of a dream,
passing out of the bright precincts of attention
like cigarette smoke passing through a window screen?

All late readers know this sinking feeling of falling
into the liquid of sleep and then rising again
to the call of a voice that you are holding in your hands,

as if pulled from the sea back into a boat
where a discussion is raging on some subject or other,
on Patagonia or Thoroughbreds or the nature of war.

Is there a better method of departure by night
than this quiet bon voyage with an open book,
the sole companion who has come to see you off,

to wave you into the dark waters beyond language?
I can hear the rush and sweep of fallen leaves outside
where the world lies unconscious, and I can feel myself

dissolving, drifting into a story that will never be written,
letting the book slip to the floor where I will find it
in the morning when I surface, wet and streaked with daylight.

—*Billy Collins*

PRESENTING THE POEM:

Chapter One

BY MARK AIELLO

SETTING THE STAGE: Here's a poem that illustrates what I spoke of yesterday. Mark Aiello takes on an unusual poetic topic: the experience of reading the first chapter of a novel. I think he nails it—what an author of fiction does to invite us inside the setting, characters, and plot.

SOME FEATURES TO NOTICE:
- The personification: *passages / that lead us . . .*
- The imagery and its accuracy: author as the *kind host*; a character as *the lady of the house*, etc.
- The humor and truth of the last stanza

RESPONSE STANCE: Please go back into "Chapter One" and mark the lines you *get*, as a reader of novels.

BENEDICTION: Here's today's invitation to you as poets: can you write about your experience as a novel reader? Consider such approaches as your relationship with main characters; your response to endings—a sad ending, a satisfying one, or one that's unsatisfying; your predictions about plot; the range of emotions you experience during a great read; or what hapens with a novel you decide to abandon.

Chapter One

I love how books begin; those passages
that lead us by the hand across
the luxurious lawns, that portage us
gently up the gravel drive,
toward the manor house.

The author is still a kind host here,
anxious that we mingle
with the other weekend guests, that we note
how even the banisters are polished for us,
that we feel free to walk out
with the lady of the house and smoke
a cigarette, down the grand alley of elms.

We're not expected to have things down pat
yet, like the family tree, or the route to the old Abbey.
Nothing really happens now,
beyond the delivery of breakfast trays.
It's not scheduled to rain
for two more chapters, and no one
who matters to us has died yet.

  —Mark Aiello

"Chapter One," © September 2002. by Mark Aiello and The Poetry Foundation

PRESENTING THE POEMS:

The Mechanic

BY DAVID FISHER

&

Kidnap Poem

BY NIKKI GIOVANNI

SETTING THE STAGE: In today's poems, the poets fantasize. In both their fantasies, they're still poets; it's their *power* as poets that's the subject of their make believe. Prepare for two great what-ifs.

**SOME FEATURES TO NOTICE—
"THE MECHANIC":**
- The visual imagery of the first three stanzas
- The humor
- The dialogue about a poem that parallels and parodies a discussion about an automobile under repair
- The strong conclusion, with its emphasis on the word *works* and its theme that poetry, too, is functional, is *useful*

SOME FEATURES TO NOTICE—"KIDNAP POEM":
- How giovanni forgoes most capitals and punctuation
- How she turns nouns into verbs (e.g., *meter you to jones beach*)
- How she transforms the vocabulary of poetry into terms of endearment
- How breaking *kid/ nap* in the final stanza slows it down
- The humor

RESPONSE STANCE: Please go back into one of these two poems, in which a poet imagines a new potential for poetry, and mark the words and lines that surprise you, as well as the ones you want to talk about.

BENEDICTION: What fantasy can you imagine fulfilling as a poet, or through one of your poems? What power or control might you assume, by virtue of the fact that you're a poet, too?

The Mechanic

As I give my last dime
to a pirate in coveralls,
as he stands smiling,
wiping his greasy, insolent hands,
a dream comes over me.

And I am dreaming of the day
when this same rich, greasy man
will come to me, clean and trembling,
bearing a Poem.

Now he explains to me
what he thinks is wrong,
and I look contemptuous,
and he begins to stammer.

And I say: "I'm sorry, but
you'll have to leave your Poem
overnight."

The next day he comes to me
and he says: "How is my Poem?"
And I say: "I can't tell a thing
'til we tear the whole thing down
and strip it," and he asks:
"How much will it cost?"
And I shrug, and I let that
settle in, and then I say:
"But it doesn't look good."

This haunted man
now telephones me daily,
and I put him off,
he is at my mercy,
he does not know
the first thing about poems.
For example, I say:

"Well I almost had it back together
when I noticed you had blown a verb,
so of course I had to strip the whole
thing down again. You don't want
to ruin the Poem with a verb that way,
do you? Call me tomorrow.

After a week or so, I give him back
his Poem.

Poor and dreaming
I stand in his filthy garage
and I am sure of it:
someday even this man will need a Poem that
works.

    —David Fisher

Kidnap Poem

ever been kidnapped
by a poet
if i were a poet
i'd kidnap you
put you in my phrases and meter
you to jones beach
or maybe coney island
or maybe just to my house
lyric you in lilacs
dash you in the rain
blend into the beach
to complement my see
play the lyre for you
ode you with my love song
anything to win you
wrap you in the red Black green
show you off to mama
yeah if i were a poet i'd kid
nap you

    —nikki giovanni

PRESENTING THE POEM:

Rescued

BY CARL JOHANSON

SETTING THE STAGE: Carl, an eighth-grade poet, knew from experience that writing a good poem is hard work. After he almost killed himself writing a good one, he wrote another good poem about what that was like.

SOME FEATURES TO NOTICE:
- The specific and visual imagery
- The humor
- The central metaphor: a poem as a vehicle that won't start, crashes, and has to be towed
- His writing teacher as AAA: the *one person* who can help Carl, as a poet, reach home

RESPONSE STANCE: Please go back into Carl's poem and mark the lines you can identify with as a poet, plus anything Carl did in this extended metaphor that you like.

BENEDICTION: The process of writing—a poem or any genre—is a rich topic for poets. What is writing a poem *like* for you? What about a short story? A report for history? What would you *compare it to*?

Rescued

Do other poets draft their poems
without turning their brains inside out?
No time wasted trying to make that line fit,
this word work?
Is there someone out there
who can snap his fingers
and BAAM
it appears out of green smoke?
While I'm left
coughing in the clouds
with page upon page of leads,
still searching
every crevice of my mind
for an idea,
one small hint
that will give my poem the fumes
to carry it over the next hill?
But, as always,

it stalls

and rolls back to where I started,
leaving me to push it back up again,
straining my creative back,
which already feels broken
by the onslaught of words.

Finally
I make it over the hill
to glimpse the paradise
of a finished poem.
But I don't watch where I'm writing
and my poem veers off the narrow road
and crashes into a tree.

So I scramble out of the mangled mess
and wait for the one person
who can tow me
and my hissing poem
home.

—*Carl Johanson*

©2006 by Nancie Atwell from *Naming the World: A Year of Poems and Lessons*
(Portsmouth, NH: Heinemann)

PRESENTING THE POEM:

Down

BY MARGARET ATWOOD

SETTING THE STAGE: Margaret Atwood does it all. She's one of the best novelists writing today in the English language; she's an essayist; she's a literary critic; and she's a poet. Atwood is also a fierce feminist and advocate for justice—brilliant in her understanding of how the world does work and passionate in her desire that the world work more fairly, especially for women. "Down" is a tough poem by a tough-minded poet. It's also one of the most extraordinary we'll read this year.

SOME FEATURES TO NOTICE — I.:

- *They* is an allusion to the ancient Greeks, who believed the sun was carried into the underworld at night by Apollo
- How the sun—which represents everyday life or an awareness of the physical world—is replaced without warning by an emerging *underworld*: the writer's imagination, which takes over her consciousness so thoroughly that the real world—*no blue, no green*—disappears to her senses

SOME FEATURES TO NOTICE — II.:

- The *old thread, old line/ of ink* is her writing: where will her writer's imagination take her this time?

SOME FEATURES TO NOTICE — III.:

- *Mute, crying* voices call to the writer's imagination; she opens her mind and lets the pain of others in

SOME FEATURES TO NOTICE — IV.:

- Now the writer's imagination enters an underworld that's peopled with her potential characters: victims of war, starvation, beatings, political atrocities, religious fanaticism, abuse, suicide. They ask her, in her writing, to speak for them, avenge them, take their place, witness their pain; women ask her to be happy for them because they are dead—their pain is ended

SOME FEATURES TO NOTICE — V.:

- The writer is conscious again of her physical world—back in her kitchen, safe but feeling guilty (*red-handed*). She wants to cleanse herself of the anguish of her imagined world by using elements from the physical world, to rid herself of the pain she has conjured up in her writing.

RESPONSE STANCE: Literally, *what is happening* in the world of this poem? Please go back into "Down" on your own and, stanza by stanza, section by section, write notes to yourself about what you think or guess Atwood is describing in each. Then we'll unpack it together.

BENEDICTION: Writers talk sometimes about the pain of writer's block or the pain of revision. But what must it feel like for a novelist to imagine the pain of her characters, to invent people who suffer and to animate their misery, then to put down the pen or shut down the computer and return to her safe, everyday life? It's a condition I never considered before this poem. It has given me new respect for good novelists: they are the ultimate empathizers. The next time a character in a novel you're reading suffers a horrible loss and you feel devastated, you might remember "Down" and wonder what it was like for the writer, in her imagination, to experience that loss.

Down

i.

They were wrong about the sun.
It does not go down into
the underworld at night.
The sun leaves merely
and the underworld emerges.
It can happen at any moment.

It can happen in the morning,
you in the kitchen going through
your mild routines.
Plate, cup, knife.
All at once there's no blue, no green,
no warning.

ii.

Old thread, old line
of ink twisting out into the clearness
we call space
where are you leading me this time?
Past the stove, past the table,
past the daily horizontal
of the floor, past the cellar,
past the believable,
down into the darkness
where you reverse and shine.

iii.

At first you think they are angels,
these albino voices, these voices
like the unpainted eyes of statues,
these mute voices like gloves
with no hands in them,
these moth voices fluttering
and baffled around your ears,
crying to make you hear them.

What do they need?

You make a cut in yourself,
a little opening
for the pain to get in.
You set loose three drops of your blood.

iv.

This is
the kingdom of the unspoken,
the kingdom of the unspeaking:

all those destroyed by war
all those who are starving
all those beaten to death
and buried in pits, those slit apart
for reasons of expediency or money
all those howling
in locked rooms, all sacrificed
children, all murdered brides,
all suicides.

They say:
Speak for us (to whom)
Some say: *Avenge us* (on whom)
Some say: *Take our place.*
Some say: *Witness.*

Others say (and these are women):
Be happy for us.

v.

There is a staircase,
there is the sun.
There is the kitchen,
the plate with toast and strawberry jam,
your subterfuge,
your ordinary mirage.

You stand red-handed.
You want to wash yourself
in earth, in rocks and grass.

What are you supposed to do
with all this loss?

  —*Margaret Atwood*

PRESENTING THE POEMS:

The Osprey
BY MARY OLIVER

&

Did You Ever?
(For Mary Oliver)
BY MARCIA CONLEY CARTER

SETTING THE STAGE: Here's another angle on yesterday's theme. The great Mary Oliver is the poet; the topic is simple: in "The Osprey," she watches an osprey catch a fish. But if you think describing a pretty scene in pretty language is all that's required of a poet's imagination, in the words of Mary Oliver, *beware!*

SOME FEATURES TO NOTICE:
- Vocabulary:
  cupidinous means greedy or filled with desire
  a **scrim,** here, is the piece of fabric used in a theatre to create the illusion of a solid wall or backdrop
- The strong visual imagery
- The sensory diction: verbs, nouns, and adjectives
- How the poem divides in two (this is typical of Oliver): first a narrative about or description of a natural phenomenon, followed, after a turn, by Oliver's attempt to draw meaning from it
- How Oliver, at the end of the poem, becomes both the osprey and the fish; how as *the imaginer* of this scene, she must feel the experience of the fish, *swimming for [its] life*, **and** that of the osprey, *thundering this way and that way / in [its] shirt of feathers*; and how this kind of thinking is no *mild exercise* of the imagination

RESPONSE STANCE: Please go back into "The Osprey" on your own and mark two things: the language you can see, and also what feel to you like the most important lines in this poem.

BENEDICTION: Together, "Down" and "The Osprey" give me new respect for good writing. The thinking and imagining required of poets and novelists are no *mild exercise,* as Mary Oliver phrased it; it is all-consuming.

Marcia, a seventh grader, understood. She wrote a poem for Mary Oliver that's a tribute to the brain work of a poet. It's called "Did You Ever?"…

Who is a poet whose imaginative work you've come to appreciate? There may be a poem waiting in your imagination, a poem in which you celebrate, wonder about, imagine, question, or defend his or her poems, as Marcia did for Mary Oliver.

The Osprey

This morning
an osprey
with its narrow
black-and-white face

and its cupidinous eyes
leaned down
from a leafy tree
to look into the lake—it looked

a long time, then its powerful
shoulders punched out a little
and it fell,
it rippled down

into the water—
then it rose, carrying,
in the clips of its feet,
a slim and limber

silver fish, a scrim
of red rubies
on its flashing sides.
All of this

was wonderful
to look at,
so I simply stood there,
in the blue morning,

looking.
Then I walked away.
Beauty is my work,
but not my only work—

later,
when the fish was gone forever
and the bird was miles away,
I came back

and stood on the shore, thinking—
and if you think
thinking is a mild exercise,
beware!

I mean, I was swimming for my life—
and I was thundering this way and that way
in my shirt of feathers—
and I could not resolve anything long enough

to become one thing
except this: the imaginer.
It was inescapable
as over and over it flung me,

without pause or mercy it flung me
to both sides of the beautiful water—
to both sides
of the knife.

—Mary Oliver

Did You Ever?
(For Mary Oliver)

Did you ever stop and think
how hard it must have been
for her to write that poem?
To think of a subject, one
to intrigue readers, one
you could write about yourself, one
you could make sense of, one
that could reach out and touch a life?
Imagine the long hours she sat writing
before dawn at her desk,
crossing out as the sun came up and revealed the dew.
Crossing out, trying it again and again,
diving for the right word
until she can't swim another stroke,
until she can't write another word,
until she has to stop or this poem will kill her.
And then finally her poem makes it to you.
You read it and nod in satisfaction.
You like the poem—some good lines—
and you put her book back on the shelf.
But did you ever wonder
what it must have taken
for her to write that poem?

 —Marcia Conley Carter

The thinking and imagining required of poets is no mild exercise.

An Afternoon in the Stacks

BY WILLIAM STAFFORD

SETTING THE STAGE: From the time I was a little girl, I've been haunted by books—reliving in my imagination the death of Charlotte in *Charlotte's Web* or Meg's reunion with her father at the end of *A Wrinkle in Time*. The haunting feeling perseveres to this day, as the novel I finished last week continues to percolate in my consciousness, even after I've shelved it and moved on to another. A good book stays in me, somehow. William Stafford took that feeling of *somehow* and crafted it as a poem, "An Afternoon in the Stacks." *Stacks*, by the way, are the bookshelves in a library.

SOME FEATURES TO NOTICE:

- The humor of the first line
- The evocative imagery and diction
- The personification and metaphors and the simile
- How the conclusion implies that reading books has connected Stafford to all of humanity: as far away as Tibet, *a candle-flame...leans when I move* because of the impact on a reader of the words of a writer

RESPONSE STANCE: Please go back into "An Afternoon in the Stacks" and mark the words and lines you like, get, and want to talk about.

BENEDICTION: Have you been haunted? What books, what characters, what plot events have haunted you? Is there a poem in you about a book you closed, but found that you'd left a piece of your head—and heart—inside it?

An Afternoon in the Stacks

Closing the book, I find I have left my head
inside. It is dark in here, but the chapters open
their beautiful spaces and give a rustling sound,
words adjusting themselves to their meaning.
Long passages open at successive pages. An echo,
continuous from the title onward, hums
behind me. From in here the world looms,
a jungle redeemed by these linked sentences
carved out when an author traveled and a reader
kept the way open. When this book ends
I will pull it inside-out like a sock
and throw it back in the library. But the rumor
of it will haunt all that follows in my life.
A candleflame in Tibet leans when I move.

—*William Stafford*

You Know Who You Are

BY NAOMI SHIHAB NYE

SETTING THE STAGE: William Stafford was a poet's poet. His honest voice, his courage, his wit, and his clear vision inspired a generation of young poets, and when he died in 1993, many mourned him in poems of their own. Naomi Shihab Nye, who you'll remember as the author of "Famous" and "A Valentine for Ernest Mann," is a Stafford disciple. In today's poem by Nye, you're about to hear one poet thanking another poet. She never names him, but I'm convinced, from the way she describes the effect of his poems, that it's William Stafford.

SOME FEATURES TO NOTICE:
- The humor and mystery of the title
- The figurative language, especially the similes: poems *like straight-backed chairs; like a raft, logs tied together; words as something portable again,/ a cup, a newspaper, a pin*
- The conclusion: in an epiphany, Nye feels comforted, rescued, and inspired by the other poet's words

RESPONSE STANCE: Please go back into Nye's love poem on your own and mark the lines you love.

BENEDICTION: I'll ask you again to consider the poets you appreciate—who rescue, comfort, and inspire you. Is there a version of "You Know Who You Are" waiting inside you to be written?

You Know Who You Are

Why do your poems comfort me, I ask myself.
Because they are upright, like straight-backed chairs.
I can sit in them and study the world as if it too
were simple and upright.

Because sometimes I live in a hurricane of words
and not one of them can save me.
Your poems come in like a raft, logs tied together,
they float.
I want to tell you about the afternoon
I floated on your poems
all the way from Durango Street to Broadway.

Fathers were paddling on the river with their small sons.
Three Mexican boys chased each other outside the library.
Everyone seemed to have some task, some occupation,
while I wandered uselessly in the streets I claim to love.

Suddenly I felt the precise body of your poems beneath me,
like a raft, I felt words as something portable again,
a cup, a newspaper, a pin.
Everything had a light around it,
not the light of Catholic miracles,
the blunt light of a Sunday afternoon.
Light in a world that rushes forward with us or without us.
I wanted to stop and gather up the blocks behind me
in this light, but it doesn't work.
You keep walking, lifting one foot, then the other,
saying "This is what I need to remember"
and then hoping you can.

—*Naomi Shihab Nye*

PRESENTING THE POEM:

Shoplifting Poetry

BY MARTIN STEINGESSER

SETTING THE STAGE: This is an example of one poem so good it made it worth buying a whole book. I was skimming a collection by Martin Steingesser in a bookstore, and I confess that I wanted to steal this poem as soon as I read it. But, unlike the speaker and his accomplice, I had to buy it. There were just too many good lines to lift.

SOME FEATURES TO NOTICE:

- The extended metaphors: reading others' poems as stealing, or as gorging oneself via one's ears
- The humor
- The specifics: how citing the names of the poets he "shoplifts" gives the poem its authority
- The strong conclusion and the vivid final image

RESPONSE STANCE: Please go back into "Shoplifting Poetry" on your own and shoplift. What did Steingesser do, as a poet, that you like, as a poet, and wouldn't mind adding to your repertoire?

BENEDICTION: We've talked about this before: if a poem were completely original, we wouldn't be able to read it or understand it. Every poem alludes to previous poems and poets. So never be afraid to be inspired by another poet's topic, form, theme, or technique. Go right ahead and shoplift poetry, then bring your own voice and your own vision to your plunder.

Shoplifting Poetry

We're in the bookstore stealing poems,
lifting the best lines.
You cop one from Williams,
I stick my hand into Pound.
No one's looking—
I throw you a line from *The Cantos*.
It disappears in your ear like spaghetti.
We stuff ourselves with Crane,
cummings, Lowell, Voznesensky—
Neruda, Rilke, Yeats!
The goods dissolve in our brain.
Now we move from the shelves with caution.
The cashier's watching. Can she tell?
Fat! We've overeaten.
You giggle. End-rhymes leak at your lips like bubbles.
I clap a hand on your mouth.
You are holding my ears
as we fall out the door.

—*Martin Steingesser*

PRESENTING THE POEM:

The House Was Quiet and the World Was Calm

BY WALLACE STEVENS

SETTING THE STAGE: Wallace Stevens is a fascinating poet. You know him already as the author of "Thirteen Ways of Looking at a Blackbird." Stevens worked his whole adult life as an executive at an insurance company in Hartford, Connecticut—a private, gray man in a gray suit. None of his colleagues even knew, until late in his career, that he was a poet. Poetry was Stevens' secret Bohemian adventure—a kind of Paris *inside him*. The critic Frank Kermode once wrote, "No poet ever wrote so fixedly from within the human head as Wallace Stevens."

Stevens is also a difficult poet: abstract, original, philosophical; a master of exquisite verse. Many of his poems are concerned with how language and culture can shape order in the "slovenly wilderness" of life. He thought the job of a poet was to create the fictions that are necessary to "harmonize" the world. His most famous poems are about finding a style for living—for surviving—decently. Wallace Stevens wanted to show that poetry could fill the void of meaningless modern life. His philosophy about poetry, his aims for his own poems, and his style as a poet are all evident in "The House Was Quiet and the World Was Calm."

SOME FEATURES TO NOTICE:
- How the poem illustrates Stevens' theory that poetry and art give meaning to and "harmonize" existence; create *quiet* and *calm;* give humans *access* to *perfection*
- How repetition creates a cadence and moves the poem
- How repetition emphasizes the mood and theme
- The form: two-line stanzas

RESPONSE STANCE: Please go back into this poem and mark the lines that give you a sense of what Wallace Stevens believes about life, literature, and reading.

BENEDICTION: Wallace Stevens worked out his ideas about how to live a good, full life—his philosophy—in his poetry. To survive decently, people need a quiet house, a summer night, and a book. Maybe more than anything else, that's what I wish for you.

The House Was Quiet and the World Was Calm

The house was quiet and the world was calm.
The reader became the book; and summer night

Was like the conscious being of the book.
The house was quiet and the world was calm.

The words were spoken as if there was no book,
Except that the reader leaned above the page,

Wanted to lean, wanted much most to be
The scholar to whom his book is true, to whom

The summer night is like a perfection of thought.
The house was quiet because it had to be.

The quiet was part of the meaning, part of the mind:
The access of perfection to the page.

And the world was calm. The truth in a calm world,
In which there is no other meaning, itself

Is calm, itself is summer and night, itself
Is the reader leaning late and reading there.

—*Wallace Stevens*

PRESENTING THE POEM:

The Next Poem

BY BILLY COLLINS

SETTING THE STAGE: With today's poem we'll come full circle. We began reading poems about writing and reading with Billy Collins' "Reading Myself to Sleep," and we'll end the study with another poem by Billy Collins.

This one begins with a cliché. When poets are asked about their published work—when they're interviewed about the poems they have written—they often say they're not interested in talking about the old stuff. They're only concerned with "the next poem."

SOME FEATURES TO NOTICE:
- The wry humor
- The visual imagery of the *imaginary mush-room*
- How the poem turns, halfway through, on the lines *And that is probably why I have lost inter-est/ in this poem*
- How the final stanza plays with a series of metaphors; how the attitude of each metaphor is self-deprecating

RESPONSE STANCE: Please go back into "The Next Poem" and mark the lines that make you smile.

BENEDICTION: Even when his poem pokes fun at his livelihood, a poet writes like a poet. I hope this group of poems invites you to reimagine poetry, writing, and reading and their role in your life. I look forward to reading your ideas, your poems, about how writing and reading change you and transform the world.

The Next Poem

Whenever the question comes up,
the poets always say the same thing:
the only poem we're interested in is the next poem,
the one not written, the poem of tomorrow.

It's a perfect answer,
which conjures up a bit of hope
and manages to place on the higher tray
of the scale of pride a gram of modesty.

But the problem is
as soon as you start to write it,
the next poem no longer *is* the next poem,
rather just another poem you are writing,
and the next poem has become
an imaginary mushroom waiting
in the future in a dark forest of pine needles.

And that is probably why I have lost interest
in this poem, in where it is going
or how it will manage to find a way to end.

It could droop into a reverie,
maybe shift to the doctor's waiting room
where I am entering it into a notebook,
or circle back to the mushroom for all I care.

All I care about is the next poem,
not this current one,
which might even turn out to be my last—

the last orange on my miniature tree,
a shroud pulled over my baby grand,
the ultimate chirp of my canary,
or, how about this?
the final umbrella on the vacant beach of my soul.

　　　—Billy Collins

Farewell:
INTRODUCTION

No matter how I try to prepare for it, the end of the school year always feels tense, scattered, rushed, and sad. After thirty years of teaching and thirty Junes, I have learned that I can't control the chaos. Way too much has to happen in the hours before that final dismissal. I've also learned not to count on my beloved eighth graders, whose emotions run higher than ever. Their responses to graduation range from non-stop tears to non-stop giddiness.

There's much I want to say to them before they go, but there's never a moment or a forum for me to say it. But there is poetry. There are poets who have found words to convey what matters and what lasts, who can help me tell my kids: *I saw you—I know who you are. You are wonderful. You're a miracle to me. Now, make a life that's worthwhile. Understand that meaningful work is everything. And honor what we did here together. You belong to something bigger than yourself. Stand on this foundation and change the world. Remember me. Remember one another. I will never forget you.*

This last section includes poems I collected over the years to read at one of our graduation ceremonies or on the last day of class—a poem to say good-bye to my kids and to inspire them, one last time, to think about who and how they wish to be in the world. For me, these are the most *useful* poems in *Naming the World*, useful in the same sense that rituals and prayers lend comfort and give meaning.

I don't teach a lesson with a poem of farewell. I do set the stage by telling the group that this is the best—the only—way I know to say good-bye. I read the poem aloud as if these are my words, as if I'm speaking them from my heart. The benediction on the last day consists of a few sentences about the meaning I hope they'll take away from the poem and the year.

I can't control the chaos of June, but one great poem can create a lacuna long and deep enough for us to gather, to pause, and to celebrate the fact that together we named the world.

Aristotle

This is the beginning.
Almost anything can happen.
This is where you find
the creation of light, a fish wriggling onto land,
the first word of *Paradise Lost* on an empty page.
Think of an egg, the letter *A*,
a woman ironing on a bare stage
as the heavy curtain rises.
This is the very beginning.
The first-person narrator introduces himself,
tells us about his lineage.
The mezzo-soprano stands in the wings.
Here the climbers are studying a map
or pulling on their long woolen socks.
This is early on, years before the Ark, dawn.
The profile of an animal is being smeared
on the wall of a cave,
and you have not yet learned to crawl.
This is the opening, the gambit,
a pawn moving forward an inch.
This is your first night with her.
your first night without her.
This is the first part
where the wheels begin to turn,
where the elevator begins its ascent,
before the doors lurch apart.

This is the middle.
Things have had time to get complicated,
messy, really. Nothing is simple anymore.
Cities have sprouted up along the rivers
teeming with people at cross-purposes—
a million schemes, a million wild looks.
Disappointment unshoulders his knapsack
here and pitches a ragged tent.
This is the sticky part where the plot congeals,
where the action suddenly reverses
or swerves off in an outrageous direction.
Here the narrator devotes a long paragraph
to why Miriam does not want Edward's child.
Someone hides a letter under a pillow.
Here the aria rises to a pitch,
a song of betrayal, salted with revenge.
And the climbing party is stuck on a ledge
halfway up the mountain.
This is the bridge, the painful modulation.
This is the thick of things.
So much is crowded into the middle—
the guitars of Spain, piles of ripe avocados,
Russian uniforms, noisy parties,

lakeside kisses, arguments heard through a wall—
too much to name, too much to think about.

And this is the end,
the car running out of road,
the river losing its name in an ocean,
the long nose of the photographed horse
touching the white electronic line.
This is the colophon, the last elephant in the parade,
the empty wheelchair,
the pigeons floating down in evening.
Here is the stage littered with bodies,
the narrator leads the characters to their cells,
and the climbers are in their graves.
It is me hitting the period
and you closing the book.
It is Sylvia Plath in the kitchen
and St Clement with an anchor around his neck.
This is the final bit
thinning away to nothing.
This is the end, according to Aristotle,
what we have all been waiting for,
what everything comes down to,
the destination we cannot help imagining,
a streak of light in the sky,
a hat on a peg, and outside the cabin, falling leaves.

      —*Billy Collins*

The Month of June: 13 ½

As my daughter approaches graduation and
puberty at the same time, at her
own calm deliberate serious rate,
she begins to kick up her heels, jazz out her
hands, thrust out her hip-bones, chant
I'm great! I'm great! She feels 8th grade coming
open around her, a chrysalis cracking and
letting her out, it falls behind her and
joins the other husks on the ground,
7th grade, 6th grade, the
purple rind of 5th grade, the
hard jacket of 4th when she had so much pain,
3rd grade, 2nd, the dim cocoon of
1st grade back there somewhere on the path, and
kindergarten like a strip of thumb-suck blanket
taken from the actual blanket they wrapped her in at birth.
The whole school is coming off her shoulders like a
cloak unclasped, and she dances forth in her
jerky child's joke dance of
self, self, her throat tight and a
hard new song coming out of it, while her
two dark eyes shine
above her body like a good mother and a
good father who look down and
love everything their baby does, the way she
lives their love.

    —*Sharon Olds*

The Ponds

Every year
the lilies
are so perfect
I can hardly believe

their lapped light crowding
the black,
mid-summer ponds.
Nobody could count all of them—

the muskrats swimming
among the pads and the grasses
can reach out
their muscular arms and touch

only so many, they are that
rife and wild.
But what in this world
is perfect?

I bend closer and see
how this one is clearly lopsided—
and that one wears an orange blight—
and this one is a glossy cheek

half nibbled away—
and that one is a slumped purse
full of its own
unstoppable decay.

Still, what I want in my life
is to be willing
to be dazzled—
to cast aside the weight of facts

and maybe even
to float a little
above this difficult world.
I want to believe I am looking

into the white fire of a great mystery.
I want to believe that the imperfections are nothing—
that the light is everything—that it is more than the sum
of each flawed blossom rising and fading. And I do.

  —Mary Oliver

You Reading This, Be Ready

Starting here, what do you want to remember?
How sunlight creeps along a shining floor?
What scent of old wood hovers, what softened
sound from outside fills the air?

Will you ever bring a better gift for the world
than the breathing respect that you carry
wherever you go right now? Are you waiting
for time to show you some better thoughts?

When you turn around, starting here, lift this
new glimpse that you found; carry into evening
all that you want from this day. This interval you spent
reading or hearing this, keep it for life—

What can anyone give you greater than now,
starting here, right in this room, when you turn around?

   —*William Stafford*

The seven of pentacles

Under a sky the color of pea soup
she is looking at her work growing away there
actively, thickly like grapevines or pole beans
as things grow in the real world, slowly enough.
If you tend them properly, if you mulch, if you water,
if you provide birds that eat insects a home and winter food,
if the sun shines and you pick off caterpillars,
if the praying mantis comes and the ladybugs and the bees,
then the plants flourish, but at their own internal clock.

Connections are made slowly, sometimes they grow underground.
You cannot tell always by looking what is happening.
More than half a tree is spread out in the soil under your feet.
Penetrate quietly as the earthworm that blows no trumpet.
Fight persistently as the creeper that brings down the tree.
Spread like the squash plant that overruns the garden.
Gnaw in the dark and use the sun to make sugar.

Weave real connections, create real nodes, build real houses.
Live a life you can endure: make love that is loving.
Keep tangling and interweaving and taking more in,
a thicket and bramble wilderness to the outside but to us
interconnected with rabbit runs and burrows and lairs.

Live as if you liked yourself, and it may happen:
reach out, keep reaching out, keep bringing in.
This is how we are going to live for a long time: not always,
for every gardener knows that after the digging, after the planting,
after the long season of tending and growth, the harvest comes.

—*Marge Piercy*

FAREWELL | 355

Love After Love

The time will come
when, with elation,
you will greet yourself arriving
at your own door, in your own mirror,
and each will smile at the other's welcome,

and say, sit here. Eat.
You will love again the stranger who was your self.
Give wine. Give bread. Give back your heart
to itself, to the stranger who has loved you

all your life, whom you ignored
for another, who knows you by heart.
Take down the love letters from the bookshelf,

the photographs, the desperate notes,
peel your own image from the mirror.
Sit. Feast on your life.

—Derek Walcott

Wild Geese

You do not have to be good.
You do not have to walk on your knees
for a hundred miles through the desert, repenting.
You only have to let the soft animal of your body
    love what it loves.
Tell me about despair, yours, and I will tell you mine.
Meanwhile the world goes on.
Meanwhile the sun and the clear pebbles of the rain
are moving across the landscapes,
over the prairies and deep trees,
the mountains and the rivers.
Meanwhile the wild geese, high in the clean blue air,
are heading home again.
Whoever you are, no matter how lonely,
the world offers itself to your imagination,
calls to you like the wild geese, harsh and exciting—
over and over announcing your place
in the family of things.

　　—Mary Oliver

Adios

It is a good word, rolling off the tongue
no matter what language you were born with.
Use it. Learn where it begins,
the small alphabet of departure,
how long it takes to think of it,
then say it, then be heard.

Marry it. More than any golden ring,
it shines, it shines.
Wear it on every finger
till your hands dance,
touching everything easily,
letting everything, easily, go.

Strap it on your back like wings.
Or a kite-tail. The stream of air behind a jet.
If you are known for anything,
let it be the way you rise out of sight
when your work is finished.

Think of things that linger: leaves,
cartons and napkins, the damp smell of mud.

Think of things that disappear.

Think of what you love best,
what brings tears to your eyes.

Something that said *adios* to you
before you knew what it meant
or how long it was for.

Explain little, the word explains itself.
Later perhaps. Lessons following lessons,
like silence following sound.

　　　—*Naomi Shihab Nye*

To be of use

The people I love the best
jump into work head first
without dallying in the shallows
and swim off with sure strokes almost out of sight.
They seem to be natives of that element,
the black sleek heads of seals
bouncing like half-submerged balls.

I love people who harness themselves, an ox to a heavy cart,
who pull like water buffalo, with massive patience,
who strain in the mud and the muck to move things forward,
who do what has to be done, again and again.

I want to be with people who submerge
in the task, who go into the fields to harvest
and work in a row and pass the bags along,
who are not parlor generals and field deserters
but move in a common rhythm
when the food must come in or the fire be put out.

The work of the world is common as mud.
Botched, it smears the hands, crumbles to dust.
But the thing worth doing well done
has a shape that satisfies, clean and evident.
Greek amphoras for wine or oil,
Hopi vases that held corn, are put in museums
but you know they were made to be used.
The pitcher cries for water to carry
and a person for work that is real.

—*Marge Piercy*

from "Song of Myself"

52

The spotted hawk swoops by and accuses me, he complains of my gab and my loitering.

I too am not a bit tamed, I too am untranslatable,
I sound my barbaric yawp over the roofs of the world.

The last scud of day holds back for me,
It flings my likeness after the rest and true as any on the shadow'd wilds.
It coaxes me to the vapor and the dusk.

I depart as air, I shake my white locks at the runaway sun,
I effuse my flesh in eddies, and drift it in lacy jags.

I bequeath myself to the dirt to grow from the grass I love,
If you want me again look for me under your boot-soles.

You will hardly know who I am or what I mean,
But I shall be good health to you nevertheless,
And filter and fibre your blood.

Failing to fetch me at first keep encouraged,
Missing me one place search another,
I stop somewhere waiting for you.

—*Walt Whitman*

Appendices

Reading Poetry as a Critic

This year I'll ask you to enter a poem with me at the start of class each day, and we'll read and talk about it together as critics. I don't mean a critic like Ebert and Roeper— thumbs up or down or three stars out of four. But I also don't mean how you may have responded to poems in your younger years, when readers tend to react in terms of personal connections—for example, you liked a poem about a dog because you had a dog.

When I say that we'll read poetry as critics, I mean we're going to read poems and talk about the experience of reading them—what you noticed or liked about how a poem is built, how it means, how it makes you feel, and what the poet did to give rise to your feelings. This kind of close reading is what critics do. Poets call it "unpacking" a poem.

I have a theory about reading poetry as a critic that I'll ask you to adopt, and that we'll adapt together for the rest of the school year. It's based on twelve principles of literary criticism.

1. One reason we'll read poetry together as critics is to improve our ability to experience poems on our own—to enter them independently, notice their features, unpack their meanings, bring the meanings into our own lives, and cherish them.

2. Another reason we'll read poetry as critics is to learn the language of criticism—to experience, in context, what's meant by such terms as *alliteration, assonance, cadence, coded language, diction, form, imagery, line break* and *stanza break, metaphor, personification, rhyme scheme, simile, symbol,* and *theme*.

3. A third reason we'll read poetry as critics is to improve our ability to write poems that matter to our lives, poems that work as good poetry and that other readers will want to experience—for example, to learn the difference between a word that's good enough and one that's precise and *right*.

4. One reader will respond differently to a poem than another. So another reason we'll read poetry as critics is to discover which of our responses are inspired and supported by specific things a poet has done, and which are personal and idiosyncratic, e.g., "This poem about a dog is good 'cause I have a dog."

5. Our responses to a poem are affected by our past experiences with poetry. The more and longer we read and unpack poetry, the better we read it, understand it, and respond to it.

6. One reader's response to a poem may be more grounded than another's. Again, the more and longer we read and unpack poetry, the more perceptively we read it.

7. Still, no reader's response is ever as good as the poem itself, ever "says" what the poem "says." For example, no matter how well someone can explain all the words, images, and references in Robert Frost's "Nothing Gold Can Stay," its meaning is complete only in the poem.

8. Because of the coded nature of the language of poetry, some poems need multiple readings to discover how and what they mean. Writing can help a reader unpack a poem, as can a dictionary. The best poems can be read a hundred times and still yield pleasures and surprises.

9. "How does a poem mean?" is a more useful question than "What does a poem mean?" Unlike other literature, in a poem, the way the meaning is coded is more interesting and important than the meaning itself.

10. When a reader unpacks a poem, the individual words, lines, images, and metaphors of the poem need to be considered in context—that is, in relation to other words, lines, images, and metaphors in the poem. In other words, a critic can't build a theory of the meaning of a poem based on one line, if the theory doesn't fit all the other lines of the poem.

11. Some words, lines, images, and metaphors in a poem are more important than others. They carry a greater weight of meaning. A productive approach to experiencing a poem is to look for its most important words, lines, images, or metaphors. *Conclusions* are especially important.

12. Poems refer or allude to other poems—to all of literature, for that matter. No poem is completely original; if it were, we wouldn't be able to read or understand it. This isn't an argument for plagiarism. It is a reminder that critics might discuss a poem in relation to other poetry.

Preparing to Present a Poem

Choose a poem you love: one that calls your name, one you can begin to talk about, one others can begin to talk about and might love, too, and one that's memorable.

Tell me the title of the poem and the name of the poet, and get your name on the schedule.

Be sure the poet's name and the source appear on your copy of the poem, then make sufficient clean photocopies for everyone in your class, plus one for you and one for me.

Then, read the poem aloud to yourself, and annotate it for oral reading:

- Mark places where the meaning is supported by a pause (with a dash or slash?).

- Mark where the meaning of the poem needs your voice to keep going, from the end of one line or stanza to the beginning of the next (a long arrow?).

- Mark places where you'll help support the meaning of the poem by going softer with your voice (a circle?) or louder (an underline?), by slowing down (dashes?) or speeding up (arrows?).

- Write a note to yourself in the margin about the emotion or tone you want your voice to convey at different points in the poem, e.g., sad, surprised, wondering, nostalgic, sarcastic, serious, naïve, angry, rueful, amazed, bitter, delighted.

- Look up every word you don't know how to pronounce, define, or explain.

- Mark any metaphors, similes, and personifications, as well as instances of alliteration, assonance, and imagery.

- Mark the rhyme scheme if there is one (e.g., ABAB) or the form if there is one (e.g., stanzas of five lines each, or repeating words or lines).

- Mark the *turn* if there is one: a point in the poem where the tone, voice, topic, or meaning shifts.

- Decide how you'll set the stage for the poem and invite others to enter it with you. See the next list for possibilities, and choose the way in that seems most appropriate for this poem and most inviting to other readers.

- Decide how you'll ask the group to respond to the poem and make sense of it. See the third list for possibilities. Choose a response stance appropriate to this poem: to what the poem does, how it means, and what it means.

©2006 by Nancie Atwell from *Naming the World: A Year of Poems and Lessons* (Portsmouth, NH: Heinemann)

Setting the Stage for a Poem: Some Options for Student Presenters

Tap your personal experience and tell:

- what attracted you to the poem or the poet

- what about the poem made you love it

- how you read it the first time through

- how it makes you feel

- what it makes you think about

- what other poem or poet it reminds you of

- what you see, hear, smell, feel, or taste as you read the poem

- what the poem makes you remember

Ask readers to tap relevant personal experiences (e.g., Who remembers a time when…? Who has ever…? Who has seen or heard…?).

Provide background: tell readers what they need to know, or ask what they already know, about:

- a subject

- an event

- a phenomenon

- a historical period

- a theory or belief

- a social tradition

- a story or myth

- a literary tradition

- a poetic form

- the poet's life, attitudes, or other poems

Ask readers for help: tell them you know there's more to this poem than you're getting, that you're intrigued by it, and that you want them to collaborate with you in unpacking it.

Ask readers what they think the title might mean or refer to.

Ask readers to close their eyes and ride on the cadence of the words as you read them.

Response Stances: Some Options for Student Presenters

- Mark the lines you want to talk about.
- Mark the lines you *need* to talk about.
- Mark your favorite lines.
- Mark the lines you can see—that create strong visual images.
- Mark the lines you can feel, smell, or hear.
- Mark the words that surprise you.
- Mark the lines that surprise you.
- Mark the lines that tickle your funny bone.
- Mark the lines that give you a strong feeling.
- Mark the lines that knock you out.
- Mark the lines you wish you had written.
- Mark the lines that make you want to read more of this poet's poetry.
- Mark the lines that confuse you.
- Mark what you think are the most important lines in the poem.
- Notice how this poem begins.
- Notice how this poem ends.
- Notice the form of this poem: see if you can figure it out.
- Mark the metaphors.
- Mark the similes.
- Mark the instances of personification.
- Mark the instances of alliteration.
- Mark the instances of assonance.
- Mark the verbs you think are strongest—most sensory.
- Notice how the poet uses white space—breaks the lines and stanzas—and write a few notes about why you think he or she did this.
- What thoughts or images come to mind immediately after reading this poem? Write them down.
- How does this poem make you feel? Write a line or two describing your emotional response.
- Mark the lines where you recognize what the poet is feeling.
- What is happening, literally, in the world of this poem? Line by stanza, see if you can unpack this poem's story.
- Write in your own words what you think this poem is saying.
- Why do you think the poet might have written this poem? Write a line or two.

©2006 by Nancie Atwell from *Naming the World: A Year of Poems and Lessons* (Portsmouth, NH: Heinemann)

Figurative Language, or Two Things as Once

Literal language is true to fact. It uses words in accordance with their actual (literal) meanings.

Example: My dog is a carnivore.

Figurative language makes comparisons between unrelated objects or ideas, in order to show something about a subject.

Example: In the kitchen, when I cook dinner, my dog is a tap dancer.

Three Kinds of Figurative Language

- *Metaphor* (Greek): means, literally, *transference*. The writer transfers qualities of one thing to another thing. A metaphor has two parts: A = B: something *is* something else. The B part, the *something else,* shows how the poet feels about or perceives the A part.

  Example:

  Thumb
  The odd, friendless boy raised by four aunts.
  –Philip Dacey

- *Simile* (from the Latin *similes*: similar): a kind of metaphor that uses *like* or *as* to compare two things: A is like B.

  Example:

  Thunder threatens
  Like a sound that rolls around and around
  In a mean dog's throat.
  –Martha Sherwood

- *Personification* (from the Greek *prósopa*, meaning "face" or "mask"): a metaphor that gives human or animate qualities to an object, animal, idea, or phenomenon.

  Example:

  "The yellow fog that rubs its back upon the window-panes"
  –T.S. Eliot

Kids' Recommended Poetry Anthologies and Collections

Angelou, Maya. 1994. *The Complete Collected Poems of Maya Angelou.* New York: Random House.

Astley, Neil, ed. 2003. *Staying Alive: Real Poems for Unreal Times.* New York: Hyperion.

Atwood, Margaret. 1995. *Morning in the Burned House.* Boston: Houghton Mifflin.

Bly, Robert, James Hillman, and Michael Meade, eds. 1992. *The Rag and Bone Shop of the Heart: Poems for Men.* New York: HarperCollins.

Brooks, Gwendolyn. 1999. *Selected Poems.* New York: HarperCollins.

Brown, Kurt, ed. 1994. *Drive, They Said: Poems about Americans and Their Cars.* Minneapolis: Milkweed Editions.

Buchwald, Emilie, and Ruth Roston, eds. 1998. *This Sporting Life: Poems about Sports and Games.* Minneapolis: Milkweed Editions.

Bukowski, Charles. 1974. *Burning in Water, Drowning in Flame: Selected Poems 1955-1973.* New York: HarperCollins.

———. 1977. *Love Is a Dog from Hell: Poems 1974-1977.* New York: HarperCollins.

———. 2003. *Sifting Through the Madness for the Word, the Line, the Way: New Poems.* New York: HarperCollins.

Coghill, Shelia and Thom Tammaro, eds. 2000. *Visiting Emily: Poems Inspired by the Life and Work of Emily Dickinson.* Iowa City: University of Iowa Press.

Collins, Billy. 2001. *Sailing Alone Around the Room: New and Selected Poems.* New York: Random House.

———, ed. 2003. *Poetry 180.* New York: Random House.

———, ed. 2005. *Another 180.* New York: Random House.

Cook, Ferris, ed. 2001. *Yowl: Selected Poems about Cats.* Boston: Little, Brown.

Cooper, Jane. 1993. *Green Notebook, Winter Road.* Gardiner, ME: Tilbury House.

Cummings, E. E. 1994. *E.E. Cummings: Complete Poems 1904-1962.* New York: W. W. Norton.

Dickinson, Emily. 1960. *The Complete Poems of Emily Dickinson,* edited by Thomas H. Johnson. Boston: Little, Brown.

Dunning, Stephen, Edward Lueders, Naomi Shihab Nye, Keith Gilyard, and Demetrice A. Worley, eds. 1995. *Reflections on a Gift of Watermelon Pickle… And Other Modern Verse.* 2d ed. Glenview, IL: Scott, Foresman.

Eastman, Arthur M., ed. 1970. *The Norton Anthology of Poetry (Shorter Edition).* New York: W.W. Norton.

Frost, Robert. 1979. *The Poetry of Robert Frost.* New York: Henry Holt.

Gillan, Maria Mazziotti, ed. 1994. *Unsettling America: An Anthology of Contemporary Multicultural Poetry.* New York: Penguin.

Giovanni, Nikki. 1996. *The Selected Poems of Nikki Giovanni.* New York: William Morrow.

Graves, Donald. 1996. *Baseball, Snakes, and Summer Squash: Poems About Growing Up.* Honesdale, PA: Boyds Mills Press.

Harper, Michael S. and Anthony Walton, eds. 2000. *The Vintage Book of African American Poetry.* New York: Random House.

———, eds. 1994. *Every Shut Eye Ain't Asleep: An Anthology of Poetry by African Americans Since 1945.* Boston: Little Brown.

Harvey, Anne, ed. 2000. *In Time of War: Unforgettable Poems of the First and Second World Wars.* London: Macmillan.

Hass, Robert. 1994. *The Essential Haiku: Versions of Basho, Buson, and Issa.* Hopewell, NJ: The Ecco Press.

Heaney, Seamus. 1990. *Selected Poems: 1966–1987.* New York: Farrar, Straus and Giroux.

Hempel, Amy, and Jim Shepard, eds. 1995. *Unleashed: Poems by Writers' Dogs.* New York: Random House.

Hughes, Langston. 1994. *The Collected Poems of Langston Hughes.* New York: Random House.

Janeczko, Paul B., ed. 1993. *Looking for Your Name: A Collection of Contemporary Poems.* New York: Orchard Books.

Keillor, Garrison, ed. 2002. *Good Poems.* New York: Penguin Books.

Kenyon, Jane. 1996. *Otherwise: New and Selected Poems.* St. Paul: Graywolf Press.

Kerouac, Jack. 2003. *The Book of Haikus.* New York: Penguin Books.

Kherdian, David, ed. 1995. *Beat Voices: An Anthology of Beat Poetry.* New York: Henry Holt.

Kingsolver, Barbara. 1998. *Another America.* Seattle: Seal Press.

Kinnell, Galway. 2000. *A New Selected Poems.* Boston: Houghton Mifflin.

Knudson, R. R., and May Swenson, eds. 1988. *American Sports Poems.* New York: Orchard Books.

Kooser, Ted. 2004. *Delights and Shadows.* Port Townsend, WA: Copper Canyon Press.

Lerner, Andrea, ed. 1990. *Dancing on the Rim of the World: An Anthology of Contemporary Northwest Native American Writing.* Tucson, AZ: Sun Tracks and the University of Arizona Press.

Lyman, Henry, ed. 1995. *After Frost: An Anthology of Poetry from New England.* Amherst, MA: University of Massachusetts.

Neruda, Pablo. 1994. *Odes to Common Things.* Boston: Little, Brown.

———. 1998. *Full Woman, Fleshly Apple, Hot Moon.* New York: HarperCollins.

Nye, Naomi Shihab. 1980. *Different Ways to Pray.* Portland, OR: Breitenbush Publications.

———. 1990. *Red Suitcase.* Brockport, NY: BOA.

———, ed. 1992. *This Same Sky.* New York: Macmillan.

Olds, Sharon. 1987. *The Gold Cell.* New York: Knopf.

Oliver, Mary. 1990. *House of Light.* Boston: Beacon Press.

———. 1992. *New and Selected Poems.* Boston: Beacon Press.

———. 1996. *West Wind.* Boston: Houghton Mifflin.

———. 2002. *What Do We Know.* Cambridge, MA: DaCapo Press.

Pastan, Linda. 1982. *PM/AM: New and Selected Poems.* New York: W. W. Norton.

———. 1988. *The Imperfect Paradise.* New York: W. W. Norton.

———. 1995. *An Early Afterlife.* New York: W. W. Norton.

Piercy, Marge. 1985. *Circles on the Water.* New York: Alfred A. Knopf.

———, ed. 1987. *Early Ripening: American Women's Poetry Now.* New York: Pandora.

Pinsky, Robert, and Maggie Dietz, eds. 2000. *America's Favorite Poems.* New York: W. W. Norton.

Plath, Sylvia. 1992. *The Collected Poems.* New York: HarperCollins.

Rochelle, Belinda, ed. 2001. *Words with Wings: A Treasury of African-American Poetry and Art.* New York: HarperCollins.

Schiff, Hilda, ed. 1995. *Holocaust Poetry.* New York: St. Martin's Press.

Shakespeare, William. 1995. *Shakespeare's Sonnets.* New York: Simon and Schuster.

Stafford, William. 1991. *Passwords.* New York: HarperCollins.

———. 1992. *My Name Is William Tell.* Lewiston, ID: Confluence Press.

———. 1993. *The Darkness around Us Is Deep: Selected Poems.* New York: HarperCollins.

———. 1996. *Even in Quiet Places.* Lewiston, ID: Confluence Press.

———. 1998. *The Way It Is: New and Selected Poems.* St. Paul: Graywolf Press.

Stallworthy, Jon, ed. 1984. *The Oxford Book of War Poetry.* London: Oxford University Press.

Steele, Susanna, ed. *Mother Gave a Shout: Poems by Women and Girls.* Volcano, CA: Volcano Press.

Wakoski, Diane. 1971. *The Motorcycle Betrayal Poems.* New York: Simon and Schuster.

Whitman, Walt. 1995. *Leaves of Grass.* Amherst, NY: Prometheus Books.

Wilbur, Richard. 1988. *New and Collected Poems.* San Diego: Harcourt Brace Jovanovich.

Williams, William Carlos. 1986. *The Collected Poems of William Carlos Williams, Volume I.* New York: New Directions.

———. 1988. *The Collected Poems of William Carlos Williams, Volume II.* New York: New Directions.

Other Poems Students Loved

For a variety of reasons, I wasn't able to include in *Naming the World* all the poems that my students named as favorites. These titles round out their list.

Margaret Atwood	Bored Variations on the Word Sleep
Billy Collins	The History Teacher Introduction to Poetry The Flight of the Reader Morning Workshop Nostalgia November
Countee Cullen	Incident
E. E. Cummings	a little innocence love is more thicker than forget Buffalo Bill's anyone lived in a pretty how town who are you, little I?
Rita Dove	Fifth Grade Autobiography Three Days of Forest, a River, Free
Robert Francis	Gold
Allen Ginsberg	A Supermarket in California
Ted Kooser	Pearl Tattoo
Audre Lord	Every Traveler Has One Vermont Poem
Haki Madhubuti	Gwendolyn Brooks
Pablo Neruda	Ode to an Onion Ode to a Bar of Soap Ode to a Spoon Ode to the Watermelon
Naomi Shahib Nye	Prayer in My Boot The Art of Disappearing
Sharon Olds	First Hour
Mary Oliver	Stories Winter at Herring Cove
Linda Pastan	Nocturnal Why Are Your Poems So Dark? A New Poet Leaves Sestina at 3 AM Autumn
Victoria Redel	Bedecked
Gary Soto	Eating While Reading Stars
Richard Wilbur	Love Calls Us to the Things of This World The Writer Merlin Enthralled

A Glossary of Some Poetic Terms

alliteration – the repetition of initial sounds, usually consonants, in neighboring words

allusion – within a poem, a reference, usually brief, to a historic or literary work, event, person, or place beyond the world of the poem

anthology – a book of selected writings by a variety of poets

assonance – the repetition of vowel sounds in neighboring words

blank verse – a poem written in iambic pentameter (duhDUH five times per line) that does not rhyme, e.g., *Hamlet* or Yeats's "The Second Coming," not to be confused with *free verse* (see below)

cadence – a rhythmic pattern based on the natural rhythms, repetitions, and emphases in speech

caesura (si·ZHOOR·uh) – a slight but definite pause *within* a line of a poem, which is created by the natural rhythm of language in a long line, or by a punctuation mark, e.g., a period in the middle of a line

close form – poetry that conforms to an established pattern, e.g., sonnet, limerick, villanelle, pantoum, tritina, sestina, rondel, etc.

collection – a book of selected writings by one poet

couplet – a pair of lines, usually written in the same form

diction – a poet's choice of words and/or their arrangement

elegy – a poem of mourning or somber meditation

end-stopped line – when sense *and* grammar pause at the end of a line: a line-break at a normal pause in speech, generally at a punctuation mark

enjambed line – when the sense and grammar of a line continue from one line to the next; also called *run-on lines*

epigraph – a quotation placed at the beginning of a poem to make the writing more resonant

figurative language – comparisons between unrelated things or ideas: metaphors, similes, personification, and allusions are all types of figurative language, which reveal the familiar in new, surprising ways

free verse – poetry that doesn't have a set rhythm, line length, or rhyme scheme; it relies, instead, on the natural rhythms of speech

hyperbole –when a poet exaggerates on purpose for effect

imagery – a sensory response that the language of a poem produces in the mind of a reader; not just visual but any sensory impression—auditory, tactile, etc.—evoked by language

irony – when a poet says one thing but means another

line – a group of words in a row; the unit of a poem

line break – the most important point in a line of poetry: the breath or pause at the end of each row of words

lyric poetry – short poems (i.e., fewer than sixty lines) about personal experience or feeling, vs. *narrative poetry* (see below) or epic poetry about communal events, like *Beowulf* or the *Iliad*; most verse written and published today is lyric poetry

metaphor – from the Greek, meaning *transference*; a comparison in which the poet writes about one thing as if it is something else: A = B, and the qualities of B are transferred to A

narrative poetry – a long poem (i.e., more than sixty lines) that tells a story at a leisurely pace: a short story in verse form

open form – see *free verse*

personification – from the Greek *prosopa*, meaning face or mask: a comparison that gives human or animate qualities to an object, animal, idea, or phenomenon

prose poem – writing that has poetic features—e.g., rhythm, imagery, compression—but doesn't rhyme, conform to a set rhythm, or break into lines

rhyme scheme – the pattern of rhyming in a poem; to describe the pattern or scheme, each line is assigned a letter, and lines that rhyme are given the same letter

sensory diction – language in a poem that evokes one or more of the five senses

simile – from the Latin *similes*, meaning similar: a kind of metaphor that uses *like* or *as* to compare two things: A is like B

speaker / persona – the identity of the voice that speaks the words of a poem; not necessarily the same person as the poet

stanza – a line or group of lines in a poem separated from other groups of lines by extra white space; a division in a poem that occurs at a natural pause or at a point where the poet wants to speed up or slow down the poem, shift its tone, change the setting, introduce a new idea or character, etc.

symbol – a concrete object or action that suggests, in addition to itself, a further meaning

tone – the attitude of the speaker or the poet toward the subject of the poem

turn – a point in a poem when its meaning moves in a new and/or significant direction, or its theme emerges

Author Index

Credits

WHAT POETRY CAN DO

YOUR LIFE

IDEAS IN THINGS

GAMES

DOGS AND CATS

THE SENSES

GROWING UP

METAPHOR

THE NATURAL WORLD